SCHOOL EFFECTIVENESS AND SCHOOL IMPROVEMENT

Series Editors: David Hopkins and David Reynolds

SCHOOL EFFECTIVENESS AND SCHOOL IMPROVEMENT

Alternative Perspectives

edited by Alma Harris and Nigel Bennett

CONTINUUM

London and New York

Continuum
The Tower Building
11 York Road
London SE1 7NX

370 Lexington Avenue
New York
NY 10017-6563

First published 2001

British Library Cataloguing-in-Publication Data
A catalogue record for this book is available from the British Library.

ISBN 0-8264-5375-9 (HB)
      0-8264-5121-7 (PB)

Typeset by YHT Ltd, London
Printed and bound in Great Britain by Biddles

Contents

Series Editors' Foreword

The fields of school effectiveness and school improvement have come to prominence very rapidly in many countries, perhaps especially so in Britain. For a variety of reasons concerned both with this and the relative novelty of the fields themselves, these disciplines and the people who work within them remain somewhat controversial for those in 'mainstream' educational research, who see the involvement of school effectiveness and improvement scholars with governments and official agencies as generating further cause for concern.

This very balanced volume is therefore a very timely addition to the literature. It is also an intellectually mature invention in the debate of considerable quality, containing chapters, some by the Editors themselves, that bring a very high level of analytical thinking to bear on issues that have too often been reduced to emotion-based sloganizing. There is therefore very useful material in the volume that reviews the state of two fields of effectiveness and improvement, that brings fresh new perspectives from the fields of educational management/administration to the debate and that brings a valuable synergy between the tenets of two fields that are still often more exclusive than they should be.

This book is sure to have a highly positive impact upon the discipline of school effectiveness and school improvement itself. It is also likely to further encourage the confluence of perspectives between the two fields on which future disciplinary advance rests, and on which rests, in part, the chances of creating bodies of knowledge and practice that will give the world's children the schools they need.

David Hopkins
David Reynolds

Contributors

Nigel Bennett Senior Lecturer in the Centre for Educational Policy and Management, The Open University.

Hugh Busher Senior Lecturer in the School of Education, University of Leicester.

Alma Harris Reader in Educational Management and Leadership, University of Nottingham.

Agnes McMahon Senior Lecturer in the School of Education, University of Bristol.

Felicity Wikely Senior Lecturer in the School of Education, University of Bath.

Mike Bottery Senior Lecturer in the School of Education, University of Hull.

Brian Fidler Professor of Education, University of Reading.

Ian Jamieson Professor of Education, University of Bath.

David Reynolds Professor of Education, University of Exeter.

Acknowledgements

This book would not have been possible without the enthusiasm and support of Anthony Haynes at Continuum. We are grateful to him for his support and patience. Thanks also go to all our authors for their high-quality work and to Denise Gayson for finalizing the manuscript for publication.

In writing this book we have inevitably drawn upon the school effectiveness and school improvement research fields. We wish to acknowledge those writers, researchers and practitioners within both fields who have contributed so much to our understanding of what makes an effective school and how schools improve. The international reputation of both fields is a reflection of their commitment and hard work. In particular, we would like to acknowledge the enormous contribution made by Peter Mortimore to the school effectiveness research field. His work over the last twenty years has ensured that the field has greatly influenced both policy makers and practitioners in many countries.

We would also like to acknowledge the many teachers and schools we have worked with over our research careers. We hope that this book will be read by those within both the teaching and research communities who remain convinced that by understanding schools we have greater opportunity to improve the life chances and educational achievements of all pupils.

ALMA HARRIS AND NIGEL BENNETT

Chapter 1

Introduction

Alma Harris and Nigel Bennett

CURRENT CONTEXT

The pressure upon schools to improve and to raise achievement is unlikely to recede over the next few years. Educational policy remains firmly focused upon securing increased pupil and school performance. This would suggest that the school effectiveness and school improvement research fields are likely to remain influential with policy makers and practitioners alike. Until recently, the two research traditions have largely gone their separate ways. Differences in methodological orientation and, it could be argued, ideological position have resulted in a continued separation between both fields.

Only a small number of studies have attempted to bridge the divide. Most recently, the Improving School Effectiveness Project has drawn upon mixed methodologies from both school effectiveness and school improvement in order to investigate how schools build capacity for change (Stoll *et al.*, 2000). However, despite such examples and calls for ways of integrating the two traditions, this still remains somewhat elusive. In our own discussions about the persistence of this division we were struck by first the insularity of much of the literature within the two fields and second the relative absence of alternative perspectives on school effectiveness and school improvement. In our writing (Bennett and Harris, 1999) we argued that by using an organizational theory perspective there was an opportunity to look at the differences between the two fields in a new and illuminating way. This book is a continuation of that theme and is intended to provide an extended and expanded analysis.

ORGANIZATION OF THE BOOK

Our original idea was to produce a book on the theme of school effectiveness and school improvement that was written by researchers largely outside both research fields. The aim was to produce a book that considered school effectiveness and school improvement from the perspective of organizational theory. Consequently, contributors to the book were requested to select a particular 'frame' from organizational theory to consider the nature and relationships between both fields (Bolman and Deal, 1997). Structural, cultural, political, symbolic and contextual frames are utilized in the chapters that follow. Each frame provides a distinctive analysis of school effectiveness and school improvement and offers an alternative perspective on the future development of both fields.

The book is divided into three parts. Part One provides the background and context for the analysis and critique of school effectiveness and school improvement. Part Two uses structural, cultural and political frames to analyse the relationship between both fields. Part Three continues this analysis but focuses particularly upon the contextual frame. The chapters in this Part address issues of teacher professionalism and student learning. The last chapter considers the future challenges and possibilities for school effectiveness and school improvement. It concludes by suggesting that greater synergy could be achieved between both fields if alternative perspectives from organizational theory were considered and applied.

In Chapter 2, Alma Harris provides a contemporary overview and critique of school effectiveness and school improvement. The chapter focuses upon the reasons for the continued separation between both fields by considering the methodological and theoretical differences that persist. The chapter also proposes some possibilities for future development and closer collaboration. In Chapter 3, David Reynolds continues and develops this theme. He describes the ways in which both fields have attempted to 'move on' both intellectually and practically. The chapter outlines the contemporary thinking that has been generated by a closer relationship between the effectiveness and improvement paradigms and speculates upon the prospects for both effectiveness and improvement as a merged discipline.

In Part Two, particular perspectives or 'frames' derived from organizational theory are used in each of the chapters to analyse school effectiveness and school improvement research. These are: the *structural frame*, i.e. the bureaucratic framework of formal roles and administrative procedures; the *political frame*, i.e. the dynamic processes of negotiation and change and the *cultural frame*, i.e. the shared norms, values and beliefs held generally by people in the organization (Bolman and Deal, 1997). In Chapter 4, Brian Fidler concentrates on the structural frame. This consists of the goals, boundaries, structures, communication systems, co-ordinating mechanisms, roles and responsibilities within an organization. The chapter presents an alternative approach to school improvement based upon a structural analysis. This approach includes the

identification of the processes that contribute to superior school performance.

In Chapter 5, Hugh Busher provides a political and cultural analysis of the
nature of school change and improvement. The chapter uses a political frame
to explore how internal micro-politics influence practice and policy making.
Chapter 6, by Nigel Bennett, extends this initial discussion of culture and
revisits the structural analysis developed in Chapter 4. The chapter goes
beyond Busher's view of power as politics to suggest that power can be seen as
a dynamic force in which both structures and cultures are moving and developing rather than as static and unchanging aspects of schools as organizations.
Structure, culture and power are combined in a three-dimensional model of
schools as organizations which, Bennett argues, offers a theoretical starting
point for linking school effectiveness and improvement research.

The chapters in Part Three extend the analysis by focusing upon the
contextual frame. School effectiveness and school improvement research are
both examined within the wider political and policy context. The chapters
focus particularly upon the implications and consequences for teachers' professional development and student learning. Chapter 7, by Agnes McMahon,
commences this analysis by suggesting that the current macro-culture is
dominated by two factors – managerialism and standards. The chapter argues
that these factors are in direct conflict with messages from school effectiveness
and improvement research and, she argues, in the long term will constrain
rather than promote school improvement. Chapter 8, by Mike Bottery,
extends this argument by looking at the macro-political context and its influence upon teacher professionalism. The chapter analyses the pressures upon
teachers and schools from the macro-political environment and considers the
kinds of professionalism teachers will need in the coming decades.

Chapter 9, by Ian Jamieson and Felicity Wikely, continues the macro-
political theme but focuses upon the expectations of schools and schooling
within the current political climate. The chapter challenges a dominant discourse derived from school effectiveness research, namely that schools should
strive to become more consistent environments for pupils and teachers. Jamieson and Wikely argue that the motivation of students is the key factor that
needs to link school organization and school context. Their analysis concludes
that effective schools are most likely to be those which are able to differentiate
their structures, strategies and policies for different groups of pupils and
different learning tasks.

The final chapter, by Nigel Bennett and Alma Harris, considers the issues,
challenges and possibilities facing school effectiveness and school improvement. It outlines the contributions made by the two research traditions and
discusses a number of common themes that emerge from the book. These themes
reflect the main criticisms of school effectiveness and improvement that appear in
a number of chapters in the book. This chapter concludes by suggesting that the
perspectives from organizational theory offer a means of addressing some of
these limitations. Furthermore, it suggests that organizational theory could offer

a basis for achieving the much sought after synergy that still remains elusive to researchers in both fields.

CODA

School effectiveness and school improvement research have played a significant role in the last two decades in validating the belief that schools make a difference and in helping to illuminate those conditions and strategies that promote school improvement. This book is not an attempt to undermine these considerable achievements or to devalue the contribution made by both research fields. Rather, this book aims to provide a collection of views that, we hope, will extend the debate about how schools develop and improve. Inevitably, differences of opinion about school effectiveness and school improvement emerge in a number of chapters but the prime purpose of this book is to look at both fields using alternative perspectives.

More needs to be known and understood about the processes and conditions that support school improvement. Similarly, more needs to be known and understood about how schools become effective and remain effective over time. Over the coming years, researchers within the school improvement and school effectiveness research fields will continue to work to develop this knowledge and understanding. However, the real challenge resides in persuading researchers outside the school effectiveness and school improvement fields to collaborate in this endeavour. As this book illustrates, there is much to be gained from involving those outside the school effectiveness and school improvement research fields in discussion, reflection and debate. We hope that this debate continues, most importantly because it has the potential to generate the knowledge and understanding to change all our schools for the better.

REFERENCES

Bennett, N. and Harris, A. (1999) 'Hearing Truth from Power'. *School Effectiveness and School Improvement. An International Journal of Research Policy and Practice.* 10:4 533–50.
Bolman, L.G. and Deal, T.E. (1984) *Modern Approaches to Understanding and Managing Organizations.* San Francisco: Jossey-Bass.
Stoll, L., Macbeath, J. and Mortimore, P. (2000) 'Behind 2000: where next for effectiveness and improvement?' in Macbeath, J. and Mortimore, P. (eds) *Improving School Effectiveness.* Buckingham: Open University Press.

Part One

Chapter 2

Contemporary Perspectives on School Effectiveness and School Improvement

Alma Harris

INTRODUCTION

Since the mid-1980s there has been increasing interest in the twin fields of school effectiveness and school improvement by policy makers, academics and practitioners alike. The impetus to improve school performance and to raise standards has contributed to the prominence of both fields within the international research community. The dual levers of accountability and market competition operating in many Western countries have forced schools to seek ways of becoming more effective and of improving their performance. In an effort to achieve this, both educators and researchers have sought answers to two fundamental questions: 'What do effective schools look like?' and 'How do schools improve and become more effective?'.

The first of these questions focuses specifically upon the outcomes of schooling and the characteristics of schools that are 'effective'. The second question is concerned mainly with the processes of schooling and ways in which the quality of schooling can be enhanced. The school effectiveness research field has focused its considerable energies upon the first question over several decades. The second question has been the central concern of those within the school improvement research community over a similar time frame. Yet, despite their focus upon resolving these related questions, the two research traditions remain clearly differentiated fields of activity, regardless of efforts to establish a more synergistic relationship (Stoll, 1996). The divergence of focus and interest between the fields has meant that, to date, there have only been tenuous links between the school effectiveness and school improvement research fields.

Recently, the call for greater synergy between the two fields has been more pressing. Hopkins (1996) notes that 'one of the most encouraging recent developments in the area of school effectiveness and improvement is the seriousness with which the confluence of these two streams of enquiry is being taken'. A number of researchers have attempted to make more synergistic connections between the two fields (Reynolds *et al.*, 1993; West and Hopkins, 1995; Gray *et al.*, 1996b; Hopkins, 1996). In a number of countries projects are emerging which reflect both paradigms (Stoll, 1996; Teddlie and Reynolds, 2000). This convergence has resulted mainly from practitioners and local authority/district policy makers borrowing from both traditions, primarily because they do not share the ideological and theoretical divisions of researchers working in the respective fields. Yet, while some form of synergy is clearly possible, it still remains somewhat elusive.

This chapter focuses upon the reasons for the continued separation between both fields. It considers the historical, methodological and theoretical fissures that exist between the two research areas. It provides a contemporary overview and critique of school effectiveness and school improvement by outlining the contribution and current limitations of each field. It concludes by proposing some possibilities for future development and closer collaboration.

SCHOOL EFFECTIVENESS

School effectiveness is an academic field which has developed rapidly over the last 30 years (Creemers, 1994). In a growing number of countries research has been undertaken that has investigated the impact that schools have upon their students' educational achievements. As a research paradigm, school effectiveness is premised upon the measurement of outcomes and quantifying differences between schools. It is organizationally rather than process based and differs from school improvement in its concentration upon a very limited range of outcomes. The concept of school effectiveness is closely related to a *means–end* relationship. In the school effectiveness research the central aim is to judge whether differences in resources, processes and organizational arrangements affect pupil outcomes and, if so, in what way. In broader terms, the effectiveness research tradition is concerned with the extent to which schools differ from one another. Most recently the field has encompassed a broader range of outcomes and has made greater use of value-added measurement (Thomas and Mortimore, 1996; Sammons, 1999).

Historically, the main impetus for the development of this research field resided in responding to the pessimistic and deterministic interpretation of findings by the American researchers Coleman *et al.* (1966) and Jencks *et al.* (1972). Their research findings emphasized the role that socio-economic and family backgrounds played in facilitating educational success. They argued that a child's test scores or examination results could be predicted far more accurately from knowing the family background than from knowing which school they went to. It was concluded, therefore, that schools made relatively little, if any, difference to the ultimate achievement and attainment of pupils.

The findings of Coleman and Jencks inspired a wave of research studies concerned with measuring the 'school effect'. These studies focused upon the micro variables within the school such as pupil attitude, pupil behaviour and school climate. In reviewing early school effectiveness studies in the USA, Firestone (1991) noted that the effective schools movement was committed to the belief that all children could learn and succeed in school. In particular, the work of Edmonds (1979) embodied the core principles of equity and social justice reflected in many of the early school effectiveness studies.

In the UK the seminal research by Rutter *et al.* (1979, p. 7), demonstrated that 'schools can do much to foster good behaviour and attainment, and that even in a disadvantaged area, schools can be a force for good'. This study found that effective schools were characterized by 'the degree of academic emphasis, teacher actions in lessons, the availability of incentives and rewards, good conditions for pupils, and the extent to which children are able to take responsibility' (p. 178). These findings were subsequently supported by a number of other studies, most notably *School Matters* (Mortimore *et al.*, 1988), a study of ILEA primary schools, and *The School Effect* (Smith and Tomlinson, 1989), a study of multi-racial comprehensives. This work was subsequently followed by a range of studies in the 1980s investigating both school and departmental effects (e.g. Nuttall *et al.*, 1989; Fitz-Gibbon, 1992).

The early work on school effectiveness suggested that schools were equally effective across a range of outcomes (Rutter *et al.*, 1979). Recent work employing more refined statistical techniques has discovered significant differences among schools in their effects on pupil achievements (Wilms, 1992; Sammons *et al.*, 1997). It has also highlighted how schools perform differentially across subject areas and in different socio-economic contexts (Jesson and Gray, 1991).

Nuttall *et al.* (1989) showed large differences for different types of pupil in the relative effectiveness of schools in London. The ILEA research suggested that the difference in experience between able and less able pupils varied markedly between one school and another. The performance of schools also varied in the ways they impacted upon boys and girls, and in their effects upon students from different ethnic groups. Some schools narrowed the gap between these different groups over time and other schools widened them in both instances.

In their research report, Nuttall *et al.* (1990) noted that some schools were more effective in raising the achievement of students with high attainment at entry than that of those with low attainment at entry. They also found that some schools were more effective in raising the achievements of one or more ethnic minority groups in comparison with other schools. The ILEA research team concluded that:

> It is not appropriate to talk of the effectiveness of a single school, as though effectiveness was measured on a single dimension and as though the school was equally effective for all groups of pupils. Rather one must investigate the differential effectiveness of schools. (Nuttall *et al.*, 1990, p. 19)

School effectiveness researchers in the UK have continued to explore issues of differential effectiveness (Thomas *et al.*, 1994; Harris *et al.*, 1995) but have broadened their research agenda considerably. Contemporary studies have included:[1]

- the size of school effects (Gray *et al.*, 1990; Daly, 1991; Thomas *et al.*, 1997);
- the continuity of school effects (Sammons *et al.*, 1995);
- the nature of differential effects (Goldstein *et al.*, 1993);
- the characteristics of differentially effective departments and teachers (Creemers, 1994; Sammons *et al.*, 1997; Harris, 1999);
- the consistency of school effects on different outcomes (Thomas *et al.*, 1994; Goldstein and Sammons, 1995).

Most recent work in the UK has moved towards a focus upon the achievement of all students, not just those within lower socio-economic groups (Sammons, 1999). Student progress over time, as measured by a broad range of outcomes, has been the central concern of contemporary studies. In this latest work the crucial importance of school intake has been highlighted and increasingly attention has been drawn to measuring intake differences (Mortimore, 1991; Mortimore *et al.*, 1994; Sammons *et al.*, 1996).

School effectiveness studies have also been conducted in a growing number of countries. The field is particularly strong in the USA, The Netherlands, Australia and the UK (Mortimore *et al.*, 1988; Levine and Lezotte, 1990; Reynolds and Cuttance, 1992; Scheerens, 1992; Creemers, 1994; Sammons, 1999). In addition, school effectiveness research is becoming more common in Asia and the Third World (Riddell, 1995). As a consequence, there now exists a wealth of research evidence from the school effectiveness research field to confirm that schools matter and do have major effects upon children's development (Reynolds and Creemers, 1990).

It is important however to recognize that school effectiveness is a relative term which is dependent upon time, outcome and student group (Sammons, 1999). Judgements about relative effectiveness require careful analysis and appropriately designed studies. As Sammons (1999) notes, measures of stability in effectiveness are not perfect over time and the complexity of extracting the factors that influence school effectiveness should not be underestimated. Consequently there are some methodological limitations within school effectiveness research and its various 'deficiencies' have been acknowledged (Teddlie and Reynolds, 2000). However, the field has also made a major contribution to the educational research community and as Reynolds *et al.* (2000) observe, the field 'has emerged from virtual obscurity to a now central position in the educational discourse that is taking place within many countries' (p. 3).

CONTRIBUTION AND LIMITATIONS

In considering the contribution of school effectiveness research, a number of writers have highlighted similar achievements (Hopkins, 1994; Mortimore, 1995; Sammons, 1999). First, the school effectiveness field has assisted in demonstrating that schools do make a difference and has helped destroy the belief that schools can do little to change the society around them. At the heart of the effective schools movement is an attack on sociological determinism and individualistic theories about learning. As Hopkins (1994, p. 14) summarizes, 'The single most important contribution of the effective schools movement is that it helped push the dominant behavioural psychological model of learning off centre stage in schools throughout the world.' The net result of this has been a more optimistic conclusion that all pupils can learn irrespective of their socio-economic context.

Second, school effectiveness studies have continuously shown that effective schools are structurally, symbolically and culturally more tightly linked than less effective ones. They operate more as an organic whole and less as a loose collection of disparate sub-systems. Hence, many school improvement programmes have focused upon promoting structural and cultural change in schools (Hopkins and Harris, 1997; Harris and Hopkins, 2000). Finally, one of the most powerful and enduring lessons from this research base is that teachers are important determinants of children's educational and social achievements. Researchers within the school effectiveness field have consistently demonstrated the contribution of teacher effectiveness to educational effectiveness (Creemers, 1994).

Despite these major achievements, the school effectiveness field has been the focus of much controversy and criticism (Elliott, 1996; Slee *et al.*, 1998; Morley and Rassol, 1999). Recent critics have argued that school effectiveness research adheres to conservative values and encourages a view of school failure that 'blames' the school and the teachers (Elliott, 1996). For example, Morley and Rassol (1999) note, 'schools and teachers are either good or bad, effective or failing. Educational success has been reduced to factors that can be measured' (p. 3). They propose that school effectiveness is located within a technical–rationalist framework that reflects a discourse of failure and an obsession with performance. Also, they contend that school effectiveness research is based upon an ideology of social control and takes a narrowly mechanistic view of education as a process. Hamilton (1998) suggests that:

> Effective schooling has become a global industry. Its activities embrace four processes: research, development, marketing and sales. Research entails the construction of new prototypes; development entails the commodification of these prototypes; marketing entails the promotion of these commodities; and sales entails efforts to ensure that market returns exceed financial investment. The school effectiveness industry, therefore, stands at the intersection of educational research and social engineering. (p. 13)

Reynolds and Teddlie (2000) argue that school effectiveness research will always be 'politically controversial since it concerns the nature and purposes of schooling' (p. 322). Whatever position one takes in this latest debate, it is clear that the field has some limitations that have been readily acknowledged (Reynolds and Teddlie, 2000). First, school effectiveness research assumes that schools are rational, goal-oriented systems, that goals are clear and agreed, that goals relate to student achievement and that these achievements are measurable. The school effectiveness research tradition therefore is strongly normative. It focuses primarily upon the structural and technical aspects of the organization and neglects the process or cultural dimensions.

Second, school effectiveness studies tend to reflect a view of a school at a particular moment in time. Teddlie and Reynolds (2000) suggest that school effectiveness studies offer a 'snapshot' of a school rather than a moving picture. Given the dynamic and evolving nature of schools as organizations, this 'snapshot' approach has limited usefulness for informing school development or improvement (Gray *et al.*, 1996b). Third, the school effectiveness work has tended to neglect conditions outside the school and conditions at other layers within the organization which contribute to overall effectiveness. As Hopkins (1990) notes, 'Much of the effective schools literature appears to take such "meso level" issues as unproblematic' (p. 188).

Finally, the effectiveness research has rarely been detailed enough to provide information on what is needed for school improvement. The lack of a focus upon the conditions which foster effectiveness or improvement in a school has meant that the practical application of much of this research base in terms of school development and improvement has proved to be somewhat limited. This last point emphasizes the separateness of the two research disciplines, which is a theme that will be returned to following an overview of the school improvement research field.

SCHOOL IMPROVEMENT

In contrast to the school effectiveness field, school improvement researchers have concentrated their efforts upon the cultural dimensions of schooling (Hopkins *et al.*, 1996). They have focused attention upon the process of school level change and the improvement strategies necessary to achieve such change (Fullan, 1992). Their stance has been one of development with an emphasis upon process measures rather than achievement outcomes. School improvement researchers have been chiefly concerned with understanding how schools change and become more effective.

Within school improvement research the school is regarded as the 'centre of change' and teachers are an inherent part of the change process. Hopkins (1996) suggests that there are two senses in which the term school improvement is generally used. The first 'is a common sense meaning which relates to general efforts to make schools better places for pupils and students to learn' (p. 32). The second is a more technical or specific definition in which Hopkins defines school improvement as a 'strategy for educational change that enhances student outcomes as well as strengthening the school's capacity for managing change' (*ibid.*).

In this respect, school improvement efforts embody the core principles of the self-renewing school where change and development are owned by the school rather than imposed from outside (Hopkins *et al.*, 1996). School improvement as an approach to school self-renewal rests on a number of key assumptions (van Velzen *et al.*, 1985; Hopkins, 1987, 1990). These include the belief that schools have the capacity to improve themselves, that school improvement involves cultural change and that this is best achieved by working on the internal conditions within each individual school. In summary, school improvement is chiefly concerned with building the organizational capacity for change and growth (Hopkins *et al.*, 1994).

Over the past two decades, a large number of school improvement projects have emerged with different emphases, theoretical orientations and diverse approaches to school level change. The sheer diversity of programmes and approaches makes the task of providing an overview of school improvement developments both complex and daunting. However, it is possible to map the school improvement terrain by using a broad categorization established by Hopkins *et al.* (1994). They delineate improvement projects as *organic* or *mechanistic*. School improvement work that is *organic* suggests broad principles or general strategies within which schools are likely to flourish. Conversely, school improvement projects that are *mechanistic* provide direct guidelines and are highly specific in the strategies they prescribe. This broad classification provides a useful framework for mapping out the school improvement projects that have been most influential in the field.

In many respects, the International School Improvement Project (ISIP) laid the cornerstone for subsequent school improvement programmes (van Velzen *et al.*, 1985; Hopkins, 1987, 1995). Spanning four years from 1982 to 1986, this project co-ordinated by the OECD united fourteen countries and a wealth of expertise upon the subject of school improvement. The ISIP proposed a different way of thinking about school level change which contrasted with the 'top down' approaches of the 1970s. Taking the school as the centre of change, the project embodied the long-term goal of moving schools towards the position of self-renewal and growth. This *organic* approach to school improvement highlighted the importance of taking a multi-level perspective on school development and change.

Other highly successful school improvement projects have been formed on the basis that they promote a particular philosophy. Some of these projects have taken the form of networks where schools subscribe to a shared set of principles. In essence, these projects provide a 'school improvement club' where admission is dependent upon agreeing to a set of project rules and guidelines. James Comer's School Development Programme (Comer, 1988), the Coalition of Essential Schools (Sizer, 1992) and the League of Professional Schools at the University of Georgia led by Carl Glickman (1990) all fall into this category and have an increasing number of schools within their networks.

Another group of highly successful school improvement programmes have taken a less open-ended approach to school level change. These programmes include the Halton Project (Stoll and Fink, 1992), the Accelerated Schools Project (Levin, 1993), the IMTEC approach to institutional development in Norway (Dalin *et al.*, 1993) and certain approaches to restructuring in the USA (Elmore, 1990; Murphy and Louis, 1994). All these projects place the school at the focal point of change and engage them in the process of school growth planning. In addition, attention is also paid to the development of clear decision making structures and building collaborative cultures within schools (Stoll and Fink, 1996).

'Improving the Quality of Education for All' (IQEA) similarly focuses upon building collaborative cultures in schools. As one of the most successful school improvement projects in the UK, IQEA is premised on the view that 'without an equal focus on the development capacity, or internal conditions of the school, innovative work quickly becomes marginalized' (Hopkins and Harris, 1997, p. 3). The project has developed a number of associate 'conditions' at school and classroom level that support and sustain improvement (Ainscow *et al.*, 1994; Hopkins *et al.*, 1997). Each school within IQEA is encouraged to work upon the school level and classroom level conditions simultaneously. Essentially IQEA is a model of school change that is premised upon facilitating cultural change within schools. It is not prescriptive in terms of what schools actually do but does define the parameters for development. It provides an over-arching model for school improvement which schools subsequently adapt for their own purposes and fit to their particular needs and context. IQEA is research driven and encourages schools not only to engage in their own internal enquiry but also to utilize the external research base concerning effective teaching and learning.

Other school improvement projects which are *organic* in nature are those based upon a partnership model with schools and the local education authority (LEA). The Schools Make a Difference Project in London (Myers, 1995) and the Lewisham School Improvement Project characterize this type of approach. Both have specifically emphasized the role of the LEA in development and change. The impetus for change in these projects is locally owned, externally supported and school initiated.

At the other end of the school improvement spectrum are projects which fall into the *mechanistic* category in the respect that they advocate or prescribe a particular approach to school improvement. Early examples of such approaches include the self-managing approach to school improvement developed in the mid-1980s (Caldwell and Spinks, 1988). This approach has been widely disseminated and is based upon a management cycle that has six phases, i.e. goal setting, policy making, planning, preparation, implementation and evaluation. Although this cycle is now fairly commonplace, this 'step by step' approach has not proved successful with all schools. It is clear that this instrumental approach and others like it do not take into account the variability of schools and school context. Such *mechanistic* approaches presuppose uniformity both within the organization and across organizations.

The High Reliability Schools Project in the UK characterizes a school improvement project designed to ensure that there are high levels of conformity between schools. This project is based upon work (Stringfield, 1995) which argues that educational systems have much to learn from the organizational processes of highly reliable organizations within the corporate and state-owned sectors. The characteristics of highly reliable organizations include effective training programmes, concentration on a few goals, standard operation procedures, attention to minor detail and identifying and rectifying weak links. The project team believe that results will be dramatically improved pupil achievements and improved school quality, although as yet there is limited evidence to support this claim.

Examples of school improvement projects that are *mechanistic* and highly prescriptive are Bob Slavin's 'Success for All' project (Slavin *et al.*, 1996), Bruce Joyce's 'Models of Teaching' approach (Joyce *et al.*, 1997) and the Barclay Calvert Project (Stringfield, 1995). These approaches to school improvement have been carefully and systematically evaluated over a number of years. A substantial evidence base exists to support their positive impact on schools in the USA and in other countries (Slavin *et al.*, 1996, 1994; Joyce and Weil, 1996; Joyce *et al.*, 1997; Stringfield, 1995).

This overview of school improvement is intended to be illustrative rather than exhaustive. Many more school improvement projects exist in the field and new improvement initiatives seem to emerge daily. Unfortunately, despite the amount and range of school improvement activity, evidence concerning their effectiveness or impact is not always forthcoming. As a consequence much criticism of the school improvement field has focused upon the relative absence of evaluative evidence and it has been suggested that much school improvement work is 'little more than glorified staff development activity' (West and Hopkins, 1995). Whatever the legitimacy of this claim, there is an accumulating knowledge base about school improvement arising from the numerous projects and programmes around the world. This knowledge base has provided important insights into the process of school development and change.

THE CURRENT POSITION

The school improvement field has contributed to a better understanding of how change is initiated, implemented and institutionalized in schools (Fullan, 1991). It has provided many practical studies that have highlighted a number of important findings about the process of successful school level change. First, school improvement research has demonstrated the vital importance of teacher development in school level change. It has consistently shown that teacher development is inextricably linked to school development and is an essential part of school improvement (Hopkins *et al.*, 1994). Second, school improvement research has reinforced the importance of leadership in securing school level change. It has pointed to the limitations of singular leadership, emphasizing instead decentralized and participatory leadership rather than top-down delegation (Jackson, 2000).

Third, school improvement work has shown that there is no one blueprint for action for change or improvement in every type of school. It has directly challenged the assumption of the 'one size fits all' approach to improvement by demonstrating the importance of matching improvement strategy to school type (Hopkins *et al.*, 1997). Fourth, the school improvement movement has reinforced the necessity of relating change efforts to specific student outcomes. It has emphasized the importance of focusing attention at the student level and of improving teaching and learning conditions within the classroom (Hopkins *et al.*, 1997). Lastly, the school improvement movement has demonstrated the importance of understanding and working with school culture (Fullan and Hargreaves, 1991; Siskin, 1994). The field has consistently shown that a school culture that promotes collegiality, trust and collaborative working relation-ships and that focuses upon teaching and learning is more likely to be self renewing and responsive to improvement efforts (Hopkins, 1996).

Even though the school improvement research field has developed sub-stantially over recent years, a number of limitations within the field persist. For example, within the school improvement tradition, there tends to be an undifferentiated approach to schools of varying socio-economic circumstances (Lauder *et al.*, 1998). Little account is taken of culture, context, socio-economic status, catchment areas, the trajectory of improvement and, indeed, of all independent variables. It is only recently that the field has recognized the need to take into account contextual factors in selecting and applying school improvement strategies (Hopkins *et al.*, 1997).

Another limitation within the field concerns an overemphasis upon the school level. A number of the school improvement projects have failed to grapple with the complexity of change and development at different levels within the organization. There is a growing body of research within the school effectiveness field which points clearly to the need for school improvement to adopt a multi-level approach and to develop strategies which impact simulta-neously and consistently at whole school, department, teacher and pupil level. Teddlie and Reynolds (2000) suggest that 'those engaged in school improve-ment need urgently to pay attention to the implications of multilevel modelling procedures for their programmes' (p. 47).

It has also been suggested that the proliferation of school improvement initiatives has simply generated a proliferation of factors that 'seem to work' (Gray *et al.*, 1996a). While comparisons of various lists reveal a high degree of overlap, nonetheless there are differences of interpretation and emphasis. Until recently, cross-cultural comparisons of school improvement have been in relatively short supply. Limited evidence exists about the transferability of school improvement programmes into quite different cultural contexts (Harris and Hopkins, 2000).

Of most concern, however, is the fact that much school improvement research has tended to neglect the 'primacy of instruction' (Teddlie and Reynolds, 2000, p. 47). Despite a considerable amount of research highlighting the relationship between teacher effectiveness and school effectiveness (Creemers, 1994), few school improvement programmes have focused upon the classroom level (Teddlie and Reynolds, 2000).

In analysing the limitations of the school improvement field, a closer collaboration with school effectiveness would seem both an obvious and pragmatic solution. As Teddlie and Reynolds (2000) argue, 'the future benefits of a merger become even clearer if one considers how central the two disciplines or "paradigms" of scientific school effectiveness and humanistic school improvement are to each other' (p. 45). On the one hand, school improvement research offers an excellent testing ground for school effectiveness theory and a means of exploring the links between process and outcomes. On the other hand, school effectiveness offers school improvement a secure basis for making evaluative judgements about programme impact. Yet, despite sound arguments for a merger between the two fields, progress towards this end has been limited but possibilities for collaboration clearly exist.

TOWARDS A MERGER: POSSIBILITIES FOR COLLABORATION

While school effectiveness and school improvement research are very different in their core conceptualizations, beliefs and theoretical orientations there is evidence to suggest that their interests have started to converge. Reynolds *et al.* (2000) suggest that in the 1990s a number of projects emerged that borrowed from both the school effectiveness and school improvement literature. Projects such as 'Improving the Quality of Education for All' in the UK, the Barclay Calvert Project in the USA and the Halton Project in Canada are cited as examples of a successful blending of school effectiveness and school improvement research. They argue that these initiatives open the way for 'new wave' programmes that combine aspects of school effectiveness and school improvement research in ways appropriate 'to context, effectiveness level, culture, capacity for improvement and personal characteristics of staff employed at each school' (Reynolds and Creemer, 2000, p. 231).

While this optimism is to be welcomed, the challenge remaining for both fields is to seek ways to further collaborate and combine their respective research efforts. It is suggested that although the related fields of school effectiveness and school improvement are still in need of further research to consolidate their growing linkages, there are shared areas for future research and development. These areas provide an agenda for future collaboration and offer the potential to cross the methodological and theoretical 'divide'. The opportunities for closer collaboration between the two fields include the following:

DEVELOPING THEORY

A common source of concern amongst school effectiveness and school improvement researchers has been the theoretical development within their respective fields. Over a decade ago Scheerens and Creemers (1989) argued for the need for theory development in school effectiveness research. Angus (1993) noted 'when theory is mentioned at all, it is generally in terms of a positivist notion of incremental, empirical theory building which, consistent with the functionalist perspective of school effectiveness work, is directed at discovering "what works" (p. 335). With respect to school improvement, Brown *et al.* (1996) also highlight its theoretical limitations. They state that 'there is, nevertheless, little theory emanating from this large mass of work which directly and effectively addresses the question of how and why things work the way they do in schools, what alternatives there are for action for change and the implications of choosing among those alternatives' (p. 98).

This would suggest that in terms of theoretical development, school effectiveness and school improvement have much to gain from closer collaboration. Most recently, Sammons (1999) has endorsed this view by suggesting that it would benefit both fields greatly if there was further development to link the theoretical bases of school improvement and school effectiveness, 'particularly through the empirical testing and refinement of existing models' (p. 352).

TAKING A MULTILEVEL APPROACH

Within the school effectiveness and school improvement research communities there is a growing recognition of the need to focus attention upon different levels within the school organization. Traditionally, in both paradigms, the school level has received most attention. It has been viewed as the main unit of analysis and the centre of change. The 'whole school' approach to change and development has predominated with a few finely targeted programmes aimed at other levels within the school. However, there is an increasing volume of work that demonstrates the importance of taking a multilevel approach when considering school processes and outputs.

Within the school effectiveness field the popularity of multilevel modelling has created an interest in the 'interactions' or 'transactions' between levels (Teddlie and Stringfield, 1993). The work on measuring differential school effectiveness is now well developed and demonstrates the importance of taking a multilevel analysis of school differences (Goldstein, 1995). Similarly, within the school improvement field there has been a move towards a multilevel approach to change and intervention (Fullan, 1999). Developing differentiated strategies for change at various levels within the school organization is not yet well developed but preliminary work has been undertaken on this theme (Hopkins *et al.*, 1997; Harris, 1999; Harris and Hopkins, 2000). Closer collaboration between the fields would not only assist in the generation of differentiated school improvement strategies but would also enable evidence about the effectiveness of such strategies to be collected.

TAKING ACCOUNT OF CONTEXT

Researchers involved in both fields have been urged to take more account of context. Taking into account relevant socio-economic factors in studies of school effectiveness and school improvement has been shown to be of increasing importance. School effectiveness research has shown that certain context variables, i.e. socio-economic status of the student body, community type, governance structure, are important factors when measuring the school effect (Teddlie and Reynolds, 2000). Similarly, school improvement research has highlighted the need to take greater account of school context in selecting school improvement strategies and interventions (Hopkins, Harris and Jackson, 1997).

Sammons (1999) notes that 'overall, it appears that, at the secondary level, there is some evidence of important contextual effects related to schools' pupil composition in terms of [SES] socio-economic status, ethnicity and ability of prior attainment' (p. 94). While the impact of context variables is well established within school effectiveness research, Teddlie and Reynolds (2000) suggest that researchers should enhance the variation in context factors where possible. Within school improvement, Hopkins *et al.* (1997) have highlighted the importance of context variables in deciding upon appropriate school improvement strategies or interventions. They argue that there is an urgent need to expand knowledge and understanding of 'context specific improvement'. Consequently, further exploration of the relationship between context and effectiveness/improvement offers both fields scope for mutual research and development.

GENERATING CASE STUDIES

Within the school improvement and school effectiveness research traditions, finely grained case studies of either effective or ineffective schools or improving or failing schools are not prevalent. In the USA, there are a number of effectiveness studies that offer rich insights into the school and classroom processes within effective schools. For example, the Louisiana School Effectiveness Study by Teddlie and Stringfield (1993) offers an in-depth description of practices within schools in the study. Similarly, *Improving the Urban High School* (Louis and Miles, 1990) provides excellent case studies of process variables and remains unsurpassed. UK case studies of improving schools are emerging (Gray *et al.*, 1998) but, until recently, most case-study accounts of improving schools have tended to reside at the level of general description.

In addition, the case-study evidence that does exist has concentrated largely on effective or improving schools. With a few notable exceptions (Stoll and Myers, 1997; Sarason, 1990), 'failing' or 'sick' schools have not been at the forefront of enquiry in either field. Detailed accounts of schools in difficulty have only just begun to emerge (Stoll and Myers, 1997) along with evidence that different school improvement strategies will be needed for 'failing schools' (Hopkins *et al.*, 1997). Consequently, rich case-study explanations combining the expertise from both fields are much needed.

USING MULTIPLE OUTCOME MEASURES

School improvement research has rarely concerned itself with measuring the impact of a development or intervention in terms of student outcomes. There has been a tendency for school improvement researchers to place an emphasis upon 'process' rather than 'outcomes'. Possibly, part of this reticence lies in a 'reluctance to be explicit about the goals of their programmes' (Teddlie and Reynolds, 2000, p. 47). There are some exceptions to this dominant trend, for example Slavin's 'Success for All' project collects and makes extensive use of outcome data to measure the impact of the programme upon students' reading levels. However, for many school improvement programmes, the absence of data prevents any gauge of impact or effectiveness.

Critics of school effectiveness research have noted that to use a single outcome measure, in particular academic achievement, is an inadequate method of ascertaining the true level of effectiveness in any one school. It is now recognized by the field that multiple outcome measures are required to explore, capture and compare levels of effectiveness (Teddlie and Stringfield, 1993; Fitz-Gibbon, 1996). The challenge facing the school effectiveness field is to generate multiple outcome measures that can be used by school improvement to judge the effectiveness of a programme or intervention. In achieving this, researchers in both communities will be better placed to understand the possible causal relationships between school processes and school outcomes.

COMMENTARY

These possibilities for future collaboration remain speculative and tentative. Integrating the two knowledge bases will not be a simple or straightforward matter. As Gray *et al.* (1996b) suggest, 'there are some more fundamental barriers to linking the knowledge of "what works" from the two paradigms with their respective commitments to understanding "effectiveness" and "improvement" (p. 172). One important barrier concerns the different way in which each field conceptualizes school performance. School effectiveness typically focuses upon outcome measurement while school improvement is more concerned with internal change processes. Successful integration therefore implies encompassing both approaches within a single framework of assessment. Gray *et al.* (1996b) have made considerable progress in this area by developing a framework for integrating effectiveness and improvement. Their innovative and powerful analysis illustrates the possibility and potential of combining the two research fields.

If both fields are to make significant advances in the next decade much will depend upon closer collaboration. Areas of overlap exist and there are gaps in knowledge that demand joint exploration. Much will depend upon the willingness of researchers in both fields to combine their considerable knowledge, expertise and understanding to reconceptualize school effectiveness and school improvement (West and Hopkins, 1996). From this reconceptualization will emerge a better understanding about the practices that result in improved educational outcomes for all students.

NOTE

1. See Teddlie, C. and Reynolds, D. (2000) *The International Handbook of School Effectiveness Research* for a comprehensive overview of school effectiveness research.

REFERENCES

Ainscow, M., Hopkins, D., Southworth, G. and West, M. (1994) *Creating the Conditions for School Improvement.* London: David Fulton Publishers.
Angus, L. (1993) 'The sociology of school effectiveness', *British Journal of Sociology of Education* **14**(3): 333–45.
Berman, P. and McLaughlin, M. (1978) 'Implementation of educational innovation', *Educational Forum* **40**(3): 345–70.
Brown, S., Riddell, S. and Duffield, J. (1996) 'Possibilities and problems of small scale studies to unpack the findings of large scale studies of school effectiveness', in J. Gray, D. Reynolds, C. T. Fitz-Gibbon and D. Jesson (eds) *Merging Traditions: The Future of Research on School Effectiveness and School Improvement.* London: Cassell.
Caldwell, B. and Spinks, J. (1988) *The Self Managing School.* Lewes: Falmer Press.
Coleman, J. S., Campbell, E., Hobson, C., McPartland, J., Mood, A., Weinfield, R. and York, R. (1966) *Equality of Educational Opportunity.* Washington, DC: Government Printing Office.
Comer, J. (1988) 'Educating poor minority children', *Scientific American*, November, 42–8.
Crandall, D., Eiseman, J. and Louis, K. (1986) 'Strategic planning issues that bear on the success of school improvement efforts', *Educational Administration Quarterly* **22**(2): 21–53.
Creemers, B. P. M. (1994) *The Effective Classroom.* London: Cassell.

Dalin, P. with Rolff, H.-G. and Kleekamp, B. (1993) *Changing the School Culture.* London: Cassell.

Daly, P. (1991) 'How large are secondary school effects in Northern Ireland?', *School Effectiveness and School Improvement* 2(4): 305–23.

Edmonds, R. (1979) 'Some schools work and more can', *Social Policy* 9 28–32.

Elliott, J. (1996) 'School effectiveness research and its critics: alternative visions of schooling', *Cambridge Journal of Education* 26(2): 199–224.

Elmore, R. (1990) *Restructuring Schools.* Oakland, CA: Jossey-Bass.

Firestone, W. A. (1991) 'Introduction', in J. R. Bliss, W. A. Firestone and C. E. Richards (eds) *Rethinking Effective Schools: Research and Practice.* Englewood Cliffs, NJ: Prentice Hall.

Fitz-Gibbon, C. T. (1996) *Monitoring Education: Indicators, Quality and Effectiveness.* London and New York: Cassell.

Fitz-Gibbon, C. T. (1992) 'School effects at A level: genesis of an information system?', in D. Reynolds and P. Cuttance (eds) *School Effectiveness: Research, Policy and Practice.* London: Cassell.

Fullan, M. (1991) *The New Meaning of Educational Change.* London: Cassell.

Fullan, M. (1992) *Successful School Improvement.* Buckingham: Open University Press.

Fullan, M. (1999) *Change Forces: The Sequel.* London: Falmer Press.

Fullan, M. and Hargreaves, A. (1991) *What's Worth Fighting for? Working Together for Your School.* Toronto: Ontario Public School Teachers' Federation.

Glickman, C. (1990) 'Pushing school reforms to a new edge: the seven ironies of school empowerment', *Phi Delta Kappan,* May, 68–75.

Goldstein, H. (1995) *Multilevel Statistical Models* (2nd edn). London: Edward Arnold and New York: Halsted Press.

Goldstein, H., Rabash, J., Yang, M., Woodhouse, G., Pan, H., Nuttall, D., and Thomas, S. (1993) 'A multilevel analysis of school examination results', *Oxford Review of Education* 19 (4): 425–33.

Goldstein, H. and Sammons, P. (1995) *The Influence of Secondary and Junior Schools on Sixteen Year Examination Performance: A Cross-Classified Multilevel Analysis.* London: ISEIC, Institute of Education.

Gray, J., Goldstein, H. and Jesson, D. (1996a) 'Changes and improvement in school effectiveness: Trends over five years', *Research Papers in Education* 11(1): 35–51.

Gray, J., Jesson, D. and Simes, N. (1990) 'Estimating differences in the examination performance of secondary schools in six LEAs – A multi-level approach to school effectiveness', *Oxford Review of Education* 16(2): 137–56.

Gray, J., Reynolds, D., Fitz-Gibbon, C. T. and Jesson, D. (eds) (1996b) *Merging Traditions: The Future of Research on School Effectiveness and School Improvement.* London: Cassell.

Gray, J., Reynolds, D. and Hopkins, D. (1998) *A Longitudinal Study of School Change and Improvement (The Improving Schools Research Project),* ESRC End of Award Report R000 235864. Cambridge: Homerton College.

Hamilton, D. (1998) 'The idols of the market place', in R. Slee, G. Weiner and S. Tomlinson (eds) *School Effectiveness for Whom'.* London: Falmer Press.

Harris, A. (1999) *Teaching and Learning in the Effective School.* London: Arena Press.

Harris, A. and Hopkins, D. (2000) 'Alternative perspectives on school improvement', *School Leadership and Management* 20(1): 9–15.

Harris, A., Jamieson, I. M. and Russ, J. (1995) 'A study of "effective" departments in secondary schools', *School Organisation* 15(3): 16.

Harris, A. and Young, J. (2000) 'Comparing school improvement programmes in the United Kingdom and Canada: lessons learned', *School Leadership and Management* 17(3): 401–11.

Hopkins, D. (1987) *Improving the Quality of Schooling.* Lewes: Falmer Press.

Hopkins, D. (1990) 'The International School Improvement Project (ISIP) and effective schooling: towards a synthesis', *School Organisation* **10**(3): 129–94.

Hopkins, D. (1994) 'School improvement in an era of change', Chapter 6, in P. Ribbins and E. Burridge (eds) *Improving Education: Promoting Quality in Schools.* London: Cassell.

Hopkins, D. (1995) 'Towards effective school improvement', *School Effectiveness and School Improvement* **6**(3): 265–74.

Hopkins, D. (1996) 'Towards a theory for school improvement', in J. Gray, D. Reynolds, C. T. Fitz-Gibbon and D. Jesson (eds) *Merging Traditions: The Future of Research on School Effectiveness and School Improvement.* London: Cassell.

Hopkins, D., Ainscow, M. and West, M. (1994) *School Improvement in an Era of Change.* London: Cassell.

Hopkins, D., Ainscow, M. and West, M. (1996) 'Unravelling the complexities of school improvement: a case study of the Improving the Quality of Education for All (IQEA) Project', in Open University Course E838 reader, *Organisational Effectiveness and Improvement in Education.*

Hopkins, D. and Harris, A. (1997) 'Improving the quality of education for all', *Support for Learning* **12**(4): 147–51.

Hopkins, D., Harris, A. and Jackson, D. (1997) 'Understanding the school's capacity for development: growth states and strategies', *School Leadership and Management* **17**(3): 401–11.

Hopkins, D. and Lagerwelj, N. (1996) *Making Good Schools: Linking School Effectiveness and School Improvement,* Chapter 4. London: Routledge.

Hopkins, D. and West, M. (1994) 'Teacher development and school improvement', in D. Walling *Teachers as Learners.* Bloomington, Ind.: PDK.

Hopkins, D., West, M., Ainscow, M., Harris, A. and Beresford, J. (1997) *Creating the Conditions for Classroom Improvement.* London: David Fulton Publishers.

Jackson, D. (2000) 'The school improvement journey: perspectives on leadership', *School Leadership and Management* **20**(1): 61–79.

Jencks, C. S., Smith, D., Ackland, H., Bane, M. J., Cohen, D., Ginter, H., Heyns, B. and Michelson, S. (1972) *Inequality: A reassessment of the effect of the family and schooling in America.* New York: Basic Books.

Jesson, D. and Gray, J. (1991) 'Slants on slopes: using multi-level models to investigate differential school effectiveness and its impact on pupils' examination results', *School Effectiveness and School Improvement* **2**(3): 230–47.

Joyce, B. and Weil, M. (1996) *Models of Teaching* (4th edn). Englewood Cliffs, NJ: Prentice-Hall.

Joyce, B., Calhoun, E. and Hopkins, D. (1997) *Models of Learning: Tools for Teaching.* Buckingham: Open University Press.

Lauder, H., Jamieson, I. and Wikely, F. (1998) 'Models of effectiveness: limits and capacities', in R. Slee, G. Weiner and S. Tomlinson (eds) *School Effectiveness for Whom? Challenges to the School Effectiveness and School Improvement Movement,* pp. 51–69. London: Falmer Press.

Levin, H. (1993) 'Learning from accelerated schools', in Block, H.J., Everson, S.T. and Guskey, T. R. (eds) *Selecting and Integrating School Improvement Programs.* New York: Scholastic Books.

Levine, D. and Lezotte, L. (1990) *Unusually Effective Schools: A Review and Analysis of Research and Practice.* Madison, WI: National Centre for Effective Schools Research and Development.

Louis, K. S. and Miles, M. B. (1990) *Improving the Urban High School: What Works and Why.* New York: Teachers College Press.

Morley, L. and Rassol, N. (1999) *School Effectiveness: Fracturing the Discourse,* London: Falmer Press.

Mortimore, P. (1991) 'The nature and findings of school effectiveness research in the primary sector', in S. Riddell and S. Brown (eds) *School Effectiveness Research: Its Messages for School Improvement.* London: HMSO.

Mortimore, P. (1995) *Effective Schools: Current Impact and Future Possibilities.* The Director's Inaugural Lecture, 7 February 1995, London: Institute of Education, University of London.

Mortimore, P., Sammons, P. and Thomas, S. (1994) 'School effectiveness and value added measures', *Assessment in Education: Principles, Policy and Practice* **1**(3): 315–32.

Mortimore, P., Sammons, P., Stoll, L., Lewis, D. and Ecob, R. (1988) *School Matters: the Junior Years.* Wells, Somerset: Open Books.

Murphy, J. and Louis, K. S. (1994) *Reshaping Principalship: Insights from Transformational Reform Efforts.* Thousand Oaks: Corwin Press.

Myers, K. (ed.) (1995) *School Improvement in Practice: Schools Make a Difference Project.* London: Falmer Press.

Nuttall, D. (1990) *Differences in Examination Performance*, RS 1277/90 London, Research and Statistics Branch, ILEA.

Nuttall, D., Goldstein, H., Prosser, R. and Rabash, J. (1989) 'Differential school effectiveness', *International Journal of Educational Research* **13**: 769–76.

Reynolds, D. (1985) *Studying School Effectiveness.* Lewes: Falmer Press.

Reynolds, D. and Creemers, B. (1990) 'School effectiveness and school improvement: A mission statement', *School Effectiveness and School Improvement* **1**(1): 1–3.

Reynolds, D. and Cuttance, P. (eds) (1992) *School Effectiveness.* London: Cassell.

Reynolds, D., Hopkins, D. and Stoll, L. (1993) 'Linking school effectiveness knowledge and school improvement practice: towards a synergy', *School Effectiveness and School Improvement* **4**(1): 37–58.

Reynolds, D. and Teddlie, C. (2000) 'Linking school effectiveness and school improvement', in Teddlie, C. and Reynolds, D. (2000) *International Handbook of School Effectiveness Research.* London: Falmer Press.

Reynolds, D., Teddlie, C., Creemers, B., Scheerens, J. and Townsend, T. (2000) 'An introduction to School Effectiveness Research', in Teddlie, C. and Reynolds, D. (2000) *International Handbook of School Effectiveness Research.* London: Falmer Press.

Riddell, A. R. (1995) *School Effectiveness and School Improvement in the Third World: A Stock-Taking and Implications for the Development of Indicators.* London: Institute of Education, University of London.

Rutter, M., Maughan, B., Mortimore, P. and Ouston, J. (1979) *Fifteen Thousand Hours.* London: Open Books.

Sammons, P. (1999) *School Effectiveness Coming of Age in the Twenty-First Century.* The Netherlands: Swets and Zetlinger.

Sammons, P., Cuttance, P., Nuttall, D. and Thomas, S. (1995) 'Continuity of school effects: A longitudinal analysis of primary and secondary school effects on GCSE performance', *School Effectiveness and School Improvement* **6**(4): 285–307.

Sammons, P., Thomas, S. and Mortimore, P. (1996) 'Differential school effectiveness: departmental variations in GCSE attainment', paper presented at the School Effectiveness and Improvement Symposium of the annual conference of the American Educational Research Association, New York, 8 April 1996.

Sammons, P., Thomas, S. and Mortimore, P. (1997) *Forging Links: Effective Schools and Effective Departments.* London: Paul Chapman Publishing.

Sarason, S. (1990) *The Predictable Failure of Educational Reform.* San Francisco: Jossey-Bass.

Scheerens, J. (1992) *Effective Schooling: Research, Theory and Practice.* London: Cassell.

Scheerens, J. and Creemers, B. (1989) (eds) 'Developments in school effectiveness research', *International Journal of Educational Research* **13**(7): 23–38.

Siskin, L. S. (1994) *Realms of Knowledge: Academic Departments in Secondary Schools.* London: Falmer Press.

Sizer, T. (1992) *Horace's School.* New York: Houghton Mifflin.

Slavin, R., Madden, N. A., Dolan, L. J. and Wasik, B. A. (1996) *Every Child, Every School: Success for All.* Thousand Oaks, CA: Corwin Press.

Slavin, R., Madden, N. A., Karweit, N. L., Dolan, L., Wasik, B. A., Ross, S. M. and Smith, L. J. (1994) 'Whenever and wherever we choose: The replication of "Success for All" ', *Phi Delta Kappan,* April, 639–47.

Slee, R., Weiner, G. and Tomlinson, S. (eds) (1998) *School Effectiveness for Whom? Challenges to the School Effectiveness and School Improvement Movements.* London: Falmer Press.

Smith, D. J. and Tomlinson, S. (1989) *The School Effect: A Study of Multi-Racial Comprehensives.* London: Policy Studies Institute.

Stoll, L. (1996) 'Linking school effectiveness and school improvement: issues and possibilities', in J. Gray, D. Reynolds, C. T. Fitz-Gibbon and D. Jesson (eds) *Merging Traditions: The Future of Research on School Effectiveness and School Improvement.* London: Cassell.

Stoll, L. and Fink, D. (1992) 'Effecting school change: the Halton approach', *School Effectiveness and School Improvement* **3**(1): 19–41.

Stoll, L. and Fink, D. (1996) *Changing Our Schools: Linking School Effectiveness and School Improvement.* Buckingham: Open University Press.

Stoll, L. and Myers, K. (1997) *No Quick Fixes: Perspectives on Schools in Difficulty.* London: Falmer Press.

Stringfield, S. (1995) 'Attempting to enhance students' learning through innovative programs: the case for schools evolving into high reliability organisations', *School Effectiveness and School Improvement* **6**(1): 67–96.

Teddlie, C. and Reynolds, D. (2000) *The International Handbook of School Effectiveness Research.* London: Falmer Press.

Teddlie, C. and Stringfield, S. (1993) *Schools Do Make a Difference: Lessons Learned from a 10-year Study of School Effects.* New York: Teachers College Press.

Thomas, S. and Mortimore, P. (1996) 'Comparison of value added models for secondary school effectiveness' *Research Papers in Education* **11**(1): 5–33.

Thomas, S., Sammons, P. and Mortimore, P. (1994) 'Stability and consistency in secondary schools' effects on students' GCSE outcomes'. Paper presented at the annual conference of the British Educational Research Association, 9 September, St Anne's College, University of Oxford.

Thomas, S., Sammons, P. and Mortimore, P. (1995) 'Stability and consistency in secondary school effects on students' outcomes over 3 years'. Paper presented at ICSEI, 3–6 January, Leeuwarden, The Netherlands.

Thomas, S., Sammons, P., and Mortimore, P. and Smees, R. (1997) 'Stability and consistency in secondary schools' effects on students' GCSE outcomes over 3 years', *School Effectiveness and School Improvement* **8**(2): 169–97.

West, M. D. and Hopkins, D. (1995) 'Re-emphasising school effectiveness and school improvement'. Paper presented to the European Educational Research Association Conference, University of Bath.

West, M. D. and Hopkins, D. (1996) 'School effectiveness and school improvement: towards a reconceptualisation'. Paper presented to the American Educational Research Association Conference, New York.

Wilms, D. (1992) *Monitoring School Performance: A Guide for Educators.* London: Falmer Press.

van Velzen, W. G., Miles, M. B., Ekholm, M., Hameyer, U. and Robin, D. (1985) *Making School Improvement Work.* Leuven/Amersfoort: Academic Publishing Company.

Chapter 3

Beyond School Effectiveness and School Improvement?

David Reynolds

INTRODUCTION

The disciplines of school effectiveness and school improvement are both very young, set against the other disciplines of education such as psychology, sociology or, for that matter, research on educational policy. Neither discipline has been in existence for more than fifteen or twenty years. However, it seems that both disciplines are now quite central ones in many countries of the world and that their growth in terms of the number of persons involved in the areas, the impact of the research and the general 'reputational' criteria of the fields is impressive.

What this chapter attempts to do is threefold. It describes the historical origins of school effectiveness research and the ways in which the field has attempted recently to 'move on' to reinvent and change itself, intellectually and practically. It then describes school improvement as a field and outlines how it too has changed over time. It then attempts to outline the contemporary thinking that has been generated by the 'merger' of the school effectiveness and improvement paradigms and to speculate upon the prospects for both effectiveness and improvement continuing to make the same progress as a merged discipline that they have as separate ones.

SCHOOL EFFECTIVENESS

The first achievement of the discipline has been to invent itself, probably the most successful disciplinary invention since that of teacher effectiveness in the late 1970s. The international journal *School Effectiveness and School Improvement* began in 1991 and, judged in terms of the impact of the material it has published measured in citation counts, sits around number 30 in the international rankings, a remarkable and unprecedented achievement for such an infant publication. The field has a professional association, The International Congress for School Effectiveness and Improvement, whose meetings now regularly command four-figure attendance and whose proceedings have regularly been published as best-selling volumes. The field now exhibits all the characteristics of a mature normal science, with the publication of *The International Handbook of School Effectiveness Research* (Teddlie and Reynolds, 2000), an international review of the literally thousands of studies that have been conducted in the last twenty years.

The reasons for this success are undoubtedly due to certain organizing characteristics. In the early stages of a field, there is much evidence from other applied sciences that what generates rapid advance is the generation of a 'taken for granted' position in terms of an agreed world view. As an example, physiology made rapid progress in the last century through its alliance with clinical medicine, which forced the discipline to concentrate upon the problems that needed solution, rather than indulge in the philosophical speculation that had characterized the discipline until then. The concentration within school effectiveness upon 'problems as taken' rather than on 'problematizing problems' has prevented the kind of values debate that disabled British sociology of education in the 1970s, in which the nature of problems and of knowledge was relativized with catastrophic results.

Two other factors have been important in helping school effectiveness to advance. First, one of the distinguishing characteristics of school effectiveness is its internationalization in terms of the very wide range of countries that have been interacting. Probably 50 countries regularly send delegates to the annual meeting – probably half a dozen have research and practice communities in excess of 50 persons. Because the discipline has strength across countries and because it started as a truly internationalized group of persons, it has been able to gain considerable progress from the interaction between persons, contexts and traditions. Put simply, it had built-in variation from its inception.

Second, disciplinary advance has been furthered by the possession of an agreed methodology, which can loosely be called positivistic, that has generated a common set of judgements as to which knowledge is valid and which is invalid. There is, of course, within the discipline a range of different kinds of data that are collected and interpreted – one can find mixed methods, some historical scholarship, some qualitative research and a great deal of conventional quantitative material. What cannot be found, though, is the belief that valid knowledge should not be separated from invalid knowledge because of the difficulty of the process.

Generating a valid knowledge base

The second achievement of the discipline has been to generate normal science in terms of an agreed set of findings concerning such issues as the size of school effects, their consistency, the processes within schools and classrooms associated with effectiveness and the possible 'context specificity' of these process factors (see review in Teddlie and Reynolds, 2000). After a promising start in the publications by Brookover and colleagues (1979) and Rutter and colleagues (1979) in the late 1970s, a redirection of research subsequently took place, generating more and better designed studies in many different countries. Progress has been made and research has produced substantive findings in the following effectiveness areas:

- The development of a different range of outcome measures to measure school effects, not only in the cognitive domain and that of basic skills but also in other social and affective areas. Connected with this research base has been the development of the concept and 'technology' of added value and associated research on the stability of school outcomes over time and the consistency between school subjects in their effects.
- The size of the 'educational' effect has been discussed and established in several research projects, especially related to different levels in the educational systems (e.g. classroom, school). Useful discussion has taken place on how to present the 'effect size' and on how to show the relevance of the contributions of classrooms, schools and the other levels in the educational system to the explanation of the results.
- Important progress has been made in the conceptualization and measurement of processes at different levels of the educational system. This has made it possible to have more precision with respect to the contributions of education in general to outcomes at the different levels and to understand the factors associated with effectiveness at the different levels. Research has been carried out to examine whether the effects are causal, linear or non-linear and on the interaction between levels. Several models of these interactions have been developed and have been tested in simulation studies.
- The great majority of the research studies have continued to focus upon the factors and variables at the different levels that cause or contribute to effectiveness. Additionally, the differences between countries in the factors that explain the variance on outcomes have also been investigated. After a period of adding more and more factors and variables, these lists of variables, factors and characteristics were scrutinized, condensed and codified into blocks of characteristics and factors that might be important (e.g. as undertaken by Levine and Lezotte (1990) in the United States and by Sammons (1999) in the United Kingdom).
- The next step was to develop models that are more theoretically based or oriented, or at least to generate more 'theoretical' explanations for the differences in educational outcomes between students, classrooms, schools and contexts, both within nations and internationally. One way of doing this was to refer to learning theories, especially theories orientated towards learning in schools, like the Carroll (1963) model, or to make use of classical sociological organizational theories, especially for the school and contextual levels.

- Major progress has also been made by further development in the method-ology of research, for example in the use of qualitative methodology for case studies. In this way, it has been possible to come up with explanations and in-depth analyses of effectiveness. The development of multilevel and causal analyses has made it possible to test on larger datasets various models of effectiveness and to look for explanations of those effects. Also, the avail-ability and the development of cohort studies has made it possible, connected with the survey nature of those studies, to have much larger datasets that include information on processes, input and context.

Improving the chances of educational advance

The third contribution has been to improve the prospects of productive educational change by combating some of the pessimism that was the product of analyses in the 1970s and 1980s. It is precisely this relevance and optimism that has made school effectiveness into perhaps the most used body of knowledge in education by practitioners, certainly in the United Kingdom and perhaps elsewhere.

First, it has convincingly helped to destroy the belief that schools can do nothing to change the society around them, and has also helped to destroy the myth that the influence of family background on children's development is so strong that they are unable to be affected by school. Twenty years ago there was a widespread belief that 'schools make no difference' (Bernstein, 1968) which reflected the results of American research (e.g. Coleman *et al.*, 1966; Jencks *et al.*, 1972) and the disappointed hopes that followed from the per-ceived failure of systemic reform, enhanced expenditure and the other policies of social engineering that constituted the liberal dream of the 1960s. Addition-ally, twenty years ago there was an educational research paradigm in which the belief that families were the sole determinants of children's 'educability' and the associated belief that schools had minimal effects generated research which, in its basic research strategies and structure, reinforced the paradigm that had created it in the first place.

The second positive effect of school effectiveness research is that in addition to destroying assumptions of the impotence of education, and maybe also helping to reduce the prevalence of family background being given as an excuse for educational failure by teachers, we have taken as our defining variables the key factors of school and pupil outcomes, from which we 'back map' to look at the processes which appear to be related to positive outcomes. Not for us in school effectiveness the celebration of new policies because they are new or because practitioners like them. For us, our 'touchstone criteria' to be applied to all educational matters concern whether children learn more or less because of the policy or practice.

Third, we have in our studies continuously shown teachers to be important

determinants of children's educational and social attainments and have therefore, hopefully, managed to enhance and build professional self-esteem.

Fourth, we have begun the creation of a 'known to be valid' knowledge base
which can act as a foundation for training (see reviews in Reynolds and
Cuttance, 1992; Mortimore, 1998; Rutter, 1983; Scheerens and Bosker, 1997).
With knowledge of school and of teacher effectiveness, the latter of which has
unfortunately to be imported from North America because of the historic
antipathy towards research in this area in some countries (see Creemers, 1994),
we can avoid the necessity of the endless reinvention of the 'teaching wheel'
and can move teachers to an advanced level conceptually and practically.

The school effectiveness cutting edge

School effectiveness now exhibits increasing intellectual sophistication, as
recent reviews make clear (Teddlie and Reynolds, 2000). In two particular
areas there is interesting work taking place.

First, there are now a number of datasets across a variety of national
contexts which suggest that family background and school quality may be
related, with consequent considerable importance both for the children affected and for educational policy in general. Work in Sweden by Grosin (1993)
and in the United States by Teddlie (1996) shows that even after one has
controlled out the effects of individual pupil background factors and/or
achievement levels, there is a tendency for schools in low socio-economic
status areas to do worse than one would have predicted and for schools in
middle-class areas to do better. Particularly marked is the existence of a group
of schools 'below the regression line' in disadvantaged communities, even
though such schools have often been the source of additional financial resources to help them improve and even though they have often attracted
considerable attention from educational reformers.

What may be happening, then, is that school and home have additive effects,
a possibility also suggested in an intriguing study of male delinquency by
Farrington (1980), in which schools acted to increase the levels of delinquency
when the prediction was already for a high rate, and to lower it below
prediction when that prediction was for a low rate. From within recent writing
on dysfunctional schools noted earlier (Reynolds, 1991, 1996; Stoll *et al.*, 1996)
has also come an appreciation of the depth of problems that schools in this
category can face, an appreciation now increasingly shared by those school
improvers who are attempting to unravel the complexities of such schools
(Hopkins, 1996).

The 'additive' idea is an important one, since it might explain that most
persistent finding of all post-war educational reform – that social-class inequality in access to educational qualifications has been largely unchanged by
educational 'improvement' on both quantity and quality dimensions. It also
integrates the two literatures which have appeared to be at cross purposes,

much to the detriment of the mutual understanding of the scholars working in the two fields – that from the sociology of education which stresses the influence of social structure, and that from school effectiveness which stresses the independent effects of schools. Schools do make a difference in this formulation but that difference acts to reinforce pre-existing differences in the structure of society.

We still need to know, of course, why there is this tendency for the less effective schools to be in more disadvantaged areas. Differential quality in schools' teacher supply may be a factor, given the likelihood of a greater number of applications for jobs being in schools in advantaged areas. The 'drift' of good people to more socially advantaged settings, offering expanding job prospects because of population growth and a less stressful environment, may also be a factor, as may the tendency for high stress situations such as the education of the disadvantaged to find 'flaws' and 'weaknesses' in organizational arrangements and personnel that would not occur in the absence of the 'stressors' that are associated with disadvantage.

Second, it is obvious from all literature reviews (Scheerens and Bosker, 1997; Reynolds and Cuttance, 1992) that the study of curricular variation within and between schools has not been a focus over the last three decades of school effectiveness research. The orientation of researchers has been towards a behavioural, technicist approach in which the 'vessel' of the school is studied rather than the 'contents'. The explanation for this is that school effectiveness research has been well aware of the immense difficulties involved in measuring the variable 'curriculum'. Time allocated to curricular knowledge in general has not been difficult to measure, likewise the time allocation to different subject groups (see, for example, the results of international surveys reported in Reynolds and Farrell, 1996). However, attempts to move further and develop typologies of curriculum content and organization, along continua such as 'open/closed', 'traditional/new', or 'culturally relevant/culturally elitist' have resulted in the expenditure of considerable effort for very little reward! Indeed, perhaps the best-known attempt to organize and analyse curriculum as *knowledge*, that of Bernstein (1968), was systematically destroyed by the work of King (1983), who noted that there was in reality only perhaps a tenth of relationships between curricular variables that was in the direction predicted by Bernstein's theory of classification and framing.

Whilst the neglect of curricular issues is not surprising, there is now a recognition that such neglect may be damaging the field. Partly this is because any reluctance to think about curricular issues cuts the field off from the very widespread discussions now in progress about the most appropriate bodies of knowledge that should be in the schools of a 'post modern age' or an 'information economy and society'. As an example, metacognitive skills are currently receiving a considerable amount of attention, in which learning is seen as an active process in which students construct knowledge and skills by working with the content (Resnick *et al.*, 1992). The new metacognitive theories differ considerably from the traditional views that are on offer historically within school effectiveness research, in which teacher instruction generates the possibility of a student mastering the task, with the knowledge being mainly declarative (how it works) and procedural (how to do it). With metacognitive theorizing the focus is more upon conditional knowledge (how to decide what to do and when to do it). The old model of instruction that school effectiveness research represents aims mainly at the direct transfer and the reproduction of existing knowledge as it is defined by schools and teachers in curricula, while the new model of instruction takes the learning of strategies by students as the centre of attention. These new models see a consequent need to change the role of the teacher, since the student being responsible for his or her own learning means that the teacher is no longer the person who instructs but is rather the person who now teaches the techniques and strategies that students need to use to construct their own knowledge.

School effectiveness research is therefore now engaging with, and learning from, the new paradigms in the field of learning and instruction. Additionally, it is learning from and debating with those who argue for a new range of social or affective outcomes to be introduced that are relevant to the highly complex, fast-moving world of the new millennium (see Stoll and Fink, 1996), in which personal affective qualities become of greater importance because knowledge itself is easily accessible through information technology.

SCHOOL IMPROVEMENT

The disciplinary area of school improvement has gone through a number of phases. The first phase, which dated from the mid 1960s to the 1970s, was the emphasis on the adoption of curriculum materials. On both sides of the Atlantic, the curriculum reform movement was intended to have a major impact on student achievement through the production and dissemination of exemplary curriculum materials. Although the materials were often of high quality, being produced by teams of academics and psychologists, in the main they failed to have an impact on teaching. The reason with hindsight is obvious; teachers were not included in the production process and the in-service training that accompanied the new curricula was often perfunctory and rudimentary. Teachers simply took what they thought was of use to them from the new materials and integrated it into their own teaching. The curriculum innovation, however, was consequently subverted.

The second phase – covering most of the 1970s – was essentially one of documenting failure, the failure of the curriculum reform movement to affect practice. It became increasingly apparent from this work that 'top–down' models of change did not work, that teachers required in-service training to acquire new knowledge and skills and that implementation did not occur spontaneously as a result of legislative fiat. It was clear that implementation is an extremely complex and lengthy process that required a sensitive combination of strategic planning and individual learning and commitment to succeed.

Much was learned about implementation during this period that was to lay the basis for future work.

The third phase, roughly from the late 70s to mid 80s, was a period of success. It was during this time that the first studies of school effectiveness were published in Britain (Rutter *et al.*, 1979; Reynolds, 1976) and that a consensus was established in the United States as to the characteristics of effective schools (Purkey and Smith, 1983; Wilson and Corcoran, 1988). It was also during this period that some major large-scale studies of school improvement projects were conducted (Crandall *et al.*, 1982, 1986; Huberman and Miles, 1984; Hargreaves, 1984; Rosenholz, 1989; Louis and Miles, 1990). Much was consequently learned about the dynamics of the change process. The OECD International School Improvement Project (ISIP) was also at work at this time, producing case studies of, and developing strategies for, school improvement (for an overview see van Velzen *et al.*, 1985; Hopkins, 1987). A number of syntheses of the work during this period also appeared, of which the contributions of Fullan (1985) and Joyce (1993) are very important.

Although this creative period produced knowledge of increasing specificity about the change process and the factors influencing effective schooling, this was a necessary but not sufficient condition to improve the quality of education. As Fullan (1991) points out, clear descriptions of success are not tantamount to solving the problem of the management of change towards that success.

Managing Change, the fourth phase which was entered in the late 1980s, will prove to be the most difficult and hopefully productive of all, as researchers and practitioners struggle to relate their strategies and their research knowledge to the realities of schools in a pragmatic, systematic and sensitive way. There is indeed now a move away from the study of change as a phenomenon to actually participating in school development, and the best of the current work on educational change is coming from people who are actually studying change as they are engaged in bringing it about (e.g. Hopkins, 1995). Research knowledge and 'change theory' is being refined through action (Fullan, 1993).

Defining school improvement

School improvement approaches to educational change embody the long-term goal of moving towards the ideal type of the self-renewing school. When the school is regarded as the 'centre' of change, then strategies for change need to take this new perspective into account. This approach that centres on the school is exemplified in the work of the OECD sponsored International School Improvement Project (ISIP) and in the knowledge that emanated from it (van Velzen *et al.*, 1985; Hopkins, 1987, 1990). School improvement as an approach to educational change rests on a number of assumptions:

• the school is the centre of change. This means that external reforms need to be sensitive to the situation in individual schools, rather than assuming that all schools are the same. It also implies that school improvement efforts need to adopt a 'classroom-exceeding' perspective, without ignoring the classroom;

- a systematic approach to change. School improvement is a carefully planned and managed process that takes place over a period of several years;
- a key focus for change is the 'internal conditions' of schools. These include not only the teaching–learning activities in the school but also the schools' procedures, role allocations and resource uses that support the teaching and learning process;
- accomplishing educational goals more effectively. Educational goals reflect the particular mission of a school and represent what the school itself regards as desirable. This suggests a broader definition of outcomes than student scores on achievement tests, even though for some schools these may be pre-eminent. Schools also serve the more general developmental needs of students, the professional development needs of teachers and the needs of its community;
- a multilevel perspective. Although the school is the centre of change it does not act alone. The school is embedded in an educational system that has to work collaboratively if the highest degrees of quality are to be achieved. This means that the roles of teachers, heads, governors, parents, support staff (advisers, higher education consultants) and local authorities should be defined, harnessed and committed to the process of school improvement.
- integrated implementation strategies. This implies a linkage between 'top–down' and 'bottom–up', remembering of course that both approaches can apply at a number of different levels in the system. Ideally 'top–down' policy provides policy aims, and overall strategy, and operational plans; this is complemented by a 'bottom–up' response involving diagnosis, priority goal setting and implementation. The former provides the framework, resources and a menu of alternatives; the latter, the energy and the school-based implementation.
- the drive towards institutionalization. Change is only successful when it has become part of the natural behaviour of teachers in the school. Implementation by itself is not enough.

THE MERGER OF SCHOOL EFFECTIVENESS AND SCHOOL IMPROVEMENT

First stirrings

From the early 1990s, the voices calling for links between school effectiveness and school improvement research reached something of a chorus. Stoll (1996) argued that 'if practitioners can see and make links between school effectiveness and school improvement, surely it is time for researchers studying the two areas to do the same and to work with schools to develop a deeper and more meaningful understanding of the research and its implications for practice' (p. 31).

In these years, there emerged in a number of countries bodies of knowledge which are not *either* effectiveness based *or* school improvement orientated, as defined by the limits of the old disciplines. Much of this 'convergence' or 'synergy' between the two paradigms has in fact resulted from practitioners and local authority/district policy makers borrowing from both traditions because they do not share the ideological commitment to the one or other ways of working of researchers in the fields, whilst some has arisen through the efforts of the International Congress for School Effectiveness and Improvement in breaking down disciplinary as well as geographical boundaries.

Sometimes the adoption of ideas from research has been somewhat uncritical; for example, the numerous attempts to apply findings from one specific context to another entirely different context when research has increasingly demonstrated significant contextual differences (Hallinger and Murphy, 1986; Teddlie *et al.*, 1989). Sometimes it is clear that projects are partial in their adoption of material from both paradigms – some projects have an understanding of what makes schools effective but an absence of any 'action plan' about how to get to the 'effectiveness' destination, whilst other projects have celebrated the 'core' school improvement cultural ideas of ownership, collegiality and laterality without acknowledgement of the key importance of school process and organization.

Nevertheless, there are a number of new ways of thinking about how we improve school quality:

• Pupil outcomes in academic (and often social) areas are regarded as the key 'success criteria' rather than the measures to do with teacher perception of the innovations which were used historically.
• These outcomes are increasingly assessed by use of 'hard' quantitative data that is regarded as necessary to build commitment and confidence amongst those taking part and to measure the success or failure of the project initiative.
• Bodies of knowledge from school effectiveness, school improvement and school development are all used to resource programmes, with a problem-centred orientation being used in which philosophical judgements about the nature of appropriate strategies are suspended in favour of a 'what works' approach that is distinctly non-denominational.
• The learning level, the instructional behaviour of teachers and the classroom level are increasingly being targeted for explicit programme attention as well as the school level, a marked contrast with work from the 1980s where 'the school' was often the sole focus. It is easy to understand why the 'lever' of the school level had been historically pulled so frequently, since of course school improvement persons and school effectiveness persons have had close relationships with senior school-level personnel. Senior school-

level personnel have gone on the courses run by school effectiveness and school improvement persons. The policy discourse in most societies has concerned the school level, not the classroom level. In some societies, such as the United Kingdom, there is indeed no recent knowledge base or literature about teacher effectiveness or about practices at classroom level that can potentiate student achievement and which would lead to a balance with the past obsession with the school level. It is clear though that the historic neglect of a coherent focus upon classrooms has been very costly indeed. First, it is clear that the greatest variation is within schools by individual department, rather than between schools. Put simply, the classroom learning level has maybe two or three times more influence on student achievement than the school level does (Creemers, 1994). Additionally, the reluctance to focus upon classrooms directly or turn round interventions at school level 'downwards' in schools until they impact on classrooms has hindered the development of programmes, because within all schools teacher focal concerns are much more related to those variables that are located at the classroom level, such as teaching, pedagogy and curriculum, than they are related to activities at the school level, like management and organization. This is probably particularly the case in ineffective schools, where there may exist a majority of staff who define the role of the teacher very narrowly as being related to curriculum and instruction, rather than being more broadly related to school-level management and organizational factors. It is clear that the neglect of the classroom level and the celebration of the school level may have historically cost us valuable teacher commitment.

• Multiple 'levers' are pulled to encourage school and teacher development, with the focus upon only the school 'owning' the process of change being replaced by a concern to utilize all reinforcers and initiators of change from outside the school (the local education or district authority) and indeed the national policy agenda to stimulate and provoke change.

• It has been clear that improvement programmes historically have not been necessarily organizationally 'tight'. Because of the fact that most of the programmes have been voluntaristic since they are linked to existing ongoing school-level and individual-level continuing professional development, it is clear that there may have been a huge differential within schools in the extent to which the programmes have been taken up. Reading between the lines, it is clear that there has been a likely tendency for programmes to impact most on the competent 'leading edge' of teachers, whilst it is also clear that a more or less significant 'trailing edge' may not have participated in the programmes or, at least, may not have participated very fully. It is highly likely that there has been within schools participating in the programmes, therefore, a substantial variation in the extent to which they have permeated within schools and the extent to which organizational innovations have moved through to implementation from the initiation phase and, ultimately, to the institutionalization phase. Given there is increasing evidence within school effectiveness of the importance of organizational cohesion, consistency and constancy, a situation in which there is greater variation between members of staff in a school because of differential take-up of improvement activities could have been adversely affecting the quality of student outcomes. The new range of programmes below share commitments to enhanced 'fidelity' of implementation and to enhanced organizational reliability in the take-up of the various programme characteristics.

The contemporary cutting edge

The merger of concerns in school effectiveness and school improvement had a considerable effect in promoting intellectual advance in the two disciplines. There is every sign that this is continuing, particularly in two further areas that are now beginning to come to the fore.

First, a new area of study has emerged in both school effectiveness and school improvement research over the past few years: the study of the relationship patterns that exist within staff groups and within student groups. This relational component constitutes the third dimension of schooling, joining the more frequently studied organizational and cultural components (Reynolds, 1992a and b). There are three reasons why the relational component of schooling has not been featured much in the disciplines until now:

1. The relational patterns of faculties and teachers are difficult to measure, since questionnaires and interviews regarding school relationships may constitute 'reactive' instruments susceptible to socially desirable responses (e.g. Webb *et al.*, 1981). By contrast, sociograms are relatively non-reactive instruments designed to measure the social structure of a group and to assess the social status of each individual in the group (e.g. Borg and Gall, 1989; Moreno, 1953). The study of Teddlie and Kochan (1991) was the first within school effectiveness research to use sociograms to assess the types of relationships that exist among faculty members, although of course many researchers have used sociograms to measure student peer relationships in classes and schools, including individuals working within the school effectiveness research paradigm (e.g. Reynolds, 1976; Reynolds *et al.*, 1987). It is also important to note that in many cultures (such as, probably, The Netherlands, Scandinavia and the countries of the Pacific Rim) it would be regarded as an unwanted intrusion into aspects of teachers' lives to ask them the sorts of questions that are needed to evoke analysable data (e.g. 'Which three of your colleagues would you approach for help if you had a professional problem?').

2. The interpersonal relations of teachers and of students have been difficult to conceptualize and analyse due to the complexity of the interactions within such social groups. The analytic technique that has been used in the

handful of studies in the area is network analysis, utilizing data gleaned from the administration of sociograms to staff members.

Social network analysis is a relatively new field, dating from the work of Moreno and expanding in the late 1970s and early 1980s (e.g. Rogers and Kincaid, 1980), that appears to provide the requisite analytical and modelling tools for analysing school generated sociograms. The recent work of Durland (e.g. Durland, 1996; Durland and Teddlie, 1996) is the first in school effectiveness research to utilize network analysis to model and analyse data from sociograms administered to faculty members in schools.

3. There is a common perception that interpersonal relations within a school, especially among staff members, are very difficult to change, so researchers in the school improvement area have not been particularly interested in studying these patterns of relationships until recently.

The recent realization of the importance of the relational dimension, especially in the case of interpersonal relations among staff members (Reynolds, 1991; Reynolds and Packer, 1992; Reynolds, 1996) has been due to three factors:

• Empirical work in the United States noted above (e.g. Durland, 1996; Durland and Teddlie, 1996; Teddlie and Kochan, 1991) that has successfully linked the effectiveness levels of schools with their different patterns of interpersonal relations among staff members.

• More speculative work done both in the school effectiveness and school improvement traditions in the United Kingdom and the United States that has linked ineffective schools with the presence of dysfunctional relations among staff members (e.g. Reynolds and Packer, 1992). Reynolds (1996) has characterized these 'grossly dysfunctional relationships' in such schools as follows:

> the presence of numerous personality clashes, feuds, personal agendas and fractured interpersonal relationships within the staff group, which operate . . . to make rational decision-making a very difficult process. (p. 154)

These dysfunctional relationships arise through the unique social-psychological history of the school (Teddlie and Stringfield, 1993) and have a tendency to continue unless drastic changes (planned or not) occur. Often these relationships manifest themselves in the generation of sharply delineated subcultures (Stoll and Fink, 1996) or cliques within the school.

• Some of those in the school improvement tradition have found that the existence of relational 'shadows' or 'ghosts' of the past have had considerable influence in affecting the progress of attempts at staff professional development (Hopkins *et al.*, 1994).

Second, the study of school failure and dysfunctionality has recently become of interest. School effectiveness and school improvement research have historically taken a very different disciplinary route to that of many other 'applied' disciplines such as medicine and dentistry, in that they have largely been concerned with schools that are 'well' or effective, rather than those that are 'sick' or ineffective. Indeed, with notable exceptions in school effectiveness research (Reynolds, 1996; Stoll and Myers, 1997) and in school improvement research (Sarason, 1981), the dominant paradigm had been to study those schools already effective or 'well' and to simply propose the adoption of the characteristics of the former organizations as the goal for the less effective. In medicine, by contrast, research and study focuses upon the sick person and on their symptoms, the causes for their sickness and on the needed interventions that may be appropriate to generate health. The study of medicine does not attempt to combat illness through the study of good health, as has school effectiveness: it studies illness to combat illness.

It is, of course, easy to see why school effectiveness has studied the already 'well', or effective, schools. The failure of the experiments of social engineering in the 1970s (Reynolds, Sullivan and Murgatroyd, 1987), combined with the research and advocacy that suggested that schools make no difference (Coleman *et al.*, 1966; Jencks *et al.*, 1972; Bernstein, 1968), led to a defensiveness within the field of school effectiveness and to an unwillingness to explore the 'trailing edge' of 'sick' schools for fear of giving the educational system an even poorer public image. Access to sick schools additionally has always been more difficult than to well or effective schools, given the well-known tendency of such ineffective schools to want to isolate themselves from potential sources of criticism from the world outside. The routine involvements of professional life in education for those in the school improvement tradition have also tended to be between the good schools and the improvers, who tend to prefer to involve themselves in the successful schools rather than to put up with the toxicity, problems and organizational trauma that is the day-to-day life of the ineffective school.

The problems arising from this concentration upon the effective rather than the ineffective schools are numerous. Because the effective schools have already become effective, we do not know what factors *made* them effective over time. There may be whole areas of schooling which are central to educational life in non-effective schools that simply cannot be seen in effective schools, such as staff groups that possess 'cliques' or interpersonal conflict between staff members. To propose dropping into the context of the ineffective school those factors that exist in the effective school may be to generate simply unreachable goals for the ineffective school, since the distance between the practice of one setting and the practice of the other may be too great to be easily bridged.

If the reorientation of effectiveness/improvement research towards the study of the sick proceeds, then a number of likely events will follow. Given that these schools are likely to increasingly be the site for numerous interventions to improve them, then there will be naturally occurring experiments going on that are much more rare in the 'steady state' effective schools. The study of sickness usually necessitates a clinical audit to see which aspects of the patient are abnormal – an educational audit can perform the same function, which of course is not necessary in an effective school because there is no concern about organizational functioning. A new educational paradigm may be being born.

CONCLUSIONS

This chapter has outlined the very considerable progress that has been made by both the school effectiveness and school improvement disciplines, originally singly but now jointly in an integrated effectiveness/improvement paradigm. The kinds of progress that we can see in the creative work on relationship patterns as the 'third dimension' of schooling and in the reconceptualization of the field as needing to focus upon the remediation of 'sick' schools rather than the further advancement of 'healing' schools has not come a moment too soon, since there is a contemporary danger that school effectiveness and improvement may be being discredited as valuable knowledge. First there have been criticisms from those (e.g. Elliott, 1996) who see effectiveness and improvement as being inherently conservative in their aims, managerialist in their orientation and part of a discourse that is concerned to narrowly 'train' the teaching profession rather than broadly 'educate' it. These criticisms are being answered in the new work reported here. Second, there is a danger that the field, even with the benefits of the merger between effectiveness and improvement, may be advancing less fast than the educational professionals who have been undoubtedly influenced by it. In the United States in the 1980s, effectiveness research 'boomed and busted' when official sponsorship brought the field to the attention of educational practitioners but the field then stagnated intellectually and practitioners found it intellectually and practically unconvincing. In the United Kingdom, the central role played by school effectiveness and school improvement research in the formulation of present government policy and the co-option of persons from the effectiveness and improvement communities into government advisory and managerial roles has had similar effects in bringing the knowledge base to practitioner attention.

However, the knowledge base in the United Kingdom, just like that in the United States, may be in danger of proving too undeveloped in its formulations, particularly in areas such as:

- the absence of much study as to the possible 'context specificity' of improvement strategies in schools of different social backgrounds, levels of effectiveness and stages of development;
- the absence of help for education professionals in generating their own knowledge within individual schools, through sophisticated use of data management, information systems and evaluation procedures.

There is much work to do, in addition to that in the promising areas described here, to make the new school effectiveness and school improvement enterprise worthy of the attention it has received.

REFERENCES

Bernstein, B. (1968) 'Education cannot compensate for society', *New Society*, **387**, 344–7.

Borg, M. and Gall, W. (1989) *Educational Research* (5th edn). New York: Longman.

Brookover, W. B., Beady, C., Flood, P., Schweitzer, J. and Wisenbaker, J. (1979) *Schools, Social Systems and Student Achievement: Schools Can Make a Difference.* New York: Praeger.

Carroll, J. B. (1963) 'A model of school learning', *Teachers College Record* **64**(8): 723–33.

Coleman, J. S., Campbell, E., Hobson, C., McPartland, J., Mood, A., Weinfeld, R. and York, R. (1996) *Equality of Educational Opportunity.* Washington, DC: Government Printing Office.

Crandall, D. (1982) *People, Policies and Practice: Examining the Chain of School Improvement* (vols 1–10). Andover, MA: The Network.

Crandall, D., Eiseman, J. and Louis, K. S. (1986) 'Strategic planning issues that bear on the success of school improvement efforts', *Educational Administration Quarterly* **22**(2): 21–53.

Creemers, B. P. M. (1994) *The Effective Classroom.* London: Cassell.

Durland, M. (1996) 'The application of network analysis to the study of differentially effective schools'. Unpublished doctoral dissertation, Louisiana State University, Baton Rouge, LA.

Durland, M. and Teddlie, C. (1996) 'A network analysis of the structural dimensions of principal leadership in differentially effective schools'. Paper presented at the annual meeting of the American Educational Research Association, New York.

Elliott, J. (1996) 'School effectiveness research and its critics: alternative visions of schooling', *Cambridge Journal of Education* **26**(2): 199–224.

Farringdon, D. (1980) 'Truancy, delinquency, the home and the school', in L. Hersou and I. Berg (eds) *Out of School.* Chichester: John Wiley.

Fullan, M. G. (1985) 'Change processes and strategies at the local level', *Elementary School Journal* **85**(13): 391–421.

Fullan, M. G. (1991) *The New Meaning of Educational Change.* London: Cassell.

Fullan, M. G. (1993) *Change Forces. Probing the Depths of Educational Reform.* London/New York/Philadelphia: Falmer Press.

Grosin, L. (1993) 'School effectiveness research as a point of departure for school evaluation', *Scandinavian Journal of Educational Research* **37**, 317–30.

Hallinger, P. and Murphy, J. (1986) 'The social context of effective schools', *American Journal of Education* **94**, 328–55.

Hargreaves, D. H. (1984) *Improving Secondary Schools.* London: Inner London Education Authority.

Hopkins, D. (1987) *Improving the Quality of Schooling.* Lewes: Falmer Press.

Hopkins, D. (1990) 'The International School Improvement Project (ISIP) and effective schooling: towards a synthesis', *School Organisation* **10**(3): 129–94.

Hopkins, D. (1995) 'Towards effective school improvement', *School Effectiveness and School Improvement* **6**(3): 265–74.

Hopkins, D. (1996) 'Towards a theory for school improvement', in J. Gray, D. Reynolds and C. T. Fitz-Gibbon (eds) *Merging Traditions: The Future of Research on School Effectiveness and School Improvement.* London: Cassell.

Hopkins, D., Ainscow, M. and West, M. (1994) *School Improvement in an Era of Change.* London: Cassell.

Hopkins, D. and Harris, A. (1997) 'Understanding the school's capacity for development: growth states and dialogues', *School Leadership and Management* **17**(3): 401–11.

Huberman, M. and Miles, M. (1984) *Innovation Up Close*. New York: Plenum.

Jencks, C. S., Smith, M., Ackland, H., Bane, M. J., Cohen, D., Ginter, H., Heyns, B. and Michelson, S. (1972) *Inequality: A Reassessment of the Effect of the Family and Schooling in America*. New York: Basic Books.

Joyce, B. (1993) *The Self Renewing School*. Alexandria, VA: Association for Supervision and Curriculum Development.

King, R. (1983) *The Sociology of School Organisation*. London: Methuen.

Levine, D. U. and Lezotte, L. W. (1990) *Unusually Effective Schools: A Review and Analysis of Research and Practice*. Madison, WI: National Centre for Effective Schools Research and Development.

Louis, K. S. and Miles, M. B. (1990) *Improving the Urban High School: What Works and Why*. New York: Teachers College Press.

Moreno, J. L. (1953) *Who Will Survive?* New York: Beacon.

Mortimore, P. (1998) *The Road to Improvement*. Lisse: Swets and Zeitlinger.

Purkey, S. and Smith, M. (1983) 'Effective schools', *The Elementary School Journal* **83**, 427–52.

Resnick, L. B. and Resnick, D. P. (1992) 'Assessing the thinking curriculum', in B. R. Gifford and M. C. O'Connor (eds) *Changing Assessment: Alternative Views of Aptitude, Achievement and Instruction*. Boston, MA: Kluwer Academic Publishers.

Reynolds, D. (1976) 'The delinquent school', in P. Woods (ed.) *The Process of Schooling*. London: Routledge and Kegan Paul.

Reynolds, D. (1991) 'Changing ineffective schools', in M. Ainscow (ed.) *Effective Schools for All*. London: David Fulton.

Reynolds, D. (1992a) 'School effectiveness and school improvement', in J. Bashi and Z. Sass (eds) *School Effectiveness and Improvement: Selected Proceedings of the Third International Congress*. pp. 67–87. Jerusalem, Israel: Magnes Press.

Reynolds, D. (1992b) 'School effectiveness and school improvement: An updated review of the British literature', in D. Reynolds and P. Cuttance (eds) *School Effectiveness: Research, Policy and Practice*. London: Cassell, pp. 1–24.

Reynolds, D. (1996) 'Turning around ineffective schools: Some evidence and some speculations', in J. Gray, D. Reynolds, C. T. Fitz-Gibbon and D. Jesson (eds) *Merging Traditions: The Future of Research on School Effectiveness and School Improvement*. London: Cassell.

Reynolds, D. and Cuttance, P. (1992) *School Effectiveness: Research, Policy and Practice*. London: Cassell.

Reynolds, D. and Farrell, S. (1996) *Worlds Apart? — A Review of International Studies of Educational Achievement Involving England*. London: Her Majesty's Stationery Office for OFSTED.

Reynolds, D. and Packer, A. (1992) 'School effectiveness and school improvement in the 1990s', in D. Reynolds and P. Cuttance (eds) *School Effectiveness: Research, Policy and Practice*. London: Cassell.

Reynolds, D., Sullivan, M. and Murgatroyd, S. J. (1987) *The Comprehensive Experiment*. Lewes: Falmer Press.

Rogers, E. M. and Kincaid, D. L. (1980) *Communication Networks: Toward a New Paradigm for Research*. New York: Macmillan.

Rosenholz, S. J. (1989) *Teachers' Workplace: The Social Organization of Schools*. New York: Longman.

Rutter, M. (1983) 'School effects on pupil progress — Findings and policy implications', *Child Development* **54**(1): 1–29.

Rutter, M., Maughan, B., Mortimore, P. and Ouston, J. with Smith, A. (1979) *Fifteen Thousand Hours: Secondary Schools and Their Effects on Children*. London: Open Books and Boston, MA: Harvard University Press.

Sammons, P. (1999) *School Effectiveness: Coming of Age in the Twenty-First Century*. Lisse: Swets and Zeitlinger.

Sarason, S. (1981) *The Culture of the School and the Problem of Educational Change.* New York: Allyn & Bacon.

Scheerens, J. and Bosker, R. (1997) *The Foundations of Educational Effectiveness.* Oxford: Pergamon Press.

Stoll, L. (1996) 'Linking school effectiveness and school improvement: Issues and possibilities', in J. Gray, D. Reynolds, C. T. Fitz-Gibbon and D. Jesson (eds) *Merging Traditions: The Future of Research on School Effectiveness and School Improvement,* pp. 51–73. London: Cassell.

Stoll, L. and Fink, D. (1996) *Changing Our Schools.* Buckingham: Open University Press.

Stoll, L. and Myers, K. (1997) *No Quick Fixes: Perspectives on Schools in Difficulty.* Lewes: Falmer Press.

Stoll, L., Myers, K. and Reynolds, D. (1996) 'Understanding ineffectiveness'. Paper presented at the annual meeting of the American Educational Research Association, New York.

Teddlie, C. (1996) *School Effectiveness Indices: East Baton Rouge Parish Public Schools, Academic Years 1991–92, 1992–93, 1993–94.* Baton Rouge, LA: Louisiana State University College of Education.

Teddlie, C. and Kochan, S. (1991) 'Evaluation of a troubled high school: Methods, results, and implications'. Paper presented at the annual meeting of the American Educational Research Association, Chicago, IL.

Teddlie, C. and Reynolds, D. (2000) *The International Handbook of School Effectiveness Research.* London and New York: Falmer Press.

Teddlie, C. and Stringfield, S. (1993) *Schools Do Make a Difference: Lessons Learned from a 10–year Study of School Effects.* New York: Teachers College Press.

Teddlie, C., Kirby, P. C. and Stringfield, S. (1989) 'Effective versus ineffective schools: Observable differences in the classroom', *American Journal of Education* **97**(3): 221–36.

van Velzen, W., Miles, M., Ekholm, M., Hameyer, U. and Robin, D. (1985) *Making School Improvement Work: A Conceptual Guide to Practice.* Leuven: Belgium, ACCO.

Webb, E. J., Campbell, D. T., Schwartz, R. D., Sechrest, L. and Grove, J. B. (1981) *Nonreactive Measures in the Social Sciences.* Boston, MA: Houghton Mifflin.

Wilson, B. C. and Corcoran, T. B. (1988) *Successful Secondary Schools.* London: Falmer Press.

Part Two

Chapter 4

A Structural Critique of School Effectiveness and School Improvement

Brian Fidler

INTRODUCTION

At a British Educational Research Association conference some years ago when the school effectiveness and the school improvement research groups held their first symposium I rather naively suggested that the linking mechanism between the two was school management. Whilst what I suggested was an underestimate of the problems, nevertheless had my advice been followed there would have been an earlier realization of the 'cul-de-sac' that the two new paradigms had entered. Largely these issues have to do with precisely the problems which school management has always grappled with – the complexity of organizational dynamics.

Although it would be very convenient to believe that research could identify clear recipes for improving the performance of schools, I believe that this will always be a chimera. This is not to suggest that research cannot provide valuable ideas but rather to suggest that jejune research, although it might appeal to funders who would like quick results, is simply a distraction. Moreover this distraction has prevented a structural analysis of the areas where more sophisticated research findings might have value.

The basic, often unstated, assumption between the two paradigms is that if school effectiveness research can identify the features which make a school successful then school improvement research can provide a means by which these features could be put in place and all schools could be made effective (Figure 1). This is certainly the logic which captures the interest of practitioners and policy makers. What is rather less clear is whether those closest to the two paradigms ever envisaged such a connection. In any case, as I shall try to demonstrate, such a connection is illusory.

Not that being illusory necessarily is a disadvantage. In the course of history there have been many quests which have captured the public imagination and

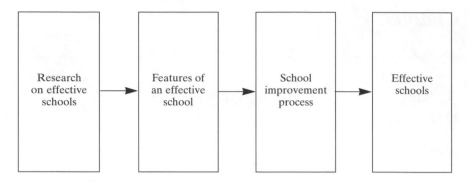

Figure 1 Policy makers' connection between school effectiveness and school improvement

appear to be able to survive the most severe rational criticisms for quite a while. Thus it would be a mistake to assume that because the golden scenario outlined above is flawed, such a vain search will be abandoned. The development of theory in the pure sciences has taught us that theories are only abandoned under two conditions, first that they are discredited empirically and second that a better and more credible theory is proposed (Kuhn, 1970). One might add a third condition for the social sciences in an increasingly media dominated age – that any replacement theory should appear new, plausible, straightforward and inexpensive to policy makers.

No one who has read Brian Rowan's provocative paper 'Shamanistic rituals in effective schools' (1984) can have failed to view the emerging school effectiveness movement in a new light. This view is echoed in Terrence Deal's welcome of the school effectiveness paradigm:

> The findings of the effective schools research may be more important as symbols than as facts. Our society presently places more faith in science than in ordinary knowledge or common sense. (Deal, 1985, p. 604)

At that early stage he appreciated the powerful symbolism that the answers provided by the effective schools movement might provide both at the policy level and also at the local level. But he also anticipated how the results might be used in ways not envisaged by the originators:

> Despite limitations of the research, local schools will use the effective schools findings to relabel old initiatives and as new labels for existing practices, as ammunition in political fights among different constituencies, and as new measures of excellence. (*ibid.*)

Whilst I recognize an equivalent need for certainty at the present time I fear that it is in overcoming this important hurdle that my suggestions will be found lacking. For I can see no easy solutions but I do believe it is possible to have a great deal more clarity about the nature of the issues. Moreover I have no illusions that research findings will yield any immediate solutions since I am convinced that judgement and leadership will remain essential ingredients in attempts to improve the performance of schools. However, the efficacy of such management can be improved by a better conceptualization of the issues.

I need to give some essential criticisms of the school effectiveness and school improvement paradigms and the connection between them before finally offering an alternative but more complicated and conditional solution. However, perhaps I first need to state the position from which I approach these issues.

Thinking about the social world is notoriously difficult – there are issues of ontology (nature of reality), epistemology (nature of knowledge), human nature and methodology (nature of research) (Burrell and Morgan, 1979). And this catalogue of important issues doesn't cover the personal difficulty of conceptualizing the external world in one's own mind – having made choices on each of the four issues, how does one conceptualize social phenomena? Any serious reflection soon reveals that there is no single way which accurately portrays reality. Any mental model we construct will be good at conceptualizing some phenomena whilst neglecting others – that is the nature of simplification. Any single perspective will be inadequate at capturing the complexity of the external world. However, the limited processing power of the human mind makes it imperative to make a personal simplified mental model of external reality if we are to make sense of the world around us.

Recognizing the lens that we use and also when we change lenses is important if we are to build up a more holistic view from a series of unidimensional perspectives. Such an explicit recognition also makes us more aware of the assumptions that we may be building into our thinking without realizing it. Thus I need to try to make clear the perspective which I shall mainly be using in this analysis. Of Bolman and Deal's (1997) four frames – structural, human relations, political and symbolic – I use the structural frame most frequently. This does not mean that I do not recognize the value of the other frames in particular situations for capturing particular aspects of organizational dynamics, but I believe that the best single frame for a variety of purposes is the structural frame. This concentrates on goals, boundaries, structures, communication systems, co-ordinating mechanisms, roles and responsibilities (Bolman and Deal, 1997). To Bennett's account of the structural perspective in Chapter 6 I would add a vitally important control mechanism – feedback – which connects input, process and outcomes. I shall return to the importance of this for school improvement research and suggest ways in which school effectiveness research might have contributed more insights.

SCHOOL EFFECTIVENESS RESEARCH

First one needs to recognize that there are two distinct threads to such research. There is the attempt to discover the factors which lead to effective schools and there is also a strand which seeks to discover the extent of the difference in student attainment between effective and ineffective schools. I shall concentrate on the former since its findings contribute to the scenario illustrated by Figure 1.

Second one needs to recognize that there are a great many criticisms which can be made of school effectiveness research. There are criticisms of principle, theory, methodology and practice.

I want to dwell on those criticisms which most impinge on the feasibility of Figure 1. It should be observed that there has been remarkably little criticism of the research in the UK until relatively recently (Preece, 1989; Elliott, 1996; Fidler *et al.*, 1996; Ouston, 1996, 1999; Slee *et al.*, 1998) compared to the USA where the criticisms were trenchant in the 1980s and the work largely sidelined by the 1990s (Purkey and Smith, 1983; Good and Brophy, 1986; Bliss *et al.*, 1991). It should also be pointed out that the vast bulk of research on school effectiveness dates from the early 1970s onwards in the USA (Levine and Lezotte, 1990; Cotton, 1995) and the sum total of research in other countries is slight by comparison, although there have been noteworthy single projects in Britain – Scotland (Willms, 1992), London (Rutter *et al.*, 1979; Mortimore *et al.*, 1988; Sammons *et al.*, 1997) and Wales (Reynolds *et al.*, 1987) with school numbers ranging from 12 to 94. The renewed interest in England has been as a result of an advance in statistical methodology – multilevel modelling – but the major problems inherent in Figure 1 remain, as I shall attempt to demonstrate.

CRITICISMS OF PRINCIPLE

There are two principal issues here which affect the value of the approach. First there is the definition of effectiveness which has been adopted and second there is the particular choice of measures for outcomes.

A recent study of school effectiveness research (Sammons *et al.*, 1995) approved a definition by Mortimore (1991) of an effective school as

> one in which pupils progress further than might be expected from consideration of its intake. (p. 9)

Essentially it is the progress of students from their attainment on entry to their attainment on leaving a particular school which is taken as the measure of effectiveness.

At first glance the use of improvement of outcomes might appear quite uncontroversial but those who are familiar with the organizational literature will know that there are competing approaches to organizational effectiveness and so it is instructive to examine the merits of these to see what the chosen definition ignores. Other approaches (Scott, 1992) recognize that the time period over which institutional effectiveness is assessed becomes important and that some indication of long-term success, rather than a measure at one point in time, is an important factor to be taken into account. Thus other approaches begin with a consideration of organizational processes and structures, particularly those related to quality assurance, and require these to be of a high standard. The argument is that where outcomes are difficult to specify, high-quality internal processes are the best guarantee of quality outcomes. The disadvantage of this approach from the perspective of those who search for an objective definition is that this opens up the prospect of judgements on essentially organizational and managerial criteria. However, the point I want to make is that by ignoring this perspective concerns about the long-term effectiveness of schools have been sacrificed. The thinking is essentially short-termism.

Ironically there is a tendency of those who have recently been introduced to the factors which have emerged from research on effective schools to use these as the defining characteristics of effective schools. As Bottery and Jamieson and Wikely point out in Chapters 8 and 9, there is a large degree of arbitrariness about these factors and they are not the ones which are likely to have emerged from alternative definitions of effectiveness cited above.

The second issue concerns the nature of the outcomes. These were originally taken to be test results on basic skills – language and numeracy in the USA – but have included GCSE results in England. Whilst these are readily measured I suspect that I am not alone in considering that the outcomes of schooling which society expects are rather broader than this. Broader in at least three senses – wider curriculum, more sophisticated intellectual and cultural skills and behavioural skills. A rounded education will include a broader range of subjects than language and number and will hope to develop more sophisticated intellectual skills than basic skills as measured by multiple-choice tests. There is also an important area of learning which covers behavioural, social and life skills which are increasingly recognized as essential for both later work performance and a satisfying adult life. The implicit assumptions in neglecting the broader aims of schooling are that (1) all schools have the same priorities and (2) effectiveness is a unidimensional concept, i.e. that effectiveness in one aspect of schooling implies effectiveness in all aspects of schooling. Both of these assumptions are likely to be open to challenge.

A further point about the restricted interpretation of achievement is that this places a great premium on ensuring that these assessments are valid indicators of higher level skills, with some concern that the reliability of the assessments is likely to decrease as the judgement of examiners is an increasing factor in assessing these more diffuse skills. There is always the ever-present concern that with high stakes assessment, teachers will teach to the tests and so decrease their indication of students' longer-term abilities.

As some commentators have pointed out the perspective from which effectiveness is viewed might be important (Slee *et al.*, 1998). Is effectiveness such a universal concept that different nations and different groups within nations can agree about its characteristics? Are the interests of society, parents and children all the same? Even if they are ultimately the same, will they be the same at all points in time? And if they are different at different points in time whose interests should predominate?

Perhaps the most worrying aspect of this area of intellectual endeavour is not the academic work itself but the expectations which have at least been allowed to grow, if not actually generated, in the minds of politicians, policy makers and practitioners. There has been no systematic investigation into what these groups ascribe to school effectiveness research but from an examination of their pronouncements and anecdotal remarks it is clear that they are unaware of the theoretical, methodological and technical limitations of the findings.

In view of the complexity and statistical nature of the work it is not easy to assess how far this misconception is based on ignorance of the details of the work or political expediency. This is reminiscent of the story of the drunk and his use of a lamp-post – is it for illumination or support? So it is with politicians. They can use research findings to illuminate policy making or they can use them, retrospectively, to legitimate their actions. Any detailed examination of these effects would need to try to assess how far school effectiveness researchers have tried to acquaint policy makers with the limitations and defects of their work.

CRITICISMS OF THEORY

At the time that most research was carried out on school effectiveness, from the late 1970s to the early 1990s, there was very little explicit theorizing. Since then there has been a little *post hoc* work although this has tended to ignore organization theory and other earlier work on effective schooling, such as Munck (1979). I shall attempt some theorizing and then examine the effects of the neglect of such work for findings on school effectiveness.

Theories of leadership since the 1960s have increasingly drawn attention to the importance of recognizing that leadership activities need to be tailored to circumstances, particularly the internal situation within an organization (Hersey and Blanchard, 1993). This is a specific example of a more general theoretical approach – contingency theory, which states that appropriate actions depend upon circumstances. There are two consequences for school effectiveness research. First, the concept of an effective school might be different according to the external context in which a school is located. One obvious variable is the socio-economic context. Even the undifferentiated evidence from the research findings on school effectiveness led Bliss (1991) and Hannaway and Talbert (1993) to make a tentative identification of two paradigms of effective schooling depending on the context – inner city and middle-class suburb. The second consequence is that effectiveness may take different forms depending on the internal conditions in the school particularly if the definition of effectiveness is wider than the present one.

A further consequence of a lack of theorizing is the oft remarked, poorly understood technology of teaching and the weak connection between cause and effect or the effects of teaching on learning (Bidwell, 1965). Whilst this is a difficulty at the level of the individual teacher and classroom, there are also similar difficulties at the organizational level. The connection between leadership activities and the practices of teachers is equally poorly understood and the precise connection between the leadership activities of the headteacher and the learning of pupils is opaque.

Here I need to explain my position. When I refer to the connections as poor I am thinking in terms of a causal connection which can be established by understanding the effect of one variable on another under precisely defined circumstances. This is not to say that leaders and others do not have their implicit theories or theories-in-use (Argyris and Schon, 1974) as to likely connections but the number of times that expectations are not fulfilled is a demonstration of the errors involved in such implicit theorizing.

The difficulty in terms of trying to identify causal connections is that there are too many variables which interact and the precise connections may be very sensitive to the initial conditions. Thus, seemingly identical situations do not yield anything like identical results – one of the precursors of chaos (Gleick, 1988). The school effectiveness research solution to this problem is to treat the school as a black box and to investigate the association of certain internal process variables with school outcomes or progress.

This has the effect of assuming that all factors operate concurrently. A more plausible assumption is that factors which create effective operations may need to be sequential and the ordering probably matters. The methodology of school effectiveness research only shows at best, the final mix. Further, although the range of factors which emerge as associated with effective schools may all be statistically significant this does not mean that they are all large enough to be important.

This approach has led to a concentration on school level variables rather than recognizing that teachers operate within classrooms which operate within schools. Whilst multilevel modelling has begun to be used to deal with levels of nested data this is still not the same as understanding causal mechanisms which bring about effects.

Although such theoretical modelling is enormously difficult there are some features which are apparent. Searching for direct causal mechanisms is unlikely to be successful as it is likely that many effects will be an indirect, rather than direct, result of actions. Thus causal modelling should seek to connect a range of intermediate effects with a final outcome (Hallinger and Heck, 1996). Such intermediate effects are likely to be interactive – one intermediate effect may affect others.

This kind of thinking suggests that there should be greater interest in structural modelling and path analysis as a way of understanding the connections between intermediate variables (Duncan, 1975; Kelloway, 1998). To date little has been attempted. There are two approaches to path analysis. One is to set up *a priori* hypotheses of relationships and to test them empirically, the second is to attempt to fit models to data retrospectively. Whilst this may be less than ideal, increasing the odds of successful prediction should not be underrated. As I shall indicate later such work may provide a connection between school effectiveness and school improvement.

CRITICISMS OF METHODOLOGY

Research in school effectiveness has been almost universally quantitative. The particular techniques used have been regression analysis and multilevel modelling to find correlates of effective schools or school level variables which appear to correlate with effectiveness. There are varying lists of such school effectiveness factors and their description seems to change to suit current opinion even though the underlying research evidence is largely the same. And as Ouston (1999), an early researcher in this field, has commented, the similarities between the findings tend to be overstated.

Multilevel modelling has enabled more accurate estimates of the contribution to progress of different components, e.g. school and classroom. Not surprisingly this has indicated a greater contribution from classroom level variables compared to school level. Whilst the use of data from individual students and multilevel modelling have been advances in technique, problems of principle remain.

The first and most substantial issue is to point out that the studies are cross-sectional studies looking at a number of schools at one point in time. Thus the results obtained are correlations and not causations. The only sense in which causal ideas have been employed is that the factors which have been examined for their relationship to effectiveness are those which educators or researchers have assumed might be so connected. In that sense they are using professional practice and, not surprisingly, little has emerged which would not have been regarded as good professional practice. If factors are not investigated, no correlations will emerge. Thus processes which might be assumed from a management perspective to be connected with effective schools, such as the work of governors, school development planning and parental participation, do not generally appear in the lists. The explanation for this is that since most of the work has been carried out in elementary schools in the USA which do not exhibit these features, they were not likely to be discovered.

This approach means that there is a degree of arbitrariness about the lists of factors which is somewhat worrying because any list of ten or so features of 'effective' schools is likely to lead to a concentration on those factors rather than others (and if there isn't such interest in the factors what is the point of the research findings?). When the list really only represents the factors which have been investigated and which have consistently appeared initially in research findings in US schools this is doubly worrying. As I have tried to explain earlier, if such practices are contextual and US schools, for example, are so different to schools in England and Wales, the list of factors may be quite misleading in terms of their importance.

Another misconception affecting the research is that effectiveness is a feature of an organization rather than a norm-referenced concept which depends upon the practices of other organizations. Indeed, a more accurate description would be 'relative effectiveness'. The methodology of assessing effectiveness is a 'zero sum game'. This means that the way effectiveness is calculated ensures that there are about as many effective schools as there are ineffective ones. All schools cannot be effective. Indeed this also means that the assessment of 'effectiveness' changes each year. It is possible for a school to be deemed effective one year and not change any of its 'effective practices' and not be deemed effective the following year. This change would not be due to any changes in the school in question but as a result of improvements in the results in other schools with whom it had no contact. This makes changes in effectiveness a rather slippery concept.

Changes in a school's effectiveness may be due to changes in its own practices, changes in other schools' practices or a combination of the two. Such a conclusion is certainly contrary to popular understanding and at variance with the way in which the school effectiveness factors are put across. These are treated as *factors*, associated with effectiveness, not as *factors whose relative quality* may be associated with effectiveness.

A final methodological issue which is endemic to school effectiveness research and about which relatively little is written is the assessment of measurement errors. First, it should be remembered that school effectiveness data uses examination and test scores of pupils. Thus all the caveats about the inaccuracies of these measures as valid assessments of a child's performance still hold true. School effectiveness research does not obviate these errors but proceeds to build upon them. This means that when likely errors are taken into account it is quite difficult to identify differences in effectiveness. Harvey Goldstein has shown examples of this on samples of school results which demonstrate that only differences in effectiveness between the 10 per cent of schools at the top of the distribution and the 10 per cent at the bottom are likely to be due to factors other than chance (Goldstein and Spiegelhalter, 1996). As Ouston (1999) comments, school effectiveness studies offer 'a very relatively weak explanation of small differences' (p. 171).

This means that for 80 per cent of schools their effectiveness is indistinguishable from each other. This finding is for schools where there are large numbers of candidates involved in calculating the effectiveness of the school. As Reynolds acknowledges in Chapter 3, when the number of pupils becomes smaller in primary schools and at classroom level the relative errors increase. Thus the potential for assessments of effectiveness of small schools and individual teachers which are not confounded by random errors becomes vanishingly small. This is not an expectation which policy makers and teachers have been prepared for and there is a danger that this problem with errors will be suppressed in order to give clear cut results.

INFLUENCE ON PRACTICE

There is just one further point that I wish to make. Are the school effectiveness results capable of informing practice? I have previously mentioned the lack of causal mechanisms and so here I am solely concerned with the clarity of the findings. How far does the term 'strong leadership' or 'professional leadership', for example, clearly identify behaviours which could be used to compare with practice in schools? Here the limitations of the quantitative research method-ology become apparent. The practices are identified on the basis of questionnaire responses. This leads to the factors being vague and, for the most part, rather obvious findings at that level of generality. In part the vagueness follows from the different ways in which the factors have been operationalized in different research studies but my conclusion is that the factors are of little practical value for those who wish to improve their practice. As Deal (1985) foresaw, the results could be used to justify a wide range of practices.

CONCLUSIONS ON SCHOOL EFFECTIVENESS

Although I have identified many criticisms of school effectiveness research I do want to highlight a major advance which it has created, which is to conceptualize and operationalize progress as a feature of a school's academic performance. The research has provided a means of identifying schools which add more value to children's attainment than other similar schools. This is valuable and could be the basis for more limited studies of the features of such schools, as I shall argue later. It is the identification of 'effectiveness factors' of which I am critical, not the research in general.

What has been gained from the school effectiveness movement and is there any harm in it? I have outlined a series of intellectual flaws in the research and so here I want to move briefly into the political and social arenas to ask 'Does it matter?' I think that it has been a distraction as it has deflected thinking from the recognition that the ends of schooling involve value judgements and that the means of obtaining those outcomes may also be dependent on the ends. It has tried to introduce a spurious certainty into the operation of schools and to downplay the need to have school leaders who are moral, wise and well-educated. Such leaders need to combine educational principles with good judgement and sound organizational understanding.

SCHOOL IMPROVEMENT

Compared to school effectiveness, school improvement is a much more diffuse concept. It is not easy to differentiate material from ideas which might appear under alternative titles in the management literature, such as management of change and organizational development. There are also areas of educational literature that are relevant such as curriculum development. Thus there are a number of competing claims for the mantle of school improvement.

This is not a new discovery. The International School Improvement Project (ISIP) in the 1980s identified the issue:

> 'School improvement' is a term many people use, but its meaning is ambiguous. Almost anything – in-service training, the adoption of an innovation, curriculum change, new teacher hiring standards, or even a national reform – can be called 'school improvement'. (Miles and Ekholm, 1985, p. 34)

Indeed in the ISIP there were groups working on school-based review (or self-evaluation), the role of principals and internal change agents, the role of external support agencies and research and evaluation as contributions to school improvement. Thus the project produced an enduring generic and widely quoted definition of school improvement as

> A systematic, sustained effort aimed at change in learning conditions and other related internal conditions in one or more schools, with the ultimate aim of accomplishing educational goals more effectively. (*ibid.*, p. 48)

This lack of precision about school improvement makes it rather more difficult to analyse with confidence than school effectiveness. There are a variety of activities which would see themselves as school improvement initiatives. Often these are practical activities in which schools, either individually or in groups, are engaged. I have devised a framework to help make sense of the range of activities which would be included in any survey of school improvement (Figure 2). The organizing variable is locus of control. This is an expression of where the power to make decisions lies and, coincidentally, the extent to which the activity is situational.

EXTERNAL INITIATIVES

I have previously likened externally initiated improvement projects to solutions searching for problems (Fidler, 1997a). A crucial discriminator is whether a school has voluntarily chosen to be involved or whether it has been mandated. At a national, state or local level an improvement initiative is formulated for implementation in schools. This ranges from E1 which can include legislation which mandates all schools to implement curricular changes such as the National Curriculum in England and Wales to E2 where externally initiated projects are financed but participation is voluntary. The distinctive difference between E1 and E2 is whether a school may choose to be involved or whether it is mandated. Much of Fullan's writing is concerned with E2

Location of control

External		Internal	
E1	E2	C	S1	S2

E1

External imposition

Sources
DfEE (1998)

E2

External invitation

Sources
van Velzen (1985)
Fullan (1991)
Hall and Hord (1987)
MacLaughlin (1990)

C

External assistance

Sources
Hopkins *et al.* (1994)
Gray (1988)

S1

Internal school improvement *process*

Sources
Hargreaves and Hopkins (1991)

S2

Internal school improvement *outcome*

Sources
Hopkins *et al.* (1996)

Figure 2 School improvement – external and internal control

activities. This distinction between E1 and E2 is not an absolute one since some E1 activities may only have an expectation that all schools of a certain type will be involved, such as the National Literacy strategy in England, whilst some E2 activities may involve substantial financial incentives to join or invitations which are difficult to refuse. There may also be differences in how obviously there is widespread support within a school to be involved compared to a decision of the headteacher alone. Similarly there may have been different levels of consultation and support from schools for the external projects before they were initiated.

The critical issues about external initiatives from a location of control perspective is that a school is required to respond to external requirements irrespective of its own requirements. Even where a school might identify a need which an external project fulfils, often timing is a compromise by which school considerations have to fit external opportunities. All too often it is the attraction of external funding which proves irresistible (McLaughlin, 1990). Research on projects of this kind in the US in the 1970s drew attention to the degree of adaptation which teachers in schools made as they implemented improvement (Hall and Hord, 1987). The degree of adaptation ranged from relatively minor to quite major distortions of the original concept, and the reasons for this included differing perceptions of what was required, and, more deliberately, using resources to meet quite different aims. Some projects prescribed certain practices which had to be implemented as a way of limiting the degree of adaptation. Considerable project resources were generally committed to training of participants and consultancy. This also had the effect of monitoring and minimizing the degree of adaptation.

INTERNAL INITIATIVES

There is a clear difference between external initiatives where schools will be working alongside other schools and an external organization and internal ones where the prerogative lies entirely with each individual school. The school development planning project (Hargreaves and Hopkins, 1991) is an example of S1 where, although there is a common planning process for development, its application in each school has major differences of content and some differences of process (MacGilchrist *et al.*, 1995). Although each school is expected to have some form of planning process, research shows that these take considerably different forms in individual schools (Glover *et al.*, 1996; Bennett *et al.*, 2000).

The category S2 covers the range of individual school activities which are targeted at particular improvements using whatever means appear appropriate. This includes activities of a very different scope and scale, ranging from individual activities in a single school department through to whole-school corporate change. These activities have the advantage of being situational in that they are tailored to the particular needs of a school. A major disadvantage from the point of view of conceptualizing and learning about school improvement is that they involve a whole series of very disparate activities which may have been devised in quite idiosyncratic ways to meet particular school needs.

Although decisions about how and what to improve are made by schools, such decisions are heavily conditioned by the external context. Since the Education Reform Act of 1988, parents in England and Wales have become much more influential, both as educational consumers and as members of governing bodies of schools. They have been provided with much more information on which to base their choice of school, such as OFSTED reports on schools and examination league tables. Thus schools have been under considerable pressure to favour certain kinds of improvement because of their possible influence on parental choice of school (Fidler, 1997a).

EXTERNAL ASSISTANCE

The intermediate category C represents the range of external assistance which schools might use to support improvement activities. This is also quite diverse and includes projects like IQEA (Improving the Quality of Education for All) which has a methodology of working but does not prescribe outcomes and claims to work with schools and not on schools (Hopkins *et al.*, 1994). The category also includes individual consultancy which schools might engage on terms specified by the school to assist improvement activities (Gray, 1988).

FIVE CHARACTERISTICS OF SCHOOL IMPROVEMENT

Sketching such an enormous range of activity, all of which might be termed 'school improvement', illustrates the difficulty which I find in trying to identify the tenets of the paradigm. Thus I shall identify what I consider to be five general tenets which characterize school improvement approaches and differentiate them from a more strategic and organizational approach which I shall propose. These tenets are somewhat diverse in keeping with the diverseness of the field.

1. Collegiality

Any writing on school improvement generally makes an assumption, either explicitly or implicitly, that it is an activity which staff work on together and engage in in a more collegial way than the hierarchical structures of schools might imply. Certainly it is not a managed activity originated by the leadership of the school. Thus there are research findings which suggest that the support of the headteacher is necessary for successful improvement but not necessarily his or her active participation (Hall and Hord, 1987). The paradigm, in pure form, appears to assume that if staff are left to get on with it they can organize themselves to carry out worthwhile improvements to teaching and learning which influence their classroom practice. How far such collegiality is genuine rather than contrived has recently been questioned (Hargreaves, 1991).

A further orientation related to collegiality is that the learning of teachers is as important as the learning of pupils. Elliott (1996) identifies the school improvement perspective as being concerned with how schools can change to become 'more *educative* institutions' (p. 221) rather than more effective ones.

The collegial orientation removes any need to consider power as a potentially distorting influence on the process. Micro-politics are assumed to be absent from decisions and actions.

2. Home-grown features

I have ascribed two related attributes to this heading. First, the work is originated by and seen only to apply to schools and second, it is atheoretical.

Writing on school improvement does not take more general ideas from other organizational writing and apply them to schools. Instead the assumption appears to be that schools are unique and need to derive their own processes from their own experience and school-based activities. Where there is any borrowing of ideas this is unconscious or at least not attributed. In some improvement projects organizational development ideas appear to have been influential. Often legitimation tends to be based on commonsense, familiar notions and accounts of what works.

It is not surprising in view of the foregoing that school improvement work is atheoretical. It does not try to assemble theoretical ideas and formulate a process from theoretical constructs, instead it takes some principles, such as collegiality and the primacy of teaching activities, to formulate a rather loose process. Often the process has to be deduced from the account of improvements which have taken place in practice.

3. Straightforwardness

There are few disagreements in the accounts of improvement other than those caused by the difficulties of grappling with the effects of teaching on the learning process. Problems are seen as educational and not organizational. Improving teaching and learning are not seen as contentious and value-laden judgements which are dependent on beliefs about the purposes of education, and beliefs about how children learn are not recognized as such. Implicitly the agreed principles are that learning is a good thing in its own right and that children learn by activity in a mainly constructivist framework.

This apparent unanimity leads me to question the rather glib phrase 'improving teaching and learning'. This should be a highly contested decision since there are very many ways of 'improving'. This can be illustrated by identifying one tension from very many. Should improvement be directed at improving current examination success or should improvement be directed at making the curriculum more relevant to future needs and acquiring skills which are more diverse than are assessed by current examinations? These are vital decisions but they are not technical decisions to be devolved to a cadre of improvers. They need widespread consultation and discussion since they will need to be pursued over a number of years and may be fundamental to the whole future direction of a school.

Value conflicts between individuals or groups do not appear because the assumptions underpinning the activity assume commonality of view on these issues and that collegial working will ensure that the staff speak with one voice that has been rationally determined within the principles underpinning the process. There are no perceived value conflicts with groups other than teachers because the process is a professional one which mainly involves teachers. Thus the views of pupils and parents may be discovered but any such input is determined in individual cases by teachers rather than being an essential part of the improvement process.

4. Deficit model

The implicit model of schooling on which school improvement operates is a deficit model. Improvement is concerned with improving current activities and putting right current failings. It does not set out to rethink or reconceptualize the learning process. In part the reason for this may be that there are few outside influences on the process – it is mainly internally generated and concerned with the technology of teaching rather than responding to external influences to change the nature of schooling because of changes in the world for which education is preparing children.

5. Independent of leadership and management

Although it is assumed that school improvement activities have the support of the headteacher it is not assumed that he or she has initiated the process nor that he or she will actively lead the process, since it is essentially concerned with classroom practice from which the headteacher is seen as remote. Thus school improvement activities are not integrated into other aspects of school management and may operate on an independent cycle from other management cycles, such as the financial.

I shall carry out the analysis of improvement under four headings: matters of principle, lack of theory, matters of methodology and practice.

1. Matters of principle

Principles behind the practice of improvement are rarely made explicit and so I shall have to infer what the principles are from the descriptions of practice. The first point is that improvement outcomes are judged by professional educators and are not seen as contested and value laden. This is consistent with the principal outcomes of improvement being concerned with teaching and learning. The process of education is seen as a neutral activity to be judged by those technically qualified: i.e. teachers. There is little recognition that there may be other views about improvement and that improving teaching has implicit assumptions about the purposes and nature of teaching. The activity does not allow for any contestation of these issues.

The second point concerns the process of improvement and ways of working together. Overwhelmingly the expectations are that these should be collegial, that groups of staff should work together closely in an interdisciplinary and non-hierarchical way. In some formulations the ways of working borrow from organizational development theory and require particularly open ways of working. There is little recognition at school level of micro-political activity and the struggle for power which goes on particularly where legitimate power has been sidelined.

It follows from this that outcomes and process of school improvement are regarded as situational only within the limitations of the principles underlying the activity – improving teaching and learning and collegial working. These principles are not subject to situational analysis.

Finally, it should be noted that the improvement initiative goes on without any obvious relationship to wider management processes in the school. Leadership of this and other activities is divided. Rather than being seen as a disadvantage this is regarded as contributing to distributed leadership and desirable. Again this is an aspect to which I shall return when school improvement research is contrasted with a strategic approach to improving schools.

2. Lack of theory

There is little theoretical or conceptual analysis of school improvement. This has a number of consequences. It impedes the creation of a coherent body of knowledge on school improvement. It means that different improvement initiatives are idiosyncratic rather than situational alternatives of a common activity. It means that systematic research is more difficult because there are insufficient clear concepts and relationships between them that might be investigated. Thus any build-up of expertise is personal to those involved in individual improvement activities rather than more publicly accessible. This impedes critical scrutiny and prevents the comparison of alternative approaches.

3. Matters of methodology

There are two aspects to methodology – methodology of *improvement* and methodology of *research* on school improvement. However, often these are combined since a research and development approach is adopted. Although this has the potential to capture the dynamic of improvement, this is difficult to discern in general terms because of the lack of conceptualization of the improvement process. Where the two are separated research on school improvement tends to be qualitative and based on case studies. Here the problem is the comparability between accounts of case studies as there is little common conceptual framework.

4. Practice

The lack of a clearly conceptualized and theorized model of school improvement reduces the value to other schools of the reported successes of an improvement initiative. The lack of a situational initial analysis means that the special factors operating in a school are not sufficiently well identified and hence similarities and differences with other settings are unclear.

Outcomes are often formulated in process terms and thus it is difficult to collect evidence to show what has been achieved in the improvement initiative. There is also no costing of the improvement effort in time and resource terms. As there is little independent evaluation and research on the process this is an area where 'good news' stories proliferate. It is difficult to know how far this is due to institutional pride and how far it is stimulated by rivalry and micropolitics with other improvement initiatives.

Finally the lack of a clear conceptualization of school improvement leaves policy makers with an inadequate understanding of what is involved. The name is appealing but without a clear understanding of what works in what situation, policy makers are left prey to a variety of approaches all called school improvement. This has similarities with the garbage can model of decision making (March and Olsen, 1979) where those with particular solutions search out politicians with problems and present their idea as the solution to whatever problems are around.

Table 1 Differences between school effectiveness and school improvement paradigms

Aspect	School Effectiveness Paradigm	School Improvement Paradigm
Implicit model	Systems model	Various including organization development
Conceptualization	Statistical	Educational
Value orientation	Objective within the choice of outcomes	Strongly collegial and professional
School outcomes	Limited	Varied
Process orientation	Static	Dynamic
Research approach	Scientific	Eclectic including action research
Generalizability of research results	High (within the paradigm)	Low
Nature of generalization	Effective school factors	Process for improving schools
Operationalization of variables	High	Low
Research data	Quantitative	Qualitative
Researchers	Academics	Practitioners
Relationship to research subjects	Sources of data	Participants
Choice of schools for research	Selected	Volunteered
Internationalization of research findings	High (within the paradigm)	Low

THE CONNECTION BETWEEN THE TWO PARADIGMS

From the foregoing discussion of the two paradigms of school effectiveness and school improvement it should be clear that they have very different orientations, as Table 1 summarizes. Even if each of them was less flawed there would be difficulties in forging links. If one accepts the two paradigms within their own terms I see the principal difficulties of connecting them as different:

1. Values orientations
2. Process orientations.

VALUES ORIENTATIONS

There are two aspects to the value positions taken by the two paradigms which make them incompatible.

School effectiveness research takes the outcomes of schooling as limited and measurable whilst school improvement researchers wish to include both the schooling process and outcomes. They also take a broad view of outcomes and reject the narrow view and its consequential findings on internal school characteristics. Thus school improvers would not accept the school effectiveness findings as valid.

The second aspect of values which contributes to incompatibility is the adherence of school improvers to a collegial style of working by teachers in schools. This would be at variance with the notion of 'strong leadership' which is one of the school effectiveness findings. In this sense some of the school effectiveness process findings have already been pre-empted by the value position of the school improvement paradigm.

PROCESS ORIENTATIONS

The final difficulty is a conceptual mismatch between the two paradigms. The school effectiveness findings give the characteristics of schools which are already effective. They do not provide any guidance about how the schools *became effective* – thus they are static in orientation rather than dynamic. There is the further concern – that the factors which have been identified as associated with effective schools may not be the ones which originally made them effective. This would not be such a handicap if the school improvement findings provided guidance about how to become effective. Here there are twin difficulties. The first is that the findings of school improvement research are weak in terms of generalizability and the second is that school improvement researchers have not studied the same outcomes as school effectiveness researchers. Thus if the school improvement findings were used to improve schools they might not lead to 'effective schools' in the terms of school effectiveness researchers.

CRITERIA FOR ANY IMPROVEMENT INITIATIVE

If the foregoing are the deficiencies of school effectiveness and school improvement, what are the alternatives? Before offering some detail on one such alternative I want first of all to propose some criteria which any appropriate approach should meet. These are:

1. Structural and systematic process

The components of the improvement process need to be well conceptualized, have a clear structural relationship to each other and include systematic operating procedures.

2. Situational orientation

Both the areas to be improved and the organizational means used to bring about improvement need to be situationally determined within the framework identified above.

3. Multiple-perspective diagnosis

The areas in need of improvement should be identified using multiple perspectives. This means involving different stakeholders and using a variety of techniques to collect their views.

4. Holistic approach

Improvement should be viewed from the perspective of the whole organization rather than being solely concerned with teaching and learning. There are organizational issues of leadership and management, staffing, resourcing and marketing which need to be integrated into thinking about improvement – both as candidates for improvement in their own right and also as contributors to improving the teaching and learning of children.

5. Long-term perspective

There needs to be an anticipation of future educational requirements of a changing world and an appreciation of the longer-term nature of significant improvement.

Senior managers in schools need to be recognized as important boundary managers. They balance internal and external demands. They are likely to be the pressure points where external demands on the school are first experienced. They should also have an overview of staffing and resources so they should be well placed to play a major role in identifying external trends and planning future staff expertise to keep pace with and take advantage of these trends. They should be able to view the organization holistically.

On the other hand I need to make clear that I am not arguing that teachers should be ignored in any decision making. They will be required to implement any changes and they have an important professional input into both the nature of these changes and how to implement them. What I am arguing for is a wider picture into which changes to teaching and learning should fit. In this way the work of the school can be more holistic. Otherwise the danger of fragmentation is that different parts of the organization might be working against each other, albeit unknowingly, rather than efforts being synchronized such that they add together rather than partially cancel each other out.

A POSSIBLE WAY FORWARD

In the introduction to this chapter I outlined the requirements for theory to progress and whilst rational criticism of existing theory was an essential element that was not sufficient. A better alternative also had to be offered. There is not space to develop an alternative here in any detail, but I have presented aspects of this alternative of which the references give further details. This solution is not without some similar flaws to the present two paradigms but it does offer an alternative and more dynamic approach to school improvement requiring leadership and management.

Although the alternative is a structural one this should not be allowed to obscure my continuing belief that the leadership and management of schools cannot be reduced to a formula. Structures and systems should be seen as supports and not as procedures to be followed unthinkingly. The most appropriate action to take at any stage will always be conditional and require interpretation of the circumstances. To take a geographical analogy, what I am seeking to provide is a better roadmap and some landmarks and signposts (see Figure 3). These will help to analyse the present position and point to indicators of ways forward to different destinations. This makes more explicit the need for leaders to have skills of organizational analysis and organizational understanding in addition to educational credentials.

The two principal existing components are strategic analysis (Fidler *et al.*, 1996, 1997b) and benchmarking (Camp, 1989; Fidler, 1999). However, I think there may be potential to use structural equation modelling and path analysis (Kelloway, 1998) to identify relationships between the structural and psychological components of an effective school. Such a framework would have a number of advantages. It could provide indicators for changes to components which contribute to effectiveness such as, for example, staff morale, staff attitudes and confidence in leadership. Such indicators could play a part in monitoring the effects of stages in improvement efforts and feed back into the change process to keep it on track (Hargreaves, 1995). A framework which could be used for both planning and researching school improvement could help build experience from case studies into more generalizable findings.

The first task for the school effectiveness strand is to identify effective schools in different situations. Although the same measure of progress may be used in each case the internal operation of the school, including the actions of teachers, must reflect these differences in their role in the education of children. Thus a series of effective schools in different external contexts and with different internal situations are needed.

The initial element in the school improvement strand is to use a strategic analysis approach (see Figure 3) to identify future needs in the organization which take account of changes in the world outside the school using the perspectives of a variety of stakeholders, to balance these with internal

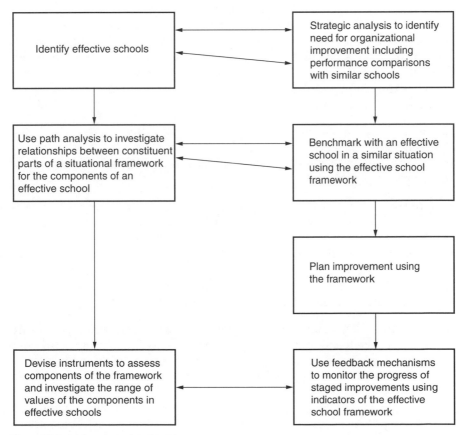

Figure 3 Model for strategic school improvement

resources and existing norms and values and to create a long-term improvement strategy which is holistic (Fidler *et al.*, 1996). This incorporates all the processes which contribute to a successful school and goes beyond the processes which directly produce outcomes for students.

The second element that identifies the processes that contribute to superior performance is benchmarking. Benchmarking is the organizational equivalent of the correlates of effective schools except that it is a process that has to be carried out by each individual improving organization rather than being universally determined (Camp, 1989). Benchmarking provides a systematic approach to improving performance of an organization by identifying and replicating better practice from other organizations. Such other organizations could be schools displaying better practice on any particular aspect of their performance. The British Government's Beacon School initiative provides the basis for this kind of operation now that schools identify some particular feature of their internal processes on which other schools might benchmark (DfEE, 2000).

More imaginatively, for some aspects of performance, schools might benchmark with non-educational organizations. For example, boarding schools might benchmark with hotels in order to improve their flexibility in terms of offering accommodation for varying periods to students rather than only full-time or weekly boarding. Educational organizations wishing to open for longer hours might benchmark with successful supermarkets which have discovered ways of extending opening hours whilst meeting financial targets.

The process consists of:

(a) Identifying superior practice in another organization;
(b) Analysing the superior practice;
(c) Translating the superior practice for use in the home organization;
(d) Implementing the superior practice.

This provides a systematic way of identifying the characteristics of superior practice in particular aspects of schooling. However, it is worth noting a number of features which demonstrate flexibility in choice of outcome, situational adaptation and the need for organization analysis and judgement for successful adaptation. If the replication is carried out superficially it is unlikely to capture the elements which lead to superior performance or could be unable to translate them and assess them for replication elsewhere.

(a) Benchmarking takes place with an organization which demonstrates the particular outcomes which are to be improved over the longer term. Thus a benchmark can be chosen for any particular outcome or process of schooling which needs to be improved rather than only using examination performance.
(b) Benchmarking takes place with another school which has as many similarities as possible with the school wishing to improve, e.g. environment, size, internal situation.

(c) The more successful school needs to be studied in order to analyse what contributes to the successful outcomes and whether and how such contributions could be introduced in the improving school. Whilst this calls for judgement it can be supplemented by a greater understanding of organizational working and more indicators to give insights into organizational well-being.

Such an approach meets all five criteria which I have adduced for a successful approach to improving schools.

CONCLUSION

Differentiating school effectiveness activities from school improvement ones will help reduce the confusion about them. It should be clear that school effectiveness has the hallmarks of a 'movement' rather than being a neutral research activity. There are believers and non-believers and endless recycling of the literature of a very few writers. School improvement, on the other hand, is extraordinarily diverse and has many competing proponents.

School effectiveness is attractive to policy makers because of the certainty and simplicity of its findings but I believe that it is fundamentally flawed in searching for generalities which could apply across all schools. I think that there are combinations of practices that can make individual schools effective. It is this dynamic of effective schools which is lacking from the current research paradigm.

School improvement is also attractive to policy makers in that it provides a way of increasing children's performance in schools by using straightforward professional knowledge in a commonsense way. Some new techniques can be introduced and employed without any need to integrate them into more holistic thinking. This attempt to compartmentalize improvement ignores possible conflicts in organizational priorities and resources and it may be trying to solve problems which individual schools don't have. Most of all, such disingenuous thinking ignores all the evidence about the difficulties of managing change and the substantial knowledge about the difficulties of leading and managing schools.

I think there is a need for more certainty about the connections between the constituent parts of good practice in schools. A research methodology to investigate these constituents and the relationships between them could increase understanding of organizational performance. The identification of core constituents and indicators of the state of these could be valuable in a number of ways. Indicators could be valuable for diagnostic purposes in planning the need for changes and also in monitoring the effects of changes. All this would provide a structural framework for school improvement and provide more secure indicators on which leaders and managers could exercise their judgement.

REFERENCES

Argyris, C. and Schon, D. A. (1974) *Theory in Practice: Increasing Professional Effectiveness.* San Francisco, CA: Jossey-Bass.

Bennett, N., Crawford, M., Levačić, R., Glover, D. and Earley, P. (2000) 'The reality of school development planning in the effective primary school: Technicist or guiding plan?', *School Leadership and Management* **20**(3): 333–51.

Bidwell, C. E. (1965) 'The school as a formal organisation', in J. G. March (ed.) *Handbook of Organizations.* Chicago, IL: Rand McNally & Co.

Bliss, J. R. (1991) 'Strategic and holistic images of effective schools', in J. R. Bliss, W. A. Firestone and C. E. Richards (eds) *Rethinking Effective School Research and Practice.* Englewood Cliffs, NJ: Prentice Hall.

Bliss, J. R., Firestone, W. A. and Richards, C. E. (eds) (1991) *Rethinking Effective School Research and Practice.* Englewood Cliffs, NJ: Prentice Hall.

Bolman, L. G. and Deal, T. E. (1997) *Reframing Organizations: Artistry, Choice and Leadership* (2nd edn). San Francisco, CA: Jossey-Bass.

Burrell, G. and Morgan. G. (1979) *Sociological Paradigms and Organisational Analysis: Elements of the Sociology of Corporate Life.* London: Heinemann Educational.

Camp, R. C. (1989) *Benchmarking: The Search for Industry Best Practices that Lead to Superior Performance.* Milwaukee, WI: American Society for Quality Control Press.

Cotton, K. (1995) *Effective Schooling Practices: A Research Synthesis 1995 Update* Portland, OR: Northwest Regional Educational Laboratory.

Deal, T. E. (1985) 'The symbolism of effective schools', *The Elementary School Journal.* **85**(5): 601–20.

Department for Education and Employment (DfEE) (1998) *The National Literacy Strategy.* London: DfEE.

Department for Education and Employment (DfEE) (2000) *Beacon Schools* (Ref: 0007/2000). London: DfEE.

Duncan, O. D. (1975) *Introduction to Structural Equation Models.* New York: Academic Press.

Elliott, J. (1996) 'School effectiveness research and its critics: alternative visions of schooling', *Cambridge Journal of Education* **26**(2): 199–224.

Fidler, B. (1997a) 'The school as a whole: School improvement and planned change', in B. Fidler, S. Russell and T. Simkins (eds) *Choices for Self-Managing Schools: Autonomy and Accountability.* London: Paul Chapman Publishing.

Fidler, B. (1997b) 'Strategic management', in B. Fidler, S. Russell and T. Simkins (eds) *Choices for Self-Managing Schools: Autonomy and Accountability.* London: Paul Chapman Publishing.

Fidler, B. (1999) 'Benchmarking and strategy', in J. Grant (ed.) *Value for Money in School Management.* York: Funding Agency for Schools.

Fidler, B. with Edwards, M., Evans, B., Mann, P. and Thomas, P. (1996) *Strategic Planning for School Improvement.* London: Pitman Publishing.

Fullan, M. G. (1991) *The New Meaning of Educational Change.* London: Cassell.

Gleick, J. (1988) *Chaos: Making a New Science.* London: William Heinemann.

Glover, D., Levačić, R. and Bennett, N. (1996) 'Leadership, planning and management in four very effective secondary schools: Part I: setting the scene', *School Organisation* **16**(2): 135–48. 'Part II: planning and performance', *School Organisation* **16**(3): 247–61.

Goldstein, H. and Spiegelhalter, D. J. (1996) 'League tables and their limitations: statistical issues in comparisons of institutional performance', *Journal of the Royal Statistical Society, Series A,* **159**(3): 385–443.

Good, T. L. and Brophy, J. E. (1986) 'School effects', in M. C. Wittrock (ed.) *Handbook of Research on Teaching* (3rd edn). New York: Macmillan.

Gray, H. L. (1988) 'Management consultancy in education: an introduction to practice', in H. L. Gray (ed.) *Management Consultancy in Schools*. London: Cassell.

Hall, G. E. and Hord, S. M. (1987) *Change in Schools: Facilitating the Process*. New York: SUNY Press.

Hallinger, P. and Heck, R. H. (1996) 'Reassessing the principal's role in school effectiveness: A review of research, 1980–1995', *Educational Administration Quarterly* **32**(1): 5–44.

Hannaway, J. and Talbert, J. E. (1993) 'Bringing context into effective schools research: Urban–suburban differences', *Educational Administration Quarterly* **29**(2): 164–86.

Hargreaves, A. (1991) 'Contrived collegiality', in J. Blase (ed.) *The Politics of School Life*. San Francisco, CA: Sage.

Hargreaves, D. H. (1995) 'Self-managing schools and development planning – chaos or control?', *School Organisation* **15**(3): 215–27.

Hargreaves, D. H. and Hopkins, D. (1991) *The Empowered School*. London: Cassell.

Hersey, P. and Blanchard, K. (1993) *Management of Organizational Behavior* (6th edn). Englewood Cliffs, NJ: Prentice-Hall.

Hopkins, D., Ainscow, M. and West, M. (1994) *School Improvement in an Era of Change*. London: Cassell.

Jesson, D., Mayston, D. and Smith, P. (1987) 'Performance assessment in the educational sector: educational and economic perspectives', *Oxford Review of Education* **13**(3): 249–66.

Kelloway, E. K. (1998) *Using LISREL for Structural Equation Modelling: A Researcher's Guide*. Thousand Oaks, CA: Sage.

Kuhn, T. S. (1970) *The Structure of Scientific Revolutions*. Chicago, IL: University of Chicago Press.

Levine, D. U. and Lezotte, L.W. (1990) *Unusually Effective Schools: A Review and Analysis of Research and Practice*. Madison, WI: The National Center for Effective Schools Research and Development.

MacGilchrist, B., Mortimore, P., Savage, J. and Beresford, C. (1995) *Planning Matters: The Impact of Development Planning in Primary Schools*. London: Paul Chapman Publishing.

McLaughlin, M. W. (1990) 'The Rand Change Agent Study revisited: macro perspectives and micro realities', *Educational Researcher* **19**(9): 11–16.

March, J. G. and Olsen, V. P. (1979) *Ambiguity and Choice in Organisations* (2nd edn). Bergen: Universitets forlaget.

Mayston, D. and Jesson, D. (1988) 'Developing models of educational accountability', *Oxford Review of Education* **14**(3): 321–39.

Miles, M. B. and Ekholm, M. (1985) 'What is School Improvement?' in W. G. van Velzen, M. B. Miles, M. Ekholm, U. Hameyer and D. Robin (eds) *Making School Improvement Work: A Conceptual Guide to Practice*. Leuven, Belgium: Academic Publishing Company.

Mortimore, P. (1991) 'The nature and findings of research on school effectiveness in the primary sector', in S. Riddell and S. Brown (eds) *School Effectiveness Research: Its Messages for School Improvement*. Edinburgh: Her Majesty's Stationery Office.

Mortimore, P., Sammons, P., Stoll, L., Lewis, D. and Ecob, R. (1988) *School Matters: The Junior Years*. Wells: Open Books.

Munck, I. M. E. (1979) *Model Building in Comparative Education* (International Association for the Evaluation of Educational Achievement Monograph Studies, No. 10). Stockholm, Sweden: Almqvist & Wiksell International.

Ouston, J. (1996) 'School effectiveness, school improvement and good schools', in P. Earley, B. Fidler and J. Ouston (eds) *Improvement through Inspection?* London: David Fulton.

Ouston, J. (1999) 'School effectiveness and school improvement: Critique of a movement', in T. Bush, L. A. Bell, R. Bolam, R. Glatter and P. M. Ribbins (eds)

Educational Management: Redefining Theory, Policy and Practice. London: Paul Chapman Publishing.

Preece, P. (1989) 'Pitfalls in research on school and teacher effectiveness', *Research Papers in Education* **4**(3): 47–69.

Purkey, S. C. and Smith, M. S. (1983) 'Effective schools: A review', *Elementary School Journal* **83**(4): 427–52.

Reynolds, D., Sullivan, M. and Murgatroyd, S. (1987) *The Comprehensive Experiment*. Lewes: Falmer Press.

Rowan, B. (1984) 'Shamanistic rituals in effective schools', *Issues in Education* **2**(1): 76–87.

Rutter, M., Maughan, B., Mortimore, P., Ouston, J. and Smith, A. (1979) *Fifteen Thousand Hours*. London: Open Books.

Sammons, P., Hillman, J. and Mortimore, P. (1995) *Key Characteristics of Effective Schools: A Review of School Effectiveness Research*. London: OFSTED.

Sammons, P., Thomas, S. and Mortimore, P. (1997) *Forging Links: Effective Schools and Effective Departments*. London: Paul Chapman Publishing.

Scott, W. R. (1992) *Organizations: Rational, Natural and Open Systems* (3rd edn). Upper Saddle River, NJ: Prentice Hall.

Slee, R., Weiner, G. with Tomlinson, S. (eds) (1998) *School Effectiveness for Whom? Challenges to the School Effectiveness and School Improvement Movements*. London: Falmer Press.

van Velzen, W. G., Miles, M. B., Ekholm, M., Hameyer, U. and Robin, D. (eds) (1985) *Making School Improvement Work: A Conceptual Guide to Practice*. Leuven, Belgium: Academic Publishing Company.

Wilms, J. D. (1992) *Monitoring School Performance*. London: Falmer Press.

Chapter 5

The Micro-Politics of Change, Improvement and Effectiveness in Schools

Hugh Busher

INTRODUCTION

Over the last 20 years or so, there has been increasing concern by central governments in the UK to describe what an effective school might look like and how schools might achieve or sustain that happy state through processes of school improvement. Despite the success of various studies in trying to characterize effective schools (Rutter *et al.*, 1977; Sammons *et al.*, 1997), little attempt has been made to locate these characteristics in their dynamic socio-political environments or to indicate how those environments interact with the internal processes of schools. At its least insightful this has led to the view that what happens inside schools is only the responsibility of those people who work inside schools so that change in schools can be brought about solely by the efforts of the staff of those schools (Barber, 1998). Yet researchers into school effectiveness, such as Mortimore (1999), acknowledge that schools make at best some 10 per cent difference to the performance of the pupils attending them, important though that difference might be.

Much of what happens in schools is caused by a multiplicity of factors that are located outside schools but are imported into schools through the semi-permeable membranes of schools' institutional boundaries by students and staff of all qualities (Busher, 1992; Barker and Busher, 1998). Staff and students in schools interact both with these external pressures and values and with each other in constructing what takes place in schools. Many of these interactions or negotiations are successful and lead to agreed ways of working and satisfactory outcomes to all parties involved. Some of these negotiations are less successful. Involved in all these negotiations are individual people who are trying to achieve their agenda, such as to teach a lesson, learn a topic or resolve a conflict with parents. These agendas are likely to be driven by overt or hidden values and beliefs about education and social order. In pursuit of these agendas, people look for symbolic and material resources and other people (who may be a resource) to help them. In other words they look for sources of power to help them implement their views and values. This suggests that schools are political arenas in which competing views of educational and social order struggle to impose the preferred values of different social groups and individual people, some of whom are more powerful and influential than others. On this basis Ball (1987) has gone some way to constructing a micro-political theory of educational organizations.

To explain how more effective schools can be created, school improvement research has largely constructed a traditional–rationalist model (Blase, 1991) on how change can be brought about. In taking for granted the power relationships in organizational processes, whether between schools and their external environments or within schools, this model overlooks the constructed and unequal nature of these relationships. Consequently the complicated socio-political dynamics of implementing or resisting change, of gaining symbolic and material resources for enacting cherished values or of losing self-esteem and peer support tend to be reduced to technicist formulae for bringing about school improvement. In practice the rational processes of planning, monitoring and evaluation complement the political dynamics of negotiation. Hoyle (1986) pointed out that:

> Micro-politics is best perceived as a continuum, one end of which is virtually indistinguishable from conventional management procedures but from which it diverges on a number of dimensions ... to the point where it constitutes almost a separate world of illegitimate, self-interested manipulation. (p. 126)

The internal processes of leading and managing school organizations can be crudely divided up into six aspects. These are the political – dynamic processes of negotiation and change; the cultural – shared norms, values and beliefs held generally by people in the organization; and the structural or bureaucratic framework of formal roles and administrative procedures. Ribbins (1985) suggests that there is a further aspect in the make-up of school institutions: the human groups and individuals. A fifth aspect is the technical, which is sustained and shaped by these other elements. This is the curriculum which teachers construct with or deliver to the students with the support of other staff. A sixth aspect is the external physical, social and economic environment which surrounds and permeates every school organization.

Micro-political processes provide the threads through which all the other aspects are interconnected and interact (Busher and Harris, 1999). Consequently they appear at the core of all the other aspects. For example, school cultures, which are discussed more fully in Chapter 6, are dynamic and created through the interactions of people. They are a nexus of shared norms and values that express how people make sense of the organization in which they work and the other people with whom they work. Although powerfully visible through various symbolic processes, organizational culture is often taken for granted by current participants in an organization who may be unaware how a particular culture has been constructed, how it might or can be changed or how it is sustained by those people in positions of power and authority.

The shaping and sustaining of an institution's culture through a variety of symbolic actions is of major concern to powerful people, such as headteachers. This is because it helps to make manifest the values and beliefs that those powerful people wish the institution to implement. Greenfield (1991) notes the importance of the moral values of headteachers in shaping the way in which they organize their schools and manage their staff and students. Thus the shaping and modifying of a school's culture, as well as of the subcultures of subject areas and student pastoral groups in it, is a political act to assert power inequitably in favour of a particular set of values and beliefs held by the most formally powerful people.

The cultural norms of a school or subject area interact with the individual agenda of participants in a school in a variety of different ways. Although the culture of a school will shape the views of new and current members of a school, perhaps through processes of induction, as Schein (1992) points out, individual people also modify the culture of school organizations. This occurs as new people join institutions or as people modify their values, beliefs and ideologies either in response to pressures external to the institution, such as central government legislation, or to developments in their own thinking or socio-economic circumstances. Such negotiations and adjustments are essentially political, being about how people sustain or modify their views and values in order to sustain their sense of self while yet remaining in, or gaining membership of, social groups which they perceive as valuable or significant either to themselves or to the people whom they represent or teach. Paechter and Head (1996) discuss how the membership of academic departments in schools and the power used within them affect teachers' senses of self-identity.

Individual people's perspectives on school organizations are of key importance since schools are made up of large numbers of individual people, although they often work in a variety of different groups and some people wield more power than others. Greenfield and Ribbins (1993) describe such individual perspectives as phenomenological. People create their own individual meanings for each social event or action in which they engage, although many of these meanings and views may be driven by professional as well as personal values. Thus for every aspect of teaching, learning or involvement in a school organizational activity each person has a different interpretation. These have to be negotiated between the people involved in the activity if that activity is to take place successfully.

Where such negotiations are unsuccessful, or staff or students decide that their needs or interests are not being met sufficiently by an activity, they are likely to resist taking part or staying part of it. For example, although people work more or less willingly in certain groups such as classes or departments for much of the time, their continuing membership is based on each person's willingness to remain part of those groups, even when the opportunities for leaving it physically are limited. At those points when people (students or staff) cannot leave a group physically, perhaps for reasons of legal contract or social pressure, they may find other ways of resisting being part of its actions (see, for example, Plant, 1987; Wolcott, 1977) or becoming disaffected with it (e.g. Willis, 1977).

The technical or curriculum aspect of a school's process is itself a constructed and a political phenomenon, representing a particular set of views and values, in both its formal or subject components and in its informal or hidden components of preferred social norms and behaviours. Armstrong (1998, p. 49) points out that what constitutes the curriculum of a school is a contested arena providing a focus for 'political, religious and philosophical debate'. Carr (1993) argues that the curriculum is:

> not a description of subject matter but a set of proposals indicating ... how subject matter is to be organised, the educational purposes it serves, the learning outcomes it is intended to achieve and the methods by which such outcomes are to be evaluated. (p. 5)

The curriculum, then, and the pedagogies used to deliver or create it are the outcomes of political processes that have been negotiated between a variety of social groups inside and outside school. Not least, the curriculum can be conceptualized as a process that is negotiated between teachers and students in the classroom although formally, in the administrative structure of the school, power is held autocratically by teachers.

Politics, then, emerges as the key element in understanding the process of shaping and changing what takes place in schools. This is because it is through processes of negotiation that people try to assert their views and values, and through the manipulation of power to gain access to material and symbolic resources that they attempt to implement them (Ball, 1987). As is usual in organizations, in schools some people are given or gain more power than others. So some people are more successful at asserting their ideologies than are others, such as the headteachers in the study by Greenfield (1991) referred to earlier. Here, politics (or micro-politics) are viewed as part of the normal processes of school organizations, not as something pathological, an indication of social malfunctioning. In this view politics are an essential part of management (Stephenson, 1985) rather than separate from or antagonistic to management (Ball, 1989).

Bringing about change or sustaining current processes depends on how people wield power. In order to try to implement particular values and beliefs people struggle to gain the material and symbolic resources that will allow them to do so (Ball, 1987). The analysis holds even when applied to disaffected students. Those students in Willis' study (1977) sought resources – time and space – to implement their preferred values in education (of not taking part in academic studies). How certain views and values, then, come to be embedded in notions of school effectiveness or celebrated in processes of school improvement can be explained by how some people at central government, university and school level have been more successful (or powerful) in asserting their views than have others.

Resistance is itself a normal part of the political process (Ganderton, 1991; van der Westhuizen, 1996). Why some people choose to resist changes, which from the perspectives of other people seem reasonable for improving school performance, can be understood in terms of what such changes might mean to those people individually or collectively or to the values that they hold on principled grounds. The changes might, for example, be perceived as an attack on some people's value systems – why should all children have to attend classes in Christian religious education, for example? Or the changes might be considered to diminish people's social status – one student wondered whether the fact that her school had been placed in Special Measures by her school's inspectors meant that she and her colleagues were worthless (Barker and Busher, 1998). Or the changes might be perceived as an incursion on time that people prefer to use for non-employment activities that they consider, none-theless, of major importance to their social lives.

A MICRO-POLITICAL ANATOMY OF PROCESSES IN SCHOOLS

A micro-political perspective offers explanations for how people co-operate in educational institutions, as well as giving insights into how people handle conflict (Ball, 1987) in the construction of these different organizational processes in schools. It offers insights into how and why one team of teachers, say an academic department in a secondary school, works better together than do others in the same school (Siskin, 1994; Paechter and Head, 1996). It recognizes that people hold a variety of different interests singly and in groups and pursue these through a variety of different strategies (Ball, 1989). Further, it does not have to make any assumptions about people being rational or needing to share the same values, which the school improvement and school effectiveness paradigms presuppose, since it allows observers to explain how people resolve conflicts, at least temporarily, in the pursuit of common goals. Thus it is about how people get things done with and through others (Blase and Anderson, 1995). It dissects the art of management and leadership, rather than offering rationalist or technicist descriptions of it that hide uncomfortable social questions about why power and resources are distributed inequitably and unequally in favour of some people and not others.

Bacharach (1988) argues that:

> Educational organisations are best conceived as political systems, both internally and in their external relationships. In educational organisations, at all levels, constant tactical power struggles occur in an effort to obtain control over real or symbolic resources . . . . Participants can be conceived of as political actors with their own needs, objectives and strategies to achieve those objectives . . . . The decision-making process is the primary arena of political conflict. Each sub-group [in a school] can be expected to approach a decision with the objective of maximising its specific interests or goals . . . . A group's efforts to have their point of view reflected in the decision outcome centres in large part around questions of authority and influence . . . . Each sub-group will have a different view of who has

the formal power (authority), who has the informal power (influence), and who should have the power to make organisational decisions. (p. 282)

A micro-political perspective focuses on the interactions between the personal, interpersonal (cultural) and formal (legitimate power and organizational structure) aspects of school organizations. Gronn (1985) maps the educational management and administration field with a matrix that sets Levinson's (1959, cited in Gronn, 1985:58–9) threefold statement about how roles and tasks are constructed – by self (intra-personally); by situation (inter-personally); by organizational structure (socially) – against Hodgkinson's (1981, cited in Gronn, 1985:58–9) taxonomy of the aspects of the field – ideas; persons; things. The micro-political perspective focuses on the point where individual participants' and stakeholders' moral philosophies and ideologies about education and society (Hodgkinson, 1991; Greenfield, 1991) – be they teachers, pupils, parents, school governors or national or local political figures – intersect and interact with the cultural norms of organizational groups in schools and powerful socio-economic imperatives from the external environment of schools. The last may derive from a variety of sources including central government legislation and local parental or business concerns and interests. The philosophies and ideologies of individual participants may be espoused and publicly proclaimed as part of a person's social and self-identity or they may be visible in how people interact with other people, singly and in groups, without necessarily being clearly articulated. Schon (1983) described this last expression of people's held views and values as theory-in-action or enacted theories.

In this conceptual framework it is possible to construe school organizational structures as merely the reified outcomes of previous power struggles between different groups of people inside and outside school organizations to implement their preferred educational values and beliefs. Cyert and March (1963) argue that organizations are essentially social constructs made up of coalitions of various individuals, work groups and social groups each, potentially, with its own values, beliefs and purposes. Organizational structures are constructed to favour or legitimate the work and views of particular and formally powerful people and office holders. Consequently they also disempower or inhibit the values and actions of other people or alter their sense of self (Foucault, 1990). Paechter and Head (1996) point out how certain women teachers were inhibited from implementing their craft knowledge in design technology lessons because male heads of department did not allocate them adequate resources for such work.

A key concept in a micro-political analysis, then, is power in organizations and how people use it (Bacharach and Lawler, 1980; Blase and Anderson, 1995) through a variety of strategies and tactics within and through an organization. In this discussion, resistance is a multiplicity of tactics that are more or less powerful in a variety of different circumstances that are used to oppose change rather than to advance it. How power might be construed and constructed is developed more fully in Chapter 6. This chapter focuses on the political process of school organizations and the strategies people use to promote and resist change and what some people call improvement.

The different facets of the micro-political process can be shown diagrammatically. Table 2 sets these out under three main headings: Manifestations of power; Organizational groups and coalitions; and Processes of negotiations. Bacharach and Lawler (1980) offered a similar division. The table is not intended to set out a hierarchy between these three different elements. That is merely a function of the printed medium. Rather the image should be that of a three-leafed clover, the three lobes or elements interacting to make up the whole model.

SUBJECT AREAS, WORKING PARTIES AND OTHER ORGANIZATIONAL GROUPS

In school organizations people fit into a variety of organizational groups. These are groups the members of which recognize that they have interests in common (Bacharach and Lawler, 1980). The extent and strength of the commonality of interest vary depending on the centrality of the group to the interests of the actors involved. In the schema in Table 2 these groups are divided up into formal organizational groups, factions (or informal groups) and networks. Hoyle (1982) simply divided them into two: the formal interest groups and informal interest sets. The latter were given this term because they were perceived as being only loose associations. However in research on the politics of school decision-making (Busher, 1992) there was clear evidence of three types. Into the first category fitted most of those formal organizational groups, such as academic departments, year groups, curriculum working parties and governors' committees. Into the second category fitted groups that had recognizable foci, functions and membership. These ranged from curriculum activity groups, such as school choirs and sports teams, to staff activity groups, such as a staff cricket team in one school and a staff football team in another, to staff study groups. In one school a group of staff met on a regular basis to take a school-based Masters degree course in education management. Into the third category fitted a number of diffuse networks. These often consisted of people who shared similar interests outside school but could not be observed to constitute a working group or active pressure group inside school.

On some issues concerning the management of a school, some of these groups may combine, i.e. form a coalition to negotiate, usually with the senior management team, about a particular issue. In many cases these coalitions last for a fairly short time, having been brought together for a single issue. In some cases these coalitions have formal organizational recognition. For example, the science departments in many secondary schools are made up of several departments, each with its own subject leader, but under the overall

Table 2 How the main political features of a school organization fit together

Manifestations of power			
Authority (formal power) ⌣ **Influence (informal power)**		**Bases** ▮	**Sources** ▮
Headship v. Leadership (Gibb, 1947)		Organizational structure; Rites, rituals, customs; Interest groups / factions	Institutional; Professional; Personal
Organizational groups and coalitions (overlapping membership)			
Formal organizational (interest) groups ▮	**Factions² (informal interest groups)** ▮		**Networks (pressure groups)** ▮
Standing¹ e.g. subject department; Ad hoc¹ e.g. working parties; Cross-institutional [¹ Poster (1976)]	Work-related; Social [² Hoyle (1982) – interest sets; Burns (1955) – cliques/ cabals]		Work-related; Social
Processes of negotiations			
Social framework ▮	**Strategies** ▮		**Sites and locations** ▮
Norms, values, beliefs; Rates of exchange; People's and group's interests (personal and professional)	Bureaucratic; Interactive; Resistant		Arenas e.g. meetings (formal and informal); Electronic networks

co-ordination of a head of science. This kind of organization Busher and Harris (1999) refer to as a federal department. The scope for intra-departmental political struggles in such departments is enormous, particularly over the allocation of resources, the particular culture to be fostered between staff and the preferred pedagogical approaches to be used with particular groups of pupils.

The construction and operation of these coalitions takes up a considerable amount of time and energy, especially for subject leaders (Busher, 1992). To achieve the interests through the formal negotiating arenas, such as heads of department meetings in a secondary school, people try to construct coalitions that wield more influence and authority than those of their opponents. A head of department in a secondary school gave this explanation of the process to show how the internal politics of a subject area were linked to whole school decision making, although he used a military metaphor:

> Coming up to a heads of departments' meeting the tempo rises and then machine guns are blazing for a couple of hours on a Tuesday night [heads of departments' meeting with the senior staff]. Then there is a gentle easing of pressure down to Friday. But it seems to occupy more or less a week . . . to gather your troops about you and get opinions for the forthcoming agenda and then to get information out

and receive responses, and follow up the discussions afterwards. (Busher, 1992, 277–8)

THE SAGA OF THE PHOTOCOPIER: A STUDY IN PRESSURE GROUP POLITICS

The following cameo, taken from Busher (1992), illustrates why and how subject leaders in a secondary school constructed a temporary coalition to sustain their preferred social and educational values, of working in collaborative cultures with their subject area colleagues to sustain cohesive subject departments. The importance of social cohesion to the effective working of subject areas is highlighted in the research of Glover *et al.* (1998) and Harris (1998).

The introduction of a new system of photocopying in a secondary school by senior staff provoked a confrontation with subject leaders when some of their key interests as subject leaders were threatened. The new photocopier was introduced for two purposes. One was to improve the quality of photocopied materials used in teaching and learning, an aim which subject leaders had sponsored for a long time. The other was to establish greater control of expenditure on this item in the school's budget. This also increased central and senior management control over the organizational processes of the school.

With the support of a formal heads of departments' meeting one of the deputy headteachers agreed a new contract with a photocopier hire company, although it increased the costs of photocopying very considerably. Under the previous system of photocopying a subject leader claimed he had spent

> sort of £19 per year out of a budget of about £1600. Now I have to allow £250 for duplicating. I can't allow open access because it is just too expensive so I have had to say everything must come through me. (Busher, 1992, 288–9)

To implement firmer control, senior staff asked subject leaders to control the access of their teaching colleagues to photocopying, using a key system – one for each subject area. The school secretariat was given oversight of the system, issuing subject leaders with a monthly audit of their accounts. This also reinforced the visible power of the senior staff and gave them the possibility of being proactive in bringing subject leaders to account for their performances.

The new system gave subject leaders greater authority as gatekeepers to subject area resources and, therefore, greater control over or management of their colleagues' pedagogic activities. In turn this encouraged greater social distance between subject leaders and their colleagues. However this was detrimental to sustaining the social cohesion of individual subject areas. Subject leaders valued highly this quality for its contribution to successful team work in their areas. So, far from encouraging subject leaders to feel more managerial and supportive of hierarchical decision-making processes, as the headteacher suggested would be the effect of the new photocopying system, many subject leaders disliked the management implications of the new system.

In large part these flowed from the costs of the new system. As they were so high subject leaders had to restrict very considerably the amount of photocopying their colleagues could do to create resources for teaching to avoid subject area budgets being drastically depleted. The new system also took up a lot of time for subject leaders to monitor.

Subject leaders gained power over their colleagues because they now had to manage and control teachers' requests for access to the photocopier. To cope with this new situation different subject leaders used a range of different strategies. These ranged from the autocratic – every piece of photocopying had to be expressly permitted by the subject leader; through the bureaucratic – ground rules were laid down within a subject area indicating under what circumstances and how much photocopying subject area staff could do, but they could access the photocopier key and sign for it themselves; through the collegial – discussing the ground rules for photocopying and considering the budget implications for the subject area at frequent meetings but leaving the photocopier key on open access; to the *laissez-faire* – leaving the photocopier key in a public place for subject area colleagues to access as they would.

Many teachers thought that heads of department used their increased power to maintain established departmental practices, as it was in their interest to do so if these were successful, rather than to support individual teachers' innovations. They were annoyed by this – illustrating how the more hierarchical management processes required by the new photocopying system threatened the social cohesion of subject areas. Many heads of department resented being brought into conflict with their colleagues, unnecessarily as they perceived it, through having to operate a more autocratic style of management than they had done formerly in order to protect the subject area budget. Such conflict was against their interests of managing a cohesive staff team.

To cope with this problem, the heads of department in the school created a temporary coalition to persuade the deputy head responsible for the photocopier contract to keep the new photocopier but to persuade the company to lease it to the school at a much lower rate. Such outcomes would meet their interests as subject leaders by keeping the improved quality of photocopied curriculum materials and reducing their need to keep a tight control on the curriculum materials activities of their colleagues.

To achieve these outcomes the heads of department decided they needed to lobby the deputy head who had negotiated the original new photocopier contract to get him to change the nature of the contract with the photocopier lending company. Lobbying involved them in going to see the deputy head during their non-contact times and talking with him at break times. One head of department explained how the heads of department collectively and informally agreed to organize this. Faced with this pressure, albeit with considerable reluctance, the deputy head renegotiated the contractual terms on which the photocopier was rented by the school. The matter never came to a formal heads of department meeting, the negotiations being completed before the next scheduled meeting was due. The change of contract was merely announced in that arena. One head of department suggested the explanation for this was that the deputy head did not want to face large-scale public disapproval of his original photocopier contract in such a public arena.

CARRYING OUT NEGOTIATIONS

Negotiations between individuals and interest groups take place within the social framework of the school. This is the culture of a school and is created by its rites, rituals, customs and language which uphold and make visible the values and beliefs preferred, by and large, by the senior staff. Embedded within this cultural milieu – Bourdieu (1990) talks about this as an habitus – are understandings about how people bargain legitimately for material and symbolic resources and what might be considered fair or reasonable rates of exchange for gaining such resources from other people (Busher, 1989). For example, one department negotiated the occasional loan of equipment from another department to teach certain aspects of their syllabus. It was not worth purchasing such equipment. In return the lending department periodically received a ream or two of duplicating paper from the borrowers (Busher, 1992).

Part of this social framework is made up of the interests of the individual people and groups in a school. Willis' (1977) group of disaffected students clearly had one such set of interests. Different departments manifest various interests in resources, beyond the usual budget negotiating round in a school. In one case, in the study by Busher (1992), an art department successfully negotiated the use of some unkempt land in a school's grounds which the science department was not using productively. The art department used the land to put up a display of pupils' sculptures, enhancing the attractiveness of the school grounds to everybody in the school and to passers-by and visitors. To borrow such a resource, the art department had to gain access to power to encourage the science department to relinquish, at least temporarily, its claim to this territory. This access to power took the form of support for this venture from the senior staff, who wanted to see the site made more attractive. Interestingly, after the sculpture exhibition was taken down at the end of the summer term, the science department became much more active in using the land which it had previously ignored, so re-asserting its claim to the territory.

The interests which teachers claim to hold, and about which they are willing to negotiate, can be divided up into professional and personal interests and into institutional interests (within the school), technical or curriculum interests, work or career-oriented interests and social interests (Busher, 1992). It is sometimes difficult to distinguish whether teachers' technical interests are actually professionally or personally driven. The most obvious example of this is of teachers who strongly prefer teaching an aspect of the curriculum and also pursue this interest in their own time outside school. The extent of these

Table 3 Examples of teachers' interests in school decision-making negotiations

Professional interests		Personal interests	
Institutional	*Technical or curriculum*	*Work or career-oriented*	*Social*
Effectiveness of school organization	Preferred pedagogic styles	Career	Many and varied: how people like to spend their leisure time
Territory – physically (e.g. which classroom) and symbolically	Preferred aspects of the curriculum to teach	Self-esteem	
Prestige of the school or the subject area	Curriculum related knowledge e.g. assessment procedures	Extra-curricular activities	
Effectiveness of pupil discipline	Particular resources available	School or subject area culture	
Relationships with senior staff	Time available for teaching preferred topics or extra-curricular activities	Job satisfaction	
How well time was managed – teaching timetable; meetings		Relationships with colleagues and pupils	
	How pupils are grouped	Educational and social values	
		Quality of informal communications	

interests is illustrated in Table 3, taken from the study by Busher (1992). A major problem for subject leaders and senior staff trying to bring about change is understanding these particular interests and trying to work with them as far as possible. Where that is not possible, they might look for a compromise through a negotiated exchange. For example, a subject leader might agree to a teacher working in a particular room in one year so long as he/she was willing to share its special facilities with other colleagues when necessary.

As might be expected, the interests of students, teachers, subject leaders and headteachers are different, if overlapping. For example, where teachers might be satisfied simply to work effectively in a classroom with their students, subject leaders may also want teachers in their area to function effectively as a team, taking part in, for example, peer review of teaching and learning strategies. Teachers might find the latter practice stressful and question its necessity, even when it has been proposed by central government (DfEE, 1998). Subject leaders, on the other hand, have a vested interest in an effectively functioning area. Esteem that is likely to be accorded to them for their professional work by a school's senior staff partially depends on this. This conflict of interest is a political matter that has to be resolved, probably through some positive-sum bargaining, i.e. everybody gains some measure of what they want, even if nobody gains exactly what they want. Bargaining tactics are discussed in more detail below.

Negotiations between teachers of whatever institutional status take place in a variety of formal and informal arenas in a school. At the most formal end of this continuum are staff and department meetings and meetings of governors and parents. At the more informal end are meetings that are called, perhaps by a subject leader for just a few minutes during a coffee break, possibly to consider a single issue. At such meetings, unlike the formally scheduled ones, minutes or notes are unlikely to be kept. Subject leaders might use such meetings to prepare themselves or others for more formal meetings or for sounding out opinion (Busher, 1992). Yet less formal meetings, but as important for sustaining communications between groups of people (be they teachers, students, or parents) as well as for sustaining the identity of particular groups, are those gatherings which take place often for some social purpose. Nonetheless these meetings provide valuable opportunities for people to engage in negotiations or simply to re-assert their shared values and purposes. Individuals who persistently absent themselves from such gatherings risk being perceived by their colleagues as distancing themselves from the group. At the least formal end of this spectrum are those contacts that happen by chance, or at least seem to happen so. In the study by Busher (1992) one subject leader in a secondary school explained where he could contact each member of his subject area staff when they were not teaching if he needed to consult them about some matter of policy or practice. Within this notion of arenas of negotiation has to be included the noticeboards in staffrooms and classrooms that convey particular values and on which people invite or warn against participation in certain activities. So too must be included the networks of electronic communication, whether telephones, e-mail or the internet. They, too, provide opportunities for people to be in contact more or less formally.

STRATEGIES FOR PROMOTING OR RESISTING CHANGE

Subject leaders and headteachers are key actors in promoting change and improvement. As post-holders in the formal organization of a school they play a variety of roles in taking change forward. As Busher and Harris (1999) argue, subject leaders exert influence through these various roles. As gatekeepers to symbolic and material resources they are able to influence strongly which initiatives receive more or less support. However, as Hoyle (1981) pointed out, teachers are also able to exert power to resist change, so no proposed or planned change can be guaranteed successful implementation without skilful attention by the innovators to the politics of bringing about change.

Whether attempting to implement change or to resist it, people in schools seem to have a variety of strategies available to them. Some of these are set out in Table 4, following a study of micro-political processes in schools by Busher (1992).

Strategies for innovation take many forms and have to be used carefully by leaders at whole school and subject or pastoral area level. The choice of strategy is situationally dependent both on the change that is intended and on the known interests and needs of the colleagues with whom the innovator has

Table 4 Strategies of innovation and resistance

Bureaucratic – use of formal authority	Interpersonal – using informal power (influence) and manipulating the culture	Resistant
Resource control	Managing the culture	Non-involvement
Job specification change	Using networks	Colonizing meetings
Changing organizational structure	Using knowledge of the organizational system	Proclaiming autonomy
Boundary management – internal and external	Collusion with colleagues	Reference to subject-based authority
Monitoring formal decision-making arenas	Displaying values through work	Filibustering
Controlling information	Positive sum bargaining	Working to contract
Co-ordinating work	Making coalitions (with powerful allies)	Using external contacts to support own position
Defining policy	Offering support	Sounding out opinion/ gleaning information
Reference to external authority	Giving rewards or recognition	Lobbying
Permitting		Appealing to traditional norms

to work to implement change. Blase (1995) points out the particular importance of effective and supportive interpersonal relationships to those leaders
wanting to introduce change and innovation, arguing that these form one of
seven major facilitative strategies. Seemingly one of the most important
aspects of the interpersonal relationships is the quality of trust and respect
between leaders and their colleagues (Blase and Blase, 1994; Busher and
Saran, 1995). It is strategies of empowering teachers and engaging them as co-
authors of processes of change that these writers argue are the most successful
in bringing about sustained change.

    For strategies to be successful, various conditions have to be met. The first of
these is that the changes proposed have to fit in with or appear to fit in with
prevailing cultural norms. Homans (1958) argues that this allows both the
instigators of change and their colleagues to perceive mutual gain in participating in the proposed processes. A second condition, that flows from the first, is
that all parties engaged in the negotiations need to believe that they can gain
from proposed changes in some way, even if they do not gain everything that
they want. Rapoport (1966) calls this a win–win negotiation. This strategy is
more likely to lead to the successful conclusion of negotiations than are 'zero-
sum' outcomes, as Bennett discusses further in Chapter 6. Therefore
innovations that are likely to succeed will promote or seem to promote the
interests of both the instigator and their colleagues, a situation in which both
parties gain something from changing their practices. In some cases this

congruity of purpose or interest may be only nominal: both parties gain from the same innovation but gain different outcomes to support different agendas.

To be more certain that innovations will succeed, instigators of change often construct coalitions of like-minded colleagues around them, as has been illustrated earlier. These coalitions are likely to be based on the parties perceiving a similarity of interest with each other and recognizing mutual gains, at least temporarily until they have achieved their particular goal. A further source of strength is for innovators to gain support from powerful people or bodies (such as key committees) inside or outside their organizations. To do so they often have to demonstrate that the proposed innovation is in the interests of the organization or of the senior staff and that it will not incur powerful opposition from other important pressure groups, such as governors, parents or particular groups of teachers.

Strategies of negotiation for implementing change cannot work without access to power. Whilst it might be important for innovators to gain support from powerful people in an institution, they also have to exercise power in their own right. Busher (1992) suggests that power derives from a variety of personal and organizational sources and can be divided into three categories: personal, professional and institutional or bureaucratic (see Table 2). These sources of power derive from who people are, the knowledge and values they hold, how they act in particular circumstances and how they use the symbolic and material resources accessible to them. These sources of power are to be distinguished from the authority (institutionally legitimated power) which is accorded to post-holders in school organizations and is often enshrined in job descriptions. Paechter and Head (1996) describe this last category of power as positional power, since it derives from the positions of authority to which people are appointed by school leaders and governors.

Personal sources of power include warmth to colleagues, reliability, being well-organized and being enthusiastic. Professional sources of power include: being part of a team; managing pupils effectively; being an effective teacher of a particular subject; understanding the workings of the school as an organizational system; having an awareness of changes in the external organizational environment and the likely impact of these on staff and students; knowing how to cope with change successfully. The ability of people to wield institutional or bureaucratic power depends on a person's status, responsibilities, access to resources and access to power and authority – legitimate or formal power (Bacharach and Lawler, 1980). The last can be crudely defined by the access which certain members of an organization have to the views of a school's senior management team. Morgan (1986) offers a similar list of sources of power in organizations. Some of these sources of power are more important for subject leaders or headteachers than they are for teachers or support staff.

RESISTANCE TO CHANGE

Among the most interesting set of political strategies are those used by people in school organizations to resist change. Hoyle (1981) pointed out that teachers could wield power against that of headteachers through a variety of different strategies. Resistance can take place for a variety of reasons but, importantly, amongst these is that of principled objection to innovation. This arises when the resisters perceive the proposed change as inimical to their espoused or enacted values and beliefs about education and social relationships through education organizations. Foucault (1990) points out how institutions shape and potentially distort people's sense of self and self-esteem. Paechter and Head (1996) point out how organizational structures, including those of schools, often exert coercive pressures on their members (teachers, pupils and governors of schools) to perform in certain ways. Resistance to such coercion is hardly surprising if attempts to exert control conflict with participants' principled values or interests, although it may not be viewed sympathetically by people in authority in a school organization, such as headteachers or school governors, who want to uphold a particular structure and culture. With students, this conflict of interests and cultures is seen most clearly when they become disaffected and behave in such ways that they are excluded from school or truant from it. Resolving such conflicts is difficult since pupils' interests have to be recognized equally with those of the teachers and with the school's cultural norms that have been transgressed (Osler, Watling and Busher, 2000).

Wolcott (1977) suggested that there was a continuum of reaction to proposed change from joyful acceptance to outright and carefully organized opposition. In doing so he made it clear that there might be little difference in practice between teachers or students who were willing, somewhat reluctantly, to engage in activities and those who wanted to question the value of particular activities. Van der Westhuizen (1996) divided resistance into three forms: passive, active and aggressive. In the last category he included subversion and sabotage, although that might not necessarily be of a violent nature. In the first category he placed negative perceptions and attitudes.

Plant (1987) thought resistance existed largely because people's interests had not been sufficiently carefully considered when other people were trying to implement change. As is shown in Table 4, Busher (1992) found a number of different strategies were used by teachers to resist change in schools. Depending on the strength of their opposition to a proposed or initiated activity they selected strategies which they thought appropriate or had at their disposal. Not all teachers or students have equal access to strategies of resistance. Ganderton (1991) suggested that organizations actually need people who resist change – he called them subversives – because they make innovators think carefully about the impact of the changes they are trying to put in place.

To counter these strategies of resistance, leaders and managers in and of schools need to engage in a variety of political activities, bringing pressure to bear on the resisters and subversives in a variety of different ways. How such ways are used, of course, is likely to depend on the political skill of the leader involved in understanding the socio-political processes of a school and in using a mixture of personal approaches, bureaucratic levers and cultural precepts. It will also depend on her or his understanding of the personal needs and interests of the resisters involved. As one subject leader explained:

> So I took a very personal interest in all aspects of the department's work as well as the wider aspects of administration and the politics in the school . . . what is happening outside of the curriculum – movements of rooms, time-tabling, personal moves, staffing moves, promotional moves . . . I've always felt that a lot of the things [in the school] were political in that decisions were often taken that affected the rest of us without us having much say in them. (Busher, 1992, p. 277)

Two cameos of action in particular circumstances, set out below, show how leaders might try to bring about change through using a variety of strategies. Some of these are rationalist strategies, for example those proposed by writers on school improvement such as Stoll and Fink (1998). Other strategies involve negotiations which take account of people's personal and professional interests and of the cultural norms of the school. These political processes to bring about change are operated more or less skilfully by leaders at various levels in a school's organization and by other people through interpersonal interactions with their colleagues.

THE DISUNITED SUBJECT TEAM

Faced with a disunited subject area a subject leader is likely to have to engage in a variety of strategies over a considerable length of time in order to create a successfully functioning team. Successful strategies are likely to meet the conditions of congruity discussed earlier and to include rationalist strategies of school improvement to promote characteristics of school effectiveness, such as those propounded by Hopkins *et al.* (1997) and Sammons *et al.* (1997). These can help to build a greater sense of team identity amongst the staff in disunited subject areas, improving professional competence by helping staff to engage in staff development and professional review. Further, through developing a clear vision or mission for the subject area that is established jointly with colleagues through consultation, subject leaders can encourage staff and students to take joint responsibility for the success of the subject area.

Nonetheless, these strategies are political strategies that try to relocate power away from individual action and towards group cohesion and process and towards shared norms of professional activity. The subject leader may well draw on symbolic and material sources to try to bring about this shift, perhaps by persuading senior staff to fund particular approaches to staff development that meet the particular needs of the staff in the subject area. In turn, this points out the importance of the subject leader gaining support from powerful people in the school organization in order to bring about change.

As the subject area team is made up of a group of individual staff, the subject leader may need to use personal strategies to build up the sense of self-worth of various members of the subject area. Blase and Blase (1994) indicate the importance of interpersonal relationships to successful leadership. Subject leaders may also need to tackle members of the subject area who continue to resist or subvert efforts to create a united team. To do this the subject leader is likely to need to find out what the particular interests of the disaffected staff are and how these might in part at least be met.

BUDGET NEGOTIATIONS

Decisions about the allocation of a school's budget are political decisions because they are about which teachers and subject areas are given what resources to implement their preferred ways of working within the compass of the preferred values of a school's budget holders. In England and Wales this group of staff is made up of senior staff, the headteacher and school governors. In this process both senior staff, subject leaders and other teaching and support staff can be seen using a variety of strategies to try to gain sufficient resources for their own educational needs and interests.

Negotiations about a school's budget are carried out within a well-known chronological framework, as one headteacher in a secondary school explained:

> Well, around about March each year, one of my deputies and myself meet every head of department or everybody who normally has spending power. We have in the back of our minds roughly what we are likely to have to allocate as we know how last year's figures went. (Busher, 1992, p. 282)

In this school, budget holders were invited to indicate their funding priorities before money was allocated to them. The headteacher and other senior staff were willing to make adjustments to the budgets normally allocated to subject areas on an historic basis to take account of current urgent projects in different parts of the school. However, as senior staff were unwilling to disclose budget figures fully to the rest of the staff, budget holders were not fully aware of the details of the school budget. So their bidding to some extent had to be based only on the resources they preferred, without taking account of what monies, realistically, were available. For senior staff this was a useful strategy for maintaining their power as it prevented teachers below the level of senior management asking fundamental questions about the distribution of the budget.

Members of the senior management justified these strategies of historic funding and restricted information on the grounds of minimizing rivalry between subject areas that might lead to confrontations between them, and to staff working less well together across the curriculum. They wanted to maintain the formal structure of the school while giving heads of department opportunity to account for their stewardship of the previous year and to bid for development projects. This allowed senior staff to evaluate the performance of each department and to decide which new proposals were most likely to help them meet their educational priorities (or interests) for promoting the success of the school. In this manner they exercised power and control over other teachers through the ways in which they managed the school.

One of the key strategies, many teachers claimed, that subject area teachers as an interest or pressure group used to assert their preferred values was to bid for about double the amount of money that they expected to receive in their budget allocation. Their bids reflected their educational priorities: that teaching should be adequately resourced without unnecessary scrimping and saving on curriculum materials. The teachers perceived the strategy of over-bidding as a means of putting pressure on senior staff. Through it they signalled how much they hoped to receive above their budget quota allocation for particular projects, if not in this budget round, then either later in the school year when the headteacher might release some contingency funding or in the next budget round.

More successful heads of department pursued strategies that allowed them to appear to senior staff as accountable and forward looking and concerned with the overall development of the school, i.e. through their actions they indicated support for the values of the most powerful staff group in the formal organization of the school. Their collection of strategies included costing out proposed developments in some detail and persuading members of the senior management team that supporting their proposals would benefit the school more than supporting other proposals. To achieve this, as several subject leaders explained in a study by Busher (1992), they had to know how to lobby senior staff and who to lobby on particular issues. In this context several subject leaders said it was of great value to departments to have members of the senior management team teaching in their subject area. Given the subject loyalties staff have as part of their professional identity (Siskin, 1994; Busher, 1992) they thought it likely that senior staff would tend to look favourably on plans put forward by their own subject areas. This was because they might understand them better than plans from other subject areas, especially if the subject leader had involved members of the department in developing the plans.

DENOUEMENT

Micro-politics provides a conceptual framework for understanding the interactions of people in schools through analysing the ways in which power is accrued, used and negotiated on principled and unprincipled grounds to try to implement the views, values and beliefs of participants and stakeholders in education. As Ball (1987) argues it provides complete explanations for processes of conflict and conflict resolution, of co-operation between participants and stakeholders in schools and between schools' internal processes and their external socio-political environments. For individual people, whether students or staff of a school, it offers explanations for how they develop and sustain their senses of self-identity and try to attain their chosen interests and goals within the social frameworks of a school's organizational culture and its existing administrative structures. It also offers explanations of how people modify these social frameworks, both of which, it is argued, are constructed through previous or historic political negotiations between former members of and stakeholders in a school organization.

A micro-political perspective offers a complementary lens to cultural, systems and individual perspectives of change and improvement in school organizations by focusing on the dynamic but unequal interpersonal processes that bring about organizational growth and development and individual personal learning. As such it offers explanations for why people promote change as well as why they resist it and how that resistance might be overcome to the mutual benefit of the resisters and their school organizations.

In a micro-political framework, definitions of school effectiveness, however far they are based on rigorous research, represent a constructed political agenda. This is to argue that definitions of effectiveness in and of schools are ontologically located in particular ideologies and cultural beliefs held by individual people and social groups about the strength of rational systems and models of organizations as sufficient explanations for organizational processes. Such definitions assume, rather than regard as problematic, the importance of the market as the key distributive mechanism in society, regardless of any fundamental differences of purpose for different types of organization between, say, private sector business, public sector services, and education. Having chosen particular parameters for whatever social philosophical reasons, it is then possible for social and educational research to uncover the characteristics of education organizations that fit with these. At present, central government in England and Wales has powerfully espoused certain ideologies about the relationship between school and society that contain within them certain definitions of school effectiveness. These in turn lead to a particular model of school organization, predicated on certain qualities of relationships between teachers, pupils, parents and the managers of schools that educational researchers have been quite successful in mapping.

Unfortunately this model overlooks the contested nature of what constitutes successful schools and successful schooling and the socio-political and ideological dynamics of interpersonal, intra-organizational and inter-organizational interactions that lead to the construction of education organizations through time. One explanation for this oversight is that it is deliberate in order to portray the model as the only one that is acceptable socially in England and Wales in the early twenty-first century. If this supposition is accurate, it is itself an example of a political strategy of how powerful organizational or social groups try to legitimate their own preferred models of organizational practice by marginalizing other possible competing models. The introduction of widespread and regular school inspection after 1993 is another example of a political strategy to put in place a particular model of school organizations. In this case a powerful social and organizational group (central government) has invested heavily in a particular process to create a framework of control by which to judge practice in schools in the light of one particular model of schooling.

Such strategies for implementing change as occur at the macro-political or state level also occur within institutions at the micro-political level. School improvement research offers education practitioners a repertoire of rational strategies for bringing about changes that fits comfortably within a micro-political model of education organizations. The threefold or clover-leafed shape of this model, as discussed earlier in this chapter (see Table 2), places such strategies within the lobe or sub-framework of micro-political processes of negotiation. However, as this chapter has argued, such rational and formal organizational strategies have to be complemented by a range of other informal interpersonal strategies and negotiative processes that allow organizational actors to take account of the broader micro-political and macro-political frameworks and processes of managing change in education organizations.

A micro-political perspective also suggests that 'school improvement' may itself be viewed as being driven by a political agenda. This is, perhaps, linked to a similar model of effective schooling that espoused by those powerful social and organizational groups which have a strong ideological investment in the currently implemented definitions of school effectiveness that are enacted in England and Wales.

The brief of the political model is wider than that of school improvement. In offering ways of understanding issues of power and authority; of organizational group and individual person interaction and transformation; of personal belief, value and interest implementation through negotiations between actors of unequal power; of change, development and resistance, it allows researchers and practitioners to understand how school organizations function internally and interact with their socio-political environments. In so doing it helps participants and stakeholders both to reflect on how to bring about change in education organizations and to enact it.

REFERENCES

Armstrong, F. (1998) 'Curriculum management and special and inclusive education', in P. Clough (ed.) *Managing Inclusive Education: From Policy to Experience*. London: Paul Chapman.

Bacharach, S. (1988) 'Notes on a political theory of educational organisations', in A. Westoby (ed.) *Culture and Power in Organizations*. Milton Keynes: Open University Press.

Bacharach, S. and Lawler, E. (1980) *Power and Politics in Organizations*. San Francisco: Jossey-Bass.

Ball, S. (1987) *'The Micro-politics of the School: Towards a Theory of School Organisation*. London: Methuen.

Ball, S. (1989) 'Micro-politics versus management', in S. Walker and L. Barton (eds) *Politics and the Processes of Schooling*. Milton Keynes: Open University Press.

Barber, M. (1998) 'The dark side of the moon: Imagining an end to failure in urban education', in L. Stoll and K. Myers (eds) *No Quick Fixes: Perspectives on Schools in Difficulty*. London: Falmer Press.

Barker, B. and Busher, H. (1998) 'External contexts and internal policies: a case–study of school improvement in its socio-political environment'. Unpublished paper given at the British Educational Research Association Annual Conference, Queens University, Belfast, August.

Blase, J. (1991) 'Introduction' in J. Blase (ed.) *The Politics of Life in Schools: Power, Conflict and Co-operation*. Newbury Park, CA: Corwin Press.

Blase, J. (1995) 'The micro-political orientation of facilitative school principals and its effects on teachers' sense of empowerment'. Paper given at the American Education Research Association Conference, San Francisco, April 1995.

Blase, J. and Anderson, G. (1995) *The Micro-politics of Educational Leadership: From Control to Empowerment*. London: Cassell.

Blase, J. and Blase, J. (1994) *Empowering Teachers: What Successful Principals Do.* Thousand Oaks, CA: Corwin.

Bourdieu, P. (1990) *In Other Words: Essays Towards a Reflexive Sociology*, trans. M. Adamson. Cambridge: Polity Press in association with Blackwells, Oxford.

Burns, T. (1955) 'The reference of conduct in small groups: cliques and cabals in occupational milieux', *Human Relations*, **8**: 467–86.

Busher, H. (1989) 'Bringing out a new publication: The role of a catalyst in the micro-politics of institutional change', *British Educational Research Journal* **15**(1): 77–87.

Busher, H. (1992) 'The politics of working in secondary schools: Some teachers' perspectives on their schools as organisations'. Unpublished PhD thesis, Leeds: School of Education, University of Leeds.

Busher, H. and Harris, A. (1999) 'Leadership of school subject areas: tensions and dimensions of managing in the middle', *School Leadership and Management* **19**(3): 305–17.

Busher, H. and Saran, R. (1995) 'Managing staff professionally', in H. Busher and R. Saran (eds) *Managing Teachers as Professionals in Schools*. London: Kogan Page.

Carr, W. (1993) 'Reconstructing the curriculum debate: an editorial introduction', *Curriculum Studies* **1**(1): 5–6.

Cyert, R. and March, J. (1963) *A Behavioural Theory of the Firm*. Englewood Cliffs, NJ: Prentice Hall.

Department for Education and Employment (DfEE) (1998) *Teachers: Meeting the Challenge of Change*. London: Her Majesty's Stationery Office.

Foucault, M. (1990) 'Foucault on education', in S. Ball (ed.) *Foucault on Education*. London: Routledge.

Ganderton, P. (1991) 'Subversion and the organisation: some theoretical considerations', *Educational Management and Administration* **19**(1): 30–6.

Gibb, C. (1947) 'The principles and traits of leadership', in C. Gibb (ed.) (1969) *Leadership*. Harmondsworth: Penguin.

Glover, D., Gleeson, D., Gough, G. and Johnson, M. (1998) 'The meaning of management: The development needs of middle managers in secondary schools', *Educational Management and Administration* **26**(3): 181–95.

Greenfield, T. and Ribbins, P. (1993) *Greenfield on Educational Administration*. London: Routledge.

Greenfield, W. D. (1991) 'Leadership in an urban elementary school', in J. Blase (ed.) *The Politics of Life in Schools: Power, Conflict and Co-operation*. Newbury Park, CA: Corwin Press.

Gronn, P. (1985) 'After T. B. Greenfield, whither educational administration?', *Educational Management and Administration,* **13**(1): 55–61.

Harris, A. (1998) 'Improving ineffective departments in secondary schools', *Educational Management and Administration* **26**(3): 269–78.
Hodgkinson, C. (1981) 'A new taxonomy of administrative processes', *Journal of Educational Administration* **19**(2): 141–52.
Hodgkinson, C. (1991) *Educational Leadership: The Moral Art.* Albany: State University of New York Press.
Homans, G. (1958) 'Social behaviour as exchange', *American Journal of Sociology* **63**(6): 597–606.
Hopkins, D., West, M., Harris, A., Ainscow, M. and Beresford, J. (1997) *Creating the Conditions for Classroom Improvement.* London: David Fulton Publishers.
Hoyle, E. (1981) 'Managerial processes in school', in *Management and the School Block 3 E323.* Buckingham: Open University Press.
Hoyle, E. (1982) 'Micro-politics of educational organisations', *Educational Management and Administration* **10**(2): 87–98.
Hoyle, E. (1986) *The Politics of School Management.* London: Hodder and Stoughton.
Levinson, D. J. (1959) 'Role, personality and social structure in the organisational setting', *Journal of Abnormal and Social Psychology* **58**: 170–80.
Morgan, C. (1986) *Images of Organizations.* Beverley Hills: Sage.
Mortimore, P. (1999) *Understanding Pedagogy and its Impact on Learning.* London: Paul Chapman.
Osler, A., Watling, R. and Busher, H. (2000) *Managing School Exclusions.* Leicester: School of Education, University of Leicester.
Paechter, C. F. and Head, J. (1996) 'Power and gender in the staffroom', *British Educational Research Journal* **22**(1): 57–69.
Plant, R. (1987) *Managing Change and Making it Stick.* London: Fontana.
Poster, C. (1976) *School Decision-making.* London: Heinemann.
Rapoport, A. (1966) *Two Person Game Theory: The Essential Ideas.* Ann Arbor: University of Michigan.
Ribbins, P. (1985) 'Organisation theory and the study of educational institutions', in M. Hughes, P. Ribbins and H. Thomas (eds) *Managing Education.* New York: Holt, Rinehart and Winston.
Rutter, M., Maughan, B., Mortimore, P. and Ouston, J. (1977) *Fifteen Thousand Hours.* Shepton Mallet: Open Books.
Sammons, P., Thomas, S. and Mortimore, P. (1997) *Forging Links: Effective Schools and Effective Departments.* London: Paul Chapman.
Schein, E. (1992) *Organizational Culture and Leadership* (2nd edition). San Francisco: Jossey-Bass.
Schon, D. (1983) *The Reflective Practitioner.* New York: Basic Books.
Siskin, L. (1994) *Realms of Knowledge.* London: Falmer Press.
Stephenson, T. (1985) *Management: A Political Activity.* London: Macmillan.
Stoll, L. and Fink, D. (1998) 'The cruising school: The unidentified ineffective school', in L. Stoll and K. Myers (eds) *No Quick Fixes: Perspectives on Schools in Difficulty.* London: Falmer Press.
van der Westhuizen, P. (1996) 'Resistance to change in educational organisations'. Paper given at the Fifth Quadrennial Research Conference of the British Educational Management and Administration Society, Robinson College, Cambridge University, UK.
Willis, P. (1977) *Learning to Labour: How Working-class Kids Get Working-class Jobs.* Farnborough: Saxon House.
Wolcott, H. (1977) *Teachers Versus Technocrats.* Eugene: University of Oregon.

Chapter 6

Power, Structure and Culture: An Organizational View of School Effectiveness and School Improvement[1]

Nigel Bennett

INTRODUCTION

Although both school effectiveness and school improvement research are concerned with schools as organizations, both pay relatively little attention to the insights that organizational theory can bring. School effectiveness research, despite strenuous attempts to move away from broad-brush statistical correlations, remains locked into a view of schools that emphasizes their structural aspects, while school improvement writing focuses on the need to change the culture of the school if improvements are to occur, so establishing an emphasis on process. The two orientations ought to complement each other but, in practice, despite a series of attempts to bring the two fields of study together, little has yet been achieved. In large part this may be due to the very characteristic of the two fields that Reynolds (Chapter 3) has claimed as their strength: their refusal to 'problematize' problems, preferring instead to take them as givens. By pursuing a 'non-denominational', 'what works' approach, the two fields of research and consultancy pursue separately defined and distinct fields of analysis and intervention, resting on quite different understandings of what 'the problems' might be, instead of seeking sources of connection between them. Creemers (e.g. 1994) has made strenuous attempts to generate a theory of effectiveness but the movements have paid insufficient attention to theorizing about what schools are – that is, organizations.

Organization theory, however, can provide a means for achieving this synergy if the view taken of the school as an organization is broadened to take account of a third, frequently ignored aspect – power. This can provide ways forward by raising alternatives to bring into consideration, challenging orthodoxies and offering new frameworks or foci for analysis – 'problematizing', to use Reynolds' term, both the problems schools face and the context in which they are to be found.

In this chapter, I will outline briefly the twin concepts of structure and culture, showing how in each case the missing concept of power can provide a dynamic element that is frequently missing. I will then bring the three elements together in a three-dimensional model of schools as organizations, and conclude by indicating briefly how this model might provide a basis for the linkage that has been sought so unsuccessfully to date.

ORGANIZATIONS

Organizations as 'systems'

The field of organization theory is enormous and one reason for this is that there is no clearly agreed view of what an organization is, nor how it should be analysed. Scott (1987) adopts a broadly systems perspective, distinguishing between 'rational', 'natural' and 'open' systems. Rational systems, he states (pp. 22–3), are 'oriented to the pursuit of relatively specific goals' and exhibit 'a relatively highly formalised' social structure. In natural systems, participants are little affected by formal structures and official goals but 'share a common interest in the survival of the system and ... engage in collective activities, informally structured, to secure this end'. Open systems are strongly influenced by their environment, which reduces the organization's structural fluidity. Nevertheless, he argues, they remain 'a coalition of shifting interest groups that develop goals by negotiation; the structure of the coalition, its activities and its outcomes are strongly influenced by environmental factors'.

Other writers, such as Hanna (1988), argue for a much tighter and more structured definition of an open system than Scott, suggesting that the key dimension of a system is the interdependence of its different parts and the complexity of the transactions that take place within it as 'inputs' become converted through a 'process' into 'outputs'. The school effectiveness movement rests on a rational open systems model. This makes it easy to see the process of educational activity as one of 'adding value' to the 'raw material' of the input. Although this way of expressing it causes offence to many in education, it is all that the debate about 'value added' and the fairness of government league tables is about. When Gray *et al.* (1999), for example, examine the basis on which we can judge the effectiveness of a school and the extent to which it can be seen as an 'improving' school, they are concerned with what it does with its 'raw material' of the children it receives each year. By seeing the organization as a rational as well as an open system, the school effectiveness movement adds an emphasis on formalized social structure and relatively specific goals to the emphasis on resource utilization and the structural interrelationship of parts of the organization. In their emphasis on a limited set of measurable outputs, as expressed in examination results, school effectiveness researchers adopt this organizational view of the school very comfortably and leave to one side a lot of process-related issues.

School improvement writers can also find much to encourage them in an open systems view of schools and colleges. Whether this is in the looser terms offered by Scott and developed more fully in the concept of the 'loosely coupled system' by Weick (1976; see also Orton and Weick, 1990) or in the tauter view expressed by Hanna (1988), there are some significant emphases that are important to school improvement efforts. First, it stresses a process as much as a product: organizational members do things to the resources that are obtained for them and without resources ('inputs') the organization cannot survive. Second, it stresses the interdependence of the different parts of an organization – sometimes referred to as its structure – but also emphasizes that this is not a fixed and unchanging arrangement. As the inputs or the processes change, so the possibility develops of changes to the structure. Third, it stresses that not only are the constituent parts of an organization interdependent, but organizations are also, to an extent, interdependent. It isn't possible for a school to strike out on its own – for example, by deciding to apply for permission to change from being an 11–16 school to an 11–18 school and start a sixth form – without affecting those around it. Related to this, and of importance in any school improvement or change effort, the open systems model sees organizations as needing to be kept in a reasonably stable condition. Consequently, when the environment becomes very turbulent, as some might describe the educational policy scene in England and Wales since 1980, an important management responsibility is to reduce the impact of that turbulence in order to create internal circumstances that do not interfere with the basic task of the organization's members. And lastly, it is important that each part of the organization is kept informed of what is going on elsewhere that might affect its work. All of this emphasizes that organizations should not be seen as static forms but as dynamic processes.

Unless they retain what Levačić *et al.* (1999) define as a strongly rational–technicist view, writers using the open systems model tend away from a mechanistic view of the organization towards one which is more organic (Burns and Stalker, 1961). However, much recent official writing about managing and leading schools as organizations has placed a strong emphasis on more mechanistic approaches, as is visible in some of the official utterances about professional development for headteachers and 'subject leaders' (e.g. Teacher Training Agency [TTA], 1998a, b). Following Taylor (1911) and Fayol (1949), mechanistic views of organizations emphasize detailed task specification, routinized work, uniform procedures and consistency, and see management as oversight, ensuring that routines are correctly adhered to and procedures (not processes) followed. It is the language of quality control rather than quality assurance; to some, perhaps, the language of OFSTED frameworks for inspecting schools (OFSTED, 1999). It is also the language of much writing on school and organizational effectiveness and of the official pronouncements that stem from it. By comparison, organic views of the organization see them as possessed of members rather than tasks and therefore capable of developing a life of their own. Organizational members who view their organization as organic see it as having the capacity to adapt and grow in relation to its environment, rather than having to be changed by management decision. Further, management becomes an activity within the organization, rather than standing more or less outside it, as the mechanistic view might sometimes suggest.

Underlying these ideas on how to think about organizations are certain basic propositions about organizations that would probably gain widespread acceptance, even if the views of organizations just outlined do not. They:

- have members;
- have a purpose, which gives rise to both the core task of the organization and the technology or technologies through which it is carried out;
- have to acquire and retain resources;
- require some sort of structure through which to ensure that the tasks are carried out and the purpose met.

Further, organizations are both identifiably similar and different. Something makes one distinguishable from another.

Examining each of these a little more can provide us with a route into a clearer discussion of the constituent elements of the model we are constructing in this chapter.

Members

If an organization must have members, then it ceases to exist without them (Greenfield, 1989). In a fundamental way, therefore, the members are the organization. Members might be volunteers, choosing to participate in its activities, and often paying for the privilege, or they might be employees, providing services to the organization in return for a reward. Goffman (1961) identified 'total organizations' as those organizations in which key members had no choice over membership or right to leave. Prisons and mental hospitals were the most obvious example but pupils might argue that schools also qualify.

Membership of any organization places certain obligations on the member, which may be written down in the shape of rules and regulations or communicated in other less formal and tangible ways. These informal norms and expectations may be officially sanctioned and universal across the whole organization or may be limited to specific tasks or areas of work. We will return to this later when we examine the concept of organizational culture.

Purpose

The clarity with which the purpose of an organization can be defined varies, as does the ease with which the core task and its associated technologies can be derived from it. At one level, organizations can be said to exist simply to survive; at another, they may exist to provide rewards to the founder or founders. Such rewards may not be financial but derive, for example, from the organization fulfilling a social need perceived or defined by the founder(s). This raises the question of how the purpose and its associated task and technologies are defined. Schein (1992) points out that organizations are artefacts: human creations, not naturally occurring phenomena. Someone starts them up. But having been started up, they may continue to exist after the founder(s) dies or moves on. Others may then take responsibility for defining the purpose and the associated tasks and technologies.

In addition, organizational purposes, tasks and technologies may be influenced, if not indeed defined, by agencies external to the organization itself. Certain activities are defined as illegal; others may not be illegal but might be regarded as inappropriate. For example, schools that progress their children from class to class according to their levels of attainment rather than their age run into difficulties in societies that expect children of similar ages to be taught together. This pressure to conform to wider societal institutional norms (Meyer and Rowan, 1977; Rowan, 1995; Ogawa and Bossert, 1997) is sometimes referred to as establishing wider legitimacy and creates pressure for organizations expressing similar purposes to conform to similar definitions of purpose, task and technology. Although they are often quite different when examined in detail, schools are widely recognizable within and indeed across societies and those that do not conform to those wider institutional norms come under enormous pressure to do so. When the Open University was created in 1969, it was a revolutionary concept of higher education that was dismissed as 'blithering nonsense' by the politician Iain Macleod who, the following year, became the new Conservative government's Chancellor of the Exchequer (quoted in Perry, 1976, p. 30). Only his death a few weeks after taking office saved it.

Resources

Resources are often understood as either financial resources or as 'raw material' to be processed. But the term can be taken more widely to include the range of expertise that can be purchased with the financial resources that are obtained. Members are also part of an organization's resources. However, obtaining such resources carries a cost and skills, knowledge and expertise can be bought cheap or bought dear, depending on their importance to the organization and their availability. Further, once obtained, they can be used more or less efficiently and this will affect the extent to which the purposes of the organization are achieved within the resources available.

Structure and tasks

The tasks involved in fulfilling the purposes of the organization have themselves to be organized. In other words, there will have to be some sort of structure that is intended to ensure that it can exploit its resources so as to deliver the activities involved in fulfilling its purposes. Structures imply that tasks and responsibilities are allocated and that resources reach the right place at the right time. They imply a means by which the activities of organizational members are influenced or directed. They also imply an accountability between members for the proper discharge of the tasks they have to complete in order to achieve the purposes of the organization.

Mechanistic views of organizations see structures as fixed, static entities that only change as the result of specific decisions by those who control them. Organic views see structures as capable of developing in an almost living way. We have to remember that, just as organizations only exist because they have members, so structures only function because of the actions of the organizational members whose work they shape. Membership can change and with it the ways in which the structures operate. Purposes can change, as can what is externally defined as legitimate, and these can affect the structuring of the core task. Technologies available to members in discharging those core tasks can also develop, placing structures under pressure. The Open University's 'revolutionary' distance learning teaching methods have now been widely replicated and superseded by new technology, with profound implications for the universities pursuing such strategies. These changes are placing traditional structures under great strain.

Structures, then, should be seen as dynamic entities, even when there is no change apparently taking place. This is what open systems theorists call 'dynamic equilibrium'. When we describe something as dynamic, we are also stating that there is something that is making it so. Hence the word 'dynamic' can be both an adjective, describing the characteristic, and a noun, identifying something or some things as giving it that dynamism. In the discussion that follows, I will try to identify both the range of structural elements that might impact on a person's work in an organization and also the dynamic that is at work, which I suggest is power. This discussion has significance, in my view, for the school effectiveness movement in that it proposes an organic relationship between organizational structures and the tasks undertaken within them, which cannot receive sufficient attention in the kind of 'snapshot' data on which effectiveness judgements are made.

STRUCTURES AS DYNAMIC ENTITIES, REFLECTING POWER DISTRIBUTION

Physical structures

Organizations use and respond to structures in a number of ways. First, there is the physical structuring of work. Secondary schools are usually created as a combination of general and specialist classrooms, workshops and other rooms. Primary schools built in the 1960s may have been constructed as a set of open-plan teaching areas and where these have expanded they may be surrounded by free-standing temporary classrooms. The main campus of the Open University has almost no formal teaching areas, since most of the 125,000 students study at home. New office blocks are usually built as open spaces, to be organized as each renting business sees fit, and some companies no longer assign individual employees to specific desks, so that they 'hot desk' wherever there is space when they need to be in the office. Those employees may do a lot of their work 'on the road', or from home, and only come into 'the office' from time to time. Such structures are deliberately constructed to organise what work is done and how it is done.

Work structures

Within that physical structure other structuring decisions are taken that affect how work is done. Secondary schools may decide to structure their pastoral work horizontally on year-group or key-stage lines or vertically through house systems. They may organize the academic teaching through departments or faculties or in some other way. Children may be organized in mixed-ability groups or banded or setted in some way according to some criteria that are determined by particular individuals or groups within the school. Primary schools may decide for some aspects of their teaching to reorganize their pupils into ability groups, or by achievement in particular areas of work, so that very bright Year 3 children may be working alongside Year 6 children some of the time or older children with special educational needs join younger children for some of their studies. All of these are structural decisions. They influence the way that organizational members do their work and the colleagues with whom they have to interact on a formal, work-related, non-social basis.

Task structures

A third, significant set of structural decisions relates to the responsibilities that individuals discharge and the tasks they carry out. Job descriptions have become major aspects of work structuring in the last fifteen years and learning how to write good job descriptions is an important part of much management training. As well as defining responsibilities and tasks, good job descriptions are supposed to demonstrate the managerial accountability of the jobholder, defining the lines of accountability and control that govern the work. Thus job descriptions tie individuals into the formal organizational chart that demonstrates how the jobs and tasks interrelate, which is what is often seen as the organization's 'structure'.

Within the area of job descriptions, some areas of work lay down strict procedural rules or protocols that are supposed to govern how the tasks are carried out. Such detailed task specification can sometimes lead to structures appearing to lose their dynamism and ossify. For example, at the beginning of the Second World War the British Army employed a time-and-motion expert to try and find ways of increasing the firing frequency of some light guns. These dated back to the Boer War but were now being used as mobile defence guns because they could be moved easily using light trucks. Among many things that puzzled the expert, he noticed that shortly before a gun was fired two of the gun crew stopped all work, stood back from the gun and stood to attention with one hand raised. No one could explain why, until eventually he found an elderly artillery officer who had served in the Boer War. This man studied the slow-motion pictures the expert had taken of the procedure and shook his head thoughtfully before suddenly saying, 'I have it! They are holding the horses!' (McLean, 1990, cited by Bate, 1994, p. 158).

Job descriptions should also state the salary of the post being described. In this way, structures also state the valuation placed upon the work being undertaken, not just in terms of its formal seniority but in terms of the resources being allocated to it. In the public sector, salary structures are frequently imposed nationally and may, therefore, restrict the freedom with which such valuations can be made. An interesting sideline on the British government's decision to introduce in 2000 a salary threshold which teachers in England will be able to cross without taking on additional responsibilities outside the classroom is that it represents the first attempt since national salary scales for teachers were introduced to make a specific statement that good teaching should be valued for itself and not rewarded by allocating additional, non-teaching responsibilities.

Structural responses to external factors

Other external structural factors also act as constraints on individual action. Legal requirements such as health and safety legislation and laws relating to child protection both place direct structural obligations on organizational decision makers and act as definitions of 'proper' behaviour by organizational members.

In all these ways, then, organizational structures define both the constraints and the formal relationships within which individual members of the organization can take action. They also demonstrate how the organization's decision makers have responded to the external constraints upon the organization, such as national salary scales or rules on the teaching of numeracy and literacy. Who those decision makers are is also defined by the structure through its definition of responsibilities in individual job descriptions.

What becomes clear from this is that organizational structures only start to have any meaning when they relate to individual actions. These take place in a network of formalized relations with colleagues that are defined by the structure of the organization. These relations define the constraints within which individuals take decisions about what they should do and how. In other words, despite their apparent rigidity and formality, the significance of organizational structures for organizational members lies in the ways in which they define their *relations* with colleagues and the *arenas* within which they are able to make decisions.

These interpersonal relations are not between equals. Earlier we stated that organizations exist for a purpose and not everyone in the organization necessarily makes an equal contribution to achieving it. Further, by virtue of the job descriptions that define responsibilities, individuals have more influence over their own areas of responsibility than do colleagues who have other responsibilities. The history teacher responsible for class 9SM may be answerable to the head of department for what is done and achieved by the class but the head of department is dependent on the history teacher for those results. He or she may direct and require certain actions but, if the teacher does not carry them out, he or she has to find ways of obtaining the teacher's will. Thus a crucial dimension of the relations which are formally defined by the structure is the power which each individual in the relationship brings to it.

We shall explore the concept of power in more detail below. For the moment, we shall take it to depend on two things. First, there is how central the individual is to the issue under consideration and the decision that has to be taken. Second, there is the extent to which the structure allows them freedom to decide how to act in response to decisions that are taken – what is usually referred to as 'discretion'. The more discretion that is created structurally – for example, by putting individuals into independent classrooms with closed doors, rather than operating in open-plan settings – the more power is held by the junior member of the relationship. How this power is used depends on how each individual then interprets the situation. Young (1981) proposed that we bring to every situation a number of elements:

- cognitive knowledge of the situation and of ways in which it might be possible to act;
- an affective valuation of the situation, leading to a judgement of the potential worth of any given action in the situation;
- the 'cathectic' sense of how we ourselves relate to the situation, interpret it and understand it: the combination, if you like, of the cognitive and affective elements;
- the directive sense of being required to decide on a course of action and take it – which might, of course, be to leave things as they are.

Young suggested that we actively deploy these four elements in a process of construction through which we come to an understanding of the situation, our freedom to act in it and our sense of what is the 'right' action in that setting. He calls this our 'assumptive world'. Since it is an active and continuous process of construction and reconstruction, it is clear that the individual assumptive world of our organizational members is another dynamic element in our organizational picture. Structural constraints, both internal to the organization and more widely derived from society or the profession to which we belong, are a major element in that understanding.

Structures, then, both create and are created by power relationships. They are dynamic: simultaneously static and fluid, fixed and changing. But exactly how an organization distributes responsibilities and responds to and prioritizes between the multitude of external pressures it faces will vary, depending upon the beliefs and assumptions of the individuals who are involved in deciding how to arrange its internal workings. In other words, as Schein (1992) would argue, the precise pattern of structural arrangements which delineate an organization's relationship with its environment and its internal workings to respond to that relationship are outgrowths of the culture of the organisation. It is to this dimension of organizations that we turn now.

CULTURES AS DYNAMIC ENTITIES, REFLECTING POWER DISTRIBUTION

What is organizational culture?

Organizational culture is taken in the literature to mean almost anything from 'the way we do things around here' (Bower, 1966) through Bolman and Deal's (1991) shared values which give rise to shared behavioural norms, to Heck and Marcoulides' (1996) proposition that it is the way that an organization solves problems to achieve its goals and maintain itself. More all-embracing concepts of organizational culture incorporate not just the norms which are supposed to govern members' actions but also the concept of what the organization is about which gives rise to them. Schein (1992) includes within an organization's culture what members believe their work involves and requires and the consequent organizational decisions that result, both structural and physical. The prior decision to found a Steiner or Montessori school thus becomes part of its culture: it involves fundamental decisions about the core technology of the school, which challenge the existing norms surrounding conventional teacher behaviour. This may be more of a problem in state schools, where disputes about educational goals and philosophy, rather than over the realization of an established philosophy in daily actions, may be more likely. Staff in independent schools are usually there because they have taken a deliberate decision to work in that sector.

Culture as distinctive rather than integrative

Most analyses of organizational culture from a management perspective focus on the norms which bind together individual behaviour into a pattern, stressing what Meyerson and Martin (1987) describe as the integrative dimension of culture (e.g. Schein, 1992; Bolman and Deal, 1991; Nias *et al.*, 1989; Wallace, 1989; Campbell, 1989). However, cultures need not be integrative: rather, they might more usefully be understood as what define organizations as distinctive from one another. Each organizational culture is unique but, as Meyerson and Martin (1987) argue, it may be a culture which differentiates sub-units and elements, producing subcultures at odds with one another, or one which accepts and copes with ambiguity, rather than attempting to relate events and actions to clearly defined goals and purposes. Each is likely to generate a different structural pattern or artefact (Schein, 1992, p. 17): a culture of differentiation, for example, is more likely to be associated with a loosely coupled structure or system (Weick, 1976) than is a culture of integration because this gives more room for variation and allows for units to 'buffer' themselves against influences of which they disapprove. Integrative cultures are more likely to be associated with tighter coupling, stronger lines of accountability and control and more emphasis on uniform practice.

Externally generated norms

The norms and rules that culturally govern the actions of organizational members derive in part from the concept of the work in which the organization is engaged. This understanding originates outside the organization, in the environment in which the organization is located. Cultural norms rest, in many cases, upon wider societal or 'institutional' definitions (Meyer and Rowan, 1977; Rowan, 1995; Ogawa, 1996). Such institutional definitions are communicated by people outside the organization, by other organizations and by organizational members themselves as a result of their training, experience and life outside the organization. For example, larger English secondary schools have tended to conform to an organizational arrangement that combines subject departments into 'faculties' or, as Busher and Harris (1999) have christened them, 'federal departments' – an example of what institutional theorists call 'isomorphism'. Nevertheless, the amount of cross-subject teaching is very varied across faculties: relatively rare in 'humanities' faculties, where history teachers are rarely asked to teach geography, but common in 'science' faculties, where physics teachers will often be found teaching chemistry to younger pupils (Bennett, 1991; 1995). Once again, this reflects the arguments of Schein (1992) and Young (1981) about the need to incorporate organizational members' views of their work and its demands within the cultural and personal definition of what is 'right'.

The culture of an organization, then, is a construct made up of a range of expectations about what are proper and appropriate actions. Such expectations are both external to the organization and internal to its members, who 'transact' them (Archer, 1980) into the culture. Just as structures generate the degree of freedom or constraint of individuals, so cultures shape how they act within those freedoms or constraints. That is to say, they shape what is seen as legitimate action in a given setting. This raises two very important questions for both school effectiveness and school improvement research: where the expectations that define legitimate action come from and how they become part of the assumptive worlds of each organizational member. Unfortunately, both areas of work largely ignore these questions, treating them as givens. For school effectiveness researchers, some version of student test scores defines the expectations and gives rise to normative understandings of teaching as being methods that improve these. School improvement researchers start from where staff are, rather than asking why they think they are there, so that it is easy for the improvement initiative to become bounded in a predefined framework.

TWO VIEWS OF POWER AS SOURCES OF NORMS: HEGEMONY AND DISCIPLINE

This outline of the institutional and environmental origins of many organizational norms reflects two major views of power in society, which it is appropriate to outline here. One is the concept of hegemony (Gramsci, 1971; Lukes, 1974) and the other is Foucault's (1977) concept of disciplinary power with its associated concept of bio-power. Hegemony is a concept that rests on the idea that domination and control rest simultaneously on both coercion and consent. This requires what Clegg (1989) describes as 'the active consent of dominated groups'. This active consent needs to be both generated and sustained, which Clegg suggests requires four key activities:

1. Taking systematic account of popular interests and demands;
2. Making compromises on secondary issues to maintain support and alliances in an inherently unstable political system (whilst maintaining essential interests);
3. Organizing support for national goals which serve the fundamental long-term interests of the dominant group;
4. Providing moral, intellectual and political leadership in order to reproduce and form a collective will or national popular outlook. (Clegg, 1989, p. 160)

Certain organizations are particularly significant in generating this active consent, notably the Church, schools, trade unions and the mass media.

This hegemonic analysis is arguably relevant to Reynolds' point, to which I referred above, that the great merit of school effectiveness research, and the reasons why it is so influential on policy makers at present, lies in its refusal to 'problematize' problems. It might be argued that by accepting the problems as given and trying to find ways of improving schools within pre-declared definitions of the purposes of schooling the school effectiveness researchers have failed to ask if schools are being asked to do what is 'right' and being given the 'right' measures of success. Instead, they are laying down externally generated norms which define what individual educators' asssumptive worlds should conform to. From this point of view, the key questions become, who defines the 'problems' in the first place that Reynolds and the school effectiveness movement try to 'solve', and who defines the criteria which will acknowledge a 'successful solution'?

Foucault's view of disciplinary power is somewhat different but again emphasizes the way in which state apparatuses are at work to control not just how individuals act but how they think. Foucault (1977) suggests that modern society has developed through techniques of surveillance. The best expression of this is Jeremy Bentham's 'panopticon', a design for a prison (or a workhouse or a school) which was intended to provide maximum surveillance of the prisoners by a minimum staff. In a panopticon, all the cells led off a central point, from which it was possible for a guard to observe what was going on in all the cells on that floor. In practice, of course, a single guard could not look along all the wings that radiated from his look-out post but this did not matter. The essence of Foucault's view of power was that it derived, not from direct surveillance, but from the fact that no prisoner could be sure that the guard was not looking along that wing. Thus the power of the prison guard lay in the potential to observe and, thence, to discipline and punish misbehaviour.

Clegg (1989) argues that disciplinary power can be seen to originate in monastic rules and systems and suggests a strong religious origin. This, of course, would strengthen the likelihood of norms and rituals becoming part of the way in which disciplinary power is exercised. The detailed regimentation and control embodied in monastic rules became characteristic of prison regimes established in the eighteenth century across Europe and the North American colonies, which gave rise to the panopticon design referred to above. At the same time, scientific developments gave rise to a view of the body as a machine. Foucault (1984) proposed that this view, allied to the increased capacity for surveillance and discipline just outlined, produced the sense that the body could be used as a vehicle for correction and control. This was largely achieved through the medical profession and schools, which identified forms of behaviour that deviated from what was seen as 'the norm'. Thus medicine and education became key vehicles through which 'bio-power' was exercised on behalf of society.

In the light of this analysis, one of the most interesting aspects of David Reynolds' chapter is his use of medical analogies and concepts. Physiology is put forward as the basis of the school effectiveness movement: we study schools that are 'well' and must find ways of understanding why those that are not 'well' are 'sick'. Further, he proposes the use of 'clinical audits' to seek out the 'dysfunc-tionalities' in the school and makes no reference to the possibility that the norms being transacted into the school may be relevant to the problems. An external reality is proposed as the basis of organizational 'health'.

An important way in which Foucault's view of power in particular differs from many others is that it does not see power as negative. Power is typically analysed in a negative way and the discussion of structure and culture so far in this chapter has used the language of constraint and control, thus appearing to link it with that view. But a view of power based on Foucault will argue that it is not concerned with delimiting and proscribing activities so much as converting the body into something both useful and docile. In this way, it relates power to the views of self-discipline that we so much admire when they result in high-quality musical or sporting achievement. It presents structures and cultures as empowering the individuals within them so that they can carry out fruitful tasks on behalf of the collectivity. (It is an interesting comment on current writing on leadership and management in education that it spends a lot of time talking about 'empowerment' without talking about 'power'.) To achieve this, according to Burrell (1998), power resides in a network of interconnected relationships. Within these relationships, power is located in the 'microphysics' of social life: 'Here, minute and diffuse power relations exist, always in tension, always in action' (*ibid.*, p. 20). It is through the day-to-day working out of these 'minute and diffuse power relations' that our organizational members' assumptive worlds are formed and influenced. (It is also appropriate to mention that an alternative reading of Foucault is more critical, seeing docility as restricting creativity and forcing conformity to group norms, thereby creating the conditions for fascism.)

POWER AND THE CREATION OF ORGANIZATIONAL CULTURE

This view of power relates comfortably to my earlier argument that saw structures as operating through relationships. It also connects easily to more traditional views of culture within organizations. These argue that the values of individual members and their concepts of the work of the organization, embedded in wider institutional contexts, may give rise to the cultural norms and so to the behavioural rules which limit individuals' freedom of action, but this does not explain how such norms are established and maintained. Schein (1992) is quite clear that they derive initially from the founder, who gathers together like-minded people who then continue to recruit similarly like-minded colleagues as the organization expands. Writers on corporate culture also see the role of the chief executive as crucial for the development of cultural norms (Deal and Kennedy, 1982; Bolman and Deal, 1991).

These views of culture creation and maintenance as a deliberate activity invest particular individuals with a great deal of power to direct the actions and behaviour of others. Deal (1985, p. 607) refers to the 'informal network of priests and priestesses [note, again, the presence of religion], gossips, story-tellers, and other cultural players' who sustain the culture of 'how we do things around here'. Such direction, as Foucault suggests, is frequently concerned with creating a strong and disciplined collectivity and need not be seen, as Ball (1987) for example would suggest, as individuals seeking power over others for their own ends. In organizational settings the power which drives and shapes the cultural and structural constraints on individual action is exercised by individuals – 'cultural players' – who possess particular forms of power resources, which they have acquired by first accepting particular norms and then developing, articulating and sustaining a particular interpretation of them.

Culture as observed is the pattern of rules and norms that derive from the basic understanding of the work that is done, and which shape the actions of those in the organization. As structures are enacted and create formal and publicly accepted rules, so cultures are also enacted and create informal and often unstated rules. Both represent forms of constraint upon the individual, and as such represent statements of power relationships between members of the organization. However, just as structures are susceptible to both direct and organic change, so cultures are not fixed either. The possibility of advocates of a new corporate culture creating a new set of norms to replace those of the old organizational culture is one potential form of change.

POWER AS THE DYNAMIC LINKING STRUCTURE AND CULTURE

I have suggested that 'cultural players' deploy power resources in order to maintain and create the organizational culture. It is necessary to explain a little more the means by which they do this. Earlier, I suggested that organizational structures were significant because they created a formalized set of relationships between the members of the organization, and that power disparities were a major influence on the way that those relationships developed. I have also suggested that the importance of organizational culture is as a further factor that shapes and defines how relationships between organizational members can be enacted. It is now suggested that we should view the acting out of relationships within organizations as an endless sequence of exchanges between parties. Each party brings a range of 'resources' to each exchange. Their distribution within the organization and the value attributed to them by the parties to each exchange are simultaneously a key determinant and consequence of culture as it is both a determinant and a consequence of structure. Even if we adopt a view of power built on Foucault's analysis, we still have to explain the particular pattern of power relationships within any given organizational setting and the results of the exchanges between parties to each relationship. I suggest that the way to do this is to examine what individuals can draw upon in their exchanges with their colleagues that cause some to be seen as more powerful than others. In other words, power in organizations becomes a resource that is brought to bear on the exchanges that make up the relationships between their members. The greater the disparity of resources between the two parties to an exchange, the more likely it is that one will be able to cause the other to act in the manner desired.

Kinds of power resources

Hales (1993) has conveniently distinguished between four kinds of power resource – physical, economic, knowledge and normative – which may be available to an individual in any exchange, and the section that follows draws heavily upon Hales' development of this idea.

Physical resource power represents the ability of one person to use physical force to coerce another to comply. *Economic* resource power rests upon the ability to provide or withhold things that someone else needs, such as a salary or the means of doing a job. In organizational terms, it is usually associated with a formal role rather than an individual. Because it rests upon the ability to call upon the formal resources of the organization, this is the form of power most closely associated with the functioning of formal structures.

Knowledge power can take two forms: administrative or technical knowledge. *Administrative* knowledge relates to the operation of the organization, whereas *technical* knowledge relates to the core of the work which the individual does. It is a resource because it can be used to provide assistance and support to a colleague who lacks it or as a counterweight to the planned exercise of economic resource power. The last form of power resource Hales identifies is *normative* power. This should be distinguished from norms in the cultural sense: rather, it is access to scarce values or desired ideas. Normative power can also rest upon personal friendships and broader reputation: the colleague who is able to persuade colleagues to do something as a personal favour calls upon normative power resources when this happens. Clearly, then, such normative power resources, like knowledge power resources, rest in individuals rather than the positions they may hold.

Compliance

The variable distribution of economic, knowledge and normative power resources accounts for the disparity in power which exists between individuals and, through the activities of individuals within them, of units within an organization. When the disparity is great, it is likely that the result will be a substantial element of what theorists of power call 'compliance' on the part of the person or persons with fewer power resources at their disposal. When there is a more equal distribution of these resources, compliance may have to be obtained through a more negotiative process. In such circumstances of relative equality, the structure is likely to provide for substantial levels of discretion for the individuals in discharging their technical activities, which makes it more difficult for managers to influence directly what they do. Economic power resources may have to fight the influence of knowledge power resources when this occurs.

Compliance may come in several forms, depending on the power resources being exercised and the legitimacy accorded to them. Normative power resources are, by definition, deemed legitimate and Hales (1993, p. 30) suggests that they result in a values-based commitment to act: compliance linked to a cognitive or emotional attachment to the task. Physical power resources, however, are non-legitimate and result in 'alienative compliance' and a search for countervailing power resources to deploy against them. Economic and knowledge resources result in a more calculative response, which might be 'cognitive compliance', wherein the person is persuaded that what is being required is correct, or 'instrumental compliance', which rests purely on a calculation of benefits and disadvantages. An important factor in the response is the availability of countervailing power resources. Economic power resources, which pass from office to office and derive from structural decisions, are likely to result in instrumental compliance, whereas knowledge power passes from person to person and is more likely to result in cognitive compliance and, since it can be reused and internalized over time, may develop into commitment.

Making the exercise of power legitimate

It is also important, when considering the nature of power within organizations and its relationship to structure and culture, to take account of the ways in which it might be deployed. Power can be deployed overtly or covertly; overt power can be direct, in the sense of an immediate action, or provisional, in the sense of a threat or promise. All methods of deployment can be positive or negative. Table 5 provides examples of these methods, using examples of economic power resources.

Thus in this formulation, power resources come in four different forms, each capable of deployment in three ways, and of being positive or negative in their use. For managers and consultants it is important to invest their power resources with as much legitimacy as possible, since only power resources deemed legitimate are likely to produce positive forms of compliance. Structures and cultures are crucial ways of attempting to provide legitimacy for power resources. Structures provide in particular the legitimation of economic resources, and the deployment of economic resources in ways not permitted by the structure is likely to be seen as corrupt and therefore non-legitimate. However, cultural norms may permit such corruption. Power resources whose deployment is legitimated through the structure of the organization tend to be used overtly.

Cultures provide the legitimation of normative and much knowledge power, since these forms of power reside in the individual rather than their office. They also provide crucial means of aligning legitimate normative and knowledge power with the wider institutional norms within which organizational members live, and which organizations have to acknowledge (Ogawa, 1996; Rowan, 1995). It is important to remember that institutional norms can be a major source of organizational cultural norms. Indeed, I argued earlier that members transact institutional norms into the culture of the organizations to which they belong. Such transactions can cause shifts in the norms embedded in organizational cultures and subcultures and, with them, changes in the power resources that are deemed legitimate. Cultures have to be continuously re-enacted and restated and the act of restatement gives room for the statement to be changed. Hence cultures live in the assumptive worlds of individual organizational members.

This process of legitimation and re-legitimation of power resources provides a tool for examining the process of cultural change and for explaining how organizational culture can be at once an agent of change and stasis. I suggest

Table 5 Examples of means of power deployment

Use of economic power resources	*Example*	*Methods of deployment*
Manager provides additional resources	'I would like you to take on this additional work and will provide you with supply cover so you can do it.'	Overt, direct, positive
Manager withholds resources	'I asked you to do this additional work and you have not done so. I am therefore penalizing your department by reallocating 50 per cent of your budget.'	Overt, direct, negative
Manager promises resources	'I would like you to take on this additional work and intend to provide you with supply cover so you can do it.'	Overt, provisional, positive
Manager threatens to withhold resources	'If you do not do the additional work I have asked you to do, then I will penalize your department by reallocating 50 per cent of your budget.'	Overt, provisional, negative
Manager implies that resources will be promised	'If you do this additional work then it is possible that I might be able to find you a responsibility point when one becomes available.'	Covert, positive
Manager implies that resources will be withheld	'I hope that you will feel able to do this. I would not like to think that you had caused a reduction of 50 per cent in your departmental budget next year.'	Covert, negative

that there is also a relationship between the kinds of power resource and their associated compliance and the issue of power disparity. The greater the power disparity, the less countervailing power can be brought to the exchange by the weaker party. Weaker parties to a relationship are more likely to possess elements of knowledge and normative power than they are economic or physical power and so are less likely to recognize economic and physical power resources as legitimate. Consequently, when economic or physical resource power is brought to bear in an exchange, the response is likely to be one of compliance rather than commitment. Indeed, a characteristic of cultural knowledge power is that it is widely shared – hence its high level of legitimacy.

It can also be suggested that attempts to apply inappropriate knowledge or normative power resources are further examples of non-legitimate uses of power. However, in the analysis offered here, whether power resources are used legitimately or non-legitimately is a judgement made at the time of the exchange in which they are deployed. Thus inappropriate knowledge would have a contested legitimacy and result in rejection or, at best, some form of calculative compliance. If the response was rejection, then a subsequent exchange might result in an attempt at coercion, leading to alienative compliance. This would have to rest on some form of physical or economic power, not the knowledge that underpinned the previous exchange. If, on the other hand, the knowledge power resources were accepted as appropriate at the time of the exchange, but subsequently found to be inappropriate, then the strength of that person's knowledge power resources would suffer in subsequent exchanges. It is important to emphasize, then, that this view of power resources sees them as being exercised repeatedly through an endless series of exchanges between individuals and therefore variable in their extent and distribution between each exchange. Thus the power resources possessed by an individual can grow or diminish through a series of exchanges or vary in an almost random way depending on the context and the parties to the exchange. Power in organizations, therefore, just like structures and cultures, is fluid and dynamic.

Power, conflict and exchange

It is easy to present this view of power as necessarily operating through conflict, as one person persuades another person to act against their will or perceived self-interest in a particular way that favours the self-interest of the more powerful partner to the exchange. Unfortunately, the term 'compliance' strengthens this interpretation. However, although it is clearly an effective analysis for conflict situations, it has relevance in other circumstances too. As was stated above, what is important to this understanding of power is not the idea of *conflict* but the principle of *exchange*, which usually but not necessarily occurs in a situation of unequal possession of resources. For example, within a rational action model, one might expect an individual's response to the exercise of power resources upon their actions to move from instrumental compliance, to cognitive compliance, to commitment, as it became clear that their interests were best served by acting in the way that the other party desired. All that is necessary for this process to begin is an uncertainty in the mind of the person complying as to what the most appropriate or desirable course of action is. Faced with uncertainty and a colleague who has greater certainty, the individual is likely to follow 'advice' or instructions.

Nor is there any reason to believe that this view of power is a 'zero-sum' perception of resources in which one party to the exchange loses power to the other as a result of compliance. Two or more colleagues may share a common understanding of the goals of the organization where they work and the actions that will fulfil them. The exchange of the economic, knowledge or normative power resources that each brings to a particular situation may result in all of them becoming better able as individuals to understand and deal with situations that arise. Thus the exchange of power resources and the forms of compliance that follow may result in strengthened understanding and greater support for individuals in complex settings, not in their turning aside from their perceived self-interest to serve someone else's.

This discussion of power, which is summarized in Table 6, has attempted to

Table 6 Characteristics of power resources in organizations

Characteristics	Power resources				
	Physical	Economic	Knowledge		Normative
Kind of resource			Administrative	Technical	
Location of resource	In the person	In the office	In the person	In the person	In the person
Status of resource	Non-legitimate	Conditional legitimacy	Conditional legitimacy	Conditional legitimacy	Legitimate by definition
Response	Alienative compliance	Instrumental (calculative) compliance	Cognitive compliance	Cognitive compliance	Moral commitment
Consequence	Search for countervailing power resources	Acknowledged only while resources are forthcoming	Growing tendency to internalize through repeated use and discovery of continuing effectiveness, leading from compliance to commitment		Moral commitment
Characteristic of organization where this predominant	←←←← Contested legitimacy		Agreed legitimacy →→→→		

demonstrate how I believe it is a crucial variable which needs to be incorporated into our analysis of structures and cultures, and why I argue that an analysis of organizations along all three dimensions is important. However, I would also stress the interconnected nature of the three dimensions. Structures can be understood as artefacts generated by the particular combination of values and assumptions that comprise the basic elements of the culture. Structures can be both formally created and informally established as networks of social relations. Cultures develop as they do because of the particular disposition of power resources among their members and the ways in which those resources are used over time. Formal and informal structures provide the vehicle through which power resources can be deployed. Legitimacy is accorded to particular forms and content of power resources depending upon the previous exercise of power resources and the extent to which they are perceived as reflecting external expectations and pressures. This interrelationship is summarized in Figure 4.

APPLYING THIS MODEL TO SCHOOL EFFECTIVENESS AND SCHOOL IMPROVEMENT

To conclude this chapter I will try to demonstrate the potential for the two schools of thought of this three-dimensional model of organizations. The model rests on the notion of relationships between individuals within organizational settings. Thus although it is concerned with organizations, it sees all organizations as collections of individual members. In this sense, it draws on the subjective theories of Greenfield (e.g. 1989; Greenfield and Ribbins, 1993). These relationships are sustained through exchanges between the parties to the relationships. How individuals respond to one another in these exchanges depends on two things: the power resources each party is seen by the other to have at their disposal and the extent to which they are deemed legitimate. These two factors shape the extent to which individuals have room to negotiate degrees of compliance and whether the response of the person with fewer power resources is one of compliance with the other's wishes or commitment to a shared course of action. Whether a set of resources are deemed legitimate will depend on the nature of the resources: economic resources are legitimated primarily by structural factors, whilst other forms of power resources are legitimated primarily by cultural factors.

School effectiveness researchers focus primarily on the structural factors that appear to correlate with effective schools as measured by quantitative measures of pupil performance. They rest on so-called rational–technicist models of schools (Levačić *et al.*, 1999). However, they do not address how changes can be brought about in the structure of a school that may create what are stated to be the structural requirements for effectiveness. This requires us to address the dynamic nature of structures and, in particular, how exchanges occur between the individuals who work within the structure. The concept of organizational power outlined here allows us to identify the resources that shape these exchanges and what legitimizes certain forms of power resources so that staff in the school move towards a committed response to pressures for change. It forces effectiveness researchers to look beyond issues of structure into questions of organizational culture and how they interpenetrate with structures. The power dimension provides a vehicle through which this can be attempted.

School improvement research has made more attempts to attend to both cultural and structural concerns. However, although it has examined ways of generating consensus among the staff, it has paid less attention to two significant concerns: how to establish the need for improvement in the first place and how to ensure that the consensus does not centre around pursuing

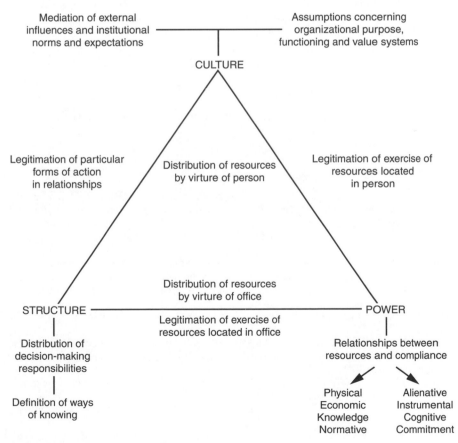

Figure 4 The three dimensions of organizational operation

practices and reforms that will strengthen actions that do not enhance effectiveness, however that is defined. A successful school improvement intervention will generate staff commitment to actions that are designed to promote greater effectiveness. The key issue related to these questions that is highlighted by the organizational model proposed in this chapter is one of legitimacy: what counts as legitimate power resources in an exchange or series of exchanges such that staff commit themselves to reforms, rather than merely complying with others' requests? A focus on the exchange process and the workings of power resources in it might allow us to identify action points in both structural and cultural terms that will make movement possible.

The conceptualization of power laid out in this chapter is not rooted in a conflict model of organizational behaviour, and allows a wide sense of the resources which individual parties to an exchange recognize as legitimate and relevant. It provides a means of understanding how structures and cultures exist and function, and how they might be altered. It can be seen that incorporating this understanding of power into both school effectiveness and school improvement analyses provides a potentially unifying dynamic for them, and begins a linkage between the structural characteristics proposed for effective schools and the cultural developments that may be needed to achieve them.

NOTE

1. Parts of this chapter draw on material previously published in *The Open University* (1996) and Bennett and Harris (1999).

REFERENCES

Archer, M. S. (1980) 'Educational politics: A model for their analysis', in P. Broadfoot, C. Brock and W. Tulasiewicz (eds) *Politics and Educational Change: An International Survey*, pp. 29–55.
Ball, S. J. (1987) *The Micropolitics of the School*. London: Methuen.
Bate, P. (1994) *Strategies for Cultural Change*. London: Butterworth-Heinemann.
Bennett, N. (1991) 'Change and continuity in school practice: A study of the influences affecting secondary school teachers' work, and the role of local and national policies within them.' Unpublished PhD thesis, Department of Government, Brunel University.
Bennett, N. (1995) *Managing Professional Teachers*. London: Paul Chapman Publishing.
Bennett, N. and Harris, A. (1999) 'Hearing truth from power? Organisation theory, school effectiveness and school improvement', *School Effectiveness and School Improvement* **10**(4): 533–50.
Bolman, L. G. and Deal, T. E. (1991) *Reframing Organizations: Artistry, Choice, Leadership*. San Francisco: Jossey-Bass.
Bower, M. (1966) *The Will to Manage: Corporate Success Through Programmed Management*. New York: McGraw-Hill.
Burns, T. and Stalker, G. M. (1961) *The Management of Innovation*. London: Tavistock.

Burrell, G. (1998) 'Modernism, postmodernism and organizational analysis: The contribution of Michel Foucault', in A. McKinlay and K. Starkey (eds) *Foucault, Management and Organization Theory*. London: Sage.

Busher, H. and Harris, A. (1999) 'Leadership of school subject areas: tensions and dimensions of managing in the middle', *School Leadership and Management* **19**(3): 305–17.

Campbell, J. (1989) 'Towards the collegial primary school', in T. Bush (ed.) *Management in Education: Theory and Practice*, pp. 57–65. Milton Keynes: Open University Press.

Clegg, S. R. (1989) *Frameworks of Power*. London: Sage.

Creemers, B. P. M. (1994) *The Effective Classroom*. London: Cassell.

Deal, T. E. (1985) 'The symbolism of effective schools', *Elementary School Journal* **85**(5): 605–20.

Deal, T. E. and Kennedy, A. A. (1982) *Corporate Cultures. The Rites and Rituals of Corporate Life*. Reading, Mass.: Addison-Wesley.

Fayol, H. (1949) *General and Industrial Management*. London: Pitman (originally published 1915).

Foucault, M. (1977) *Discipline and Punish: The Birth of the Prison*. Harmondsworth: Penguin.

Foucault, M. (1984) *The History of Sexuality: An Introduction*. Harmondsworth: Peregrine.

Goffman, E. (1961) *Asylums*. Harmondsworth: Penguin.

Gramsci, A. (1971) *Selections from the Prison Notebooks*. London: Lawrence and Wishart.

Gray, J., Hopkins, D., Reynolds, D., Wilcox, B., Farrell, S. and Jesson, D. (1999) *Improving Schools: Performance and Potential*. Buckingham: Open University Press.

Greenfield, T. B. (1989) 'Organizations as social inventions: Rethinking assumptions about change', in T. Bush (ed.) *Management in Education: Theory and Practice*, pp. 81–95. Milton Keynes: Open University Press.

Greenfield, T. and Ribbins, P. (eds) (1993) *Greenfield on Educational Administration: Towards a Humane Science*. London: Routledge.

Hales, C. (1993) *Managing Through Organisation*. London: Routledge.

Hanna, D. (1988) *Designing Organizations for High Performance*. Reading, Mass.: Addison-Wesley.

Heck, R. H. and Marcoulides, G. A. (1996) 'School culture and performance: Testing the invariance of an organisational model', *School Effectiveness and School Improvement* **7**(1): 76–95.

Levačić, R., Glover, D., Bennett, N. and Crawford, M. (1999) 'Modern headship for the rationally-managed school: Combining cerebral and insightful approaches', in T. Bush, L. Bell, R. Bolam, R. Glatter and P. Ribbins (eds) *Educational Management: Redefining Theory, Policy and Practice*. London: Paul Chapman Publishing.

Lukes, S. (1974) *Power: A Radical View*. London: Macmillan.

McLean, A. J. (1990) *Cultures at Work: How to Identify and Understand Them*. Bath: Bath Associates.

Meyer, J. W. and Rowan, B. (1977) 'Institutionalized organizations: Formal structure as myth and ceremony', *American Journal of Sociology* **83**(2): 340–63.

Meyerson, D. and Martin, J. (1987) 'Cultural change: An integration of three different views', *Journal of Management Studies* **24**(6): 623–47.

Nias, J., Southworth, G. and Yeomans, R. (1989) *Staff Relationships in the Primary School*. London: Cassell.

Office for Standards in Education (OFSTED) (1999) *Inspecting Schools – The Framework Effective from January 2000*. London: OFSTED.

Ogawa, R. T. (1996) 'The case for organisation in highly-institutionalised settings'.

Paper presented to the American Educational Research Association Annual Meeting, April, New York.

Ogawa, R. T. and Bossert, S. (1997) 'Leadership as an organizational quality', in M. Crawford, L. Kydd and C. Riches (eds) *Leadership and Teams in Educational Management*, pp. 9–23. Buckingham: Open University Press.

Orton, J. D. and Weick, K. E. (1990) 'Loosely coupled systems: A reconceptualisation', *Academy of Management Review* **15**(2): 203–23.

Perry, W. (1976) *Open University: A Personal Account by the First Vice-Chancellor.* Milton Keynes: Open University Press.

Rowan, B. (1995) 'Institutional analysis of educational organizations: Lines of theory and directions for research', in *Advances in Research and Theories of School Management*, vol. 3, pp. 1–20. Greenwich, CT: JAI Press.

Schein, E. A. (1992) *Organizational Culture and Leadership.* San Francisco: Jossey-Bass.

Scott, W. R. (1987) *Organizations: Rational, Natural and Open Systems* (2nd edn). Englewood Cliffs, NJ: Prentice-Hall.

Taylor, F. W. (1911) *Principles of Scientific Management.* New York: Harper.

Teacher Training Agency (TTA) (1998a) *National Standards for Subject Leaders.* London: Teacher Training Agency.

Teacher Training Agency (TTA) (1998b) *National Standards for Headteachers.* London: Teacher Training Agency.

The Open University (1996) *E838 Leadership and Management in Education: Study Guide.* Milton Keynes: The Open University.

Wallace, M. (1989) 'Towards a collegiate approach to curriculum management in primary and middle schools', in M. Preedy (ed.) *Approaches to Curriculum Management*, pp. 182–94. Milton Keynes: Open University Press.

Weick, K. E. (1976) 'Educational organisations as loosely-coupled systems', *Administrative Science Quarterly* **21**(1): 1–21.

Young, K. (1981) 'Discretion as an implementation problem: a framework for interpretation', in M. Adler and S. Asquith (eds) *Discretion and Welfare*, pp. 33–46. London: Heinemann.

Part Three

Chapter 7

A Cultural Perspective on School Effectiveness, School Improvement and Teacher Professional Development

Agnes McMahon

INTRODUCTION

> We know what it takes to create a good school: a strong, skilled head who understands the importance of clear leadership, committed staff and parents, high expectations of every child and above all good teaching. These characteristics cannot be put in place by altering the school structure or by legislation and financial pressure alone. Effective change in a field as dependent on human interaction as education requires millions of people to change their behaviour. That will require constant advocacy and persuasion to create a climate in which schools are constantly challenged to compare themselves to other similar schools and adopt proven ways of raising their performance. (DfEE, 1997, p. 12)

> We must replace the culture of complacency with commitment to success. (DfEE, 1997, p. 3)

These statements from the paper *Excellence in Schools,* published soon after the election of the Labour government, are a neat illustration of the paradoxes of school culture. The explicit and implicit messages here are that school cultures are holistic; that 'good' schools have a distinctive culture; and that school cultures can be changed. All these propositions are open to question. However, it is also recognized that it is difficult to change behaviour and that this cannot be fully achieved through national legislation and financial pressure. At school level the implicit strategy seems to be that leaders should create a climate that is supportive and gives people a belief that they can improve, and yet challenges them by highlighting weaknesses. This is a difficult balance to sustain, not least because it requires the leader to work with the organizational culture within the framework of a macronational culture.

The purposes of this chapter are to explore what is understood by school culture and to consider what a cultural perspective might contribute to the debate about school effectiveness and school improvement. It discusses the potential conflict between the macronational educational policy pressures on the one hand, and the messages from research on school effectiveness and school improvement on the other, and considers how this tension impacts upon school improvement initiatives, particularly teacher professional development, which are seen as central to such improvement.

SCHOOL CULTURE – A CONTESTED CONCEPT

The concept of school culture is a very slippery one. The terms culture and climate are often used to refer to the same phenomenon, although Hoyle (1986, p. 3) argues that values are central to the concept of culture and that climate focuses upon the quality of relationships between members of an organization. Questions abound about whether the culture of an organization can be viewed holistically, about how it can be identified and the extent to which it can be managed and changed. Schein's definition provides a good starting point. He argues that culture is

> a pattern of basic assumptions – invented, discovered or developed by a given group as it learns to cope with its problems of external adaptation and integration – that has worked well enough to be considered valid and, therefore has to be taught to new members as the correct way to perceive, think and feel in relation to those problems. (Schein, 1985, p. 9)

He identifies three levels to organizational culture: *artifacts* (e.g. allocation of space, use of language) which can be easily observed even if not easily understood; the *values* which individuals say are held by members of the organization, though these may be espoused rather than practised; and the *basic assumptions* guiding behaviour which are taken for granted by members of the organization and are largely unconscious and so hard for an outsider to identify. These basic assumptions are learned by a group over time, deeply held and difficult to change. Although he speaks of new members of the organization being 'taught' the culture, in so far as this is a formal process it is easier to see how it can be done in relation to espoused values rather than to basic, deeply held assumptions. Yet leaders need to gain some understanding of the culture if they are to try to manage it. The early stage of headship is a time when headteachers are socialized into the knowledge, values and behaviours that constitute the culture of a particular school. Weindling (1999, p. 98) refers to this as organizational socialization, described as '. . . a critical period when the new head's notions of headship meet the reality of a particular school'. Alvesson's definition of culture, while similar in many respects to Schein's, introduces the notion of organizational culture being represented in symbols:

> a shared and learned world of experiences, meanings, values, and understandings which inform people and which are expressed, reproduced, and communicated partly in symbolic form. (Alvesson, 1993, p. 3)

Bolman and Deal's definition of culture also notes the power of symbols: 'Our view is that every organisation develops distinctive beliefs and patterns over time. Many of these patterns or assumptions are unconscious or taken for granted. They are reflected in myths, fairy tales, stories, rituals, ceremonies, and other symbolic forms' (1991, p. 268). They argue that managers who understand the power of symbols strengthen their chances of influencing the organization.

However, Firestone and Louis, drawing on work by Swidler (1986), have argued that such definitions give too much emphasis to values and the holistic nature of organizational culture. An alternative, which they support, is to view culture as 'a tool kit that provides strategies for action that members of the culture can use in many different ways' (Firestone and Louis, 1999, p. 299). This interpretation of culture gives room for individual creativity and recognizes that the culture may not be uniform and that individuals and groups will draw differentially on what Firestone and Louis term the cultural codes. Rather than a holistic school culture there are likely to be a number of subcultures which reflect cultural differences between the various groups of people (e.g. teachers, pupils, parents) and the subgroups (e.g. the science teachers) who form the school community. The more differentiated the culture within an organization, the more difficult it is likely to be to manage and change.

Interest in the study of organizational cultures is prompted by the recognition that there is a link between the culture of an organization and its performance. Logically it would seem to follow that by developing an understanding of the culture one will gain insights into how the organization works and learns. This knowledge might then be used to manipulate the culture in some way, either to manage or change it (Alvesson, 1993). Cultures in organizations clearly change over time, people move in and out of the organization, it may be restructured, change may occur in response to internal or external challenge or pressure. However, setting out deliberately to change the culture and choosing appropriate strategies for doing this is no easy matter. Organizational theory often focuses on the role of leaders or managers as cultural change agents but their power may be limited in practice. Alvesson argues that managers are more likely to be driven by the culture and suggests that, although management will have an influence on culture, 'it is possible to be at the same time a product of a culture, to be constrained by it, and to some degree to be able to change or at least modify it' (Alvesson, 1993, p. 90).

THE MESSAGES FROM RESEARCH ON SCHOOL EFFECTIVENESS AND SCHOOL IMPROVEMENT

The policy focus on a standards agenda has meant that research on school effectiveness and improvement has come under close scrutiny. School effectiveness researchers are agreed that schools can make a difference to student outcomes and this core message has been used to provide a rationale for the drive to raise standards. The research findings are broadly in line with the conclusion reached by Creemers (1994, p. 20) that 'about 12% to 18% of the variance in student outcomes can be explained by classroom and school factors, when we take into account the background of the students.' This is sufficient to make a positive difference to pupil achievement. Research also suggests that schools in similar contexts can reach different levels of achievement, that the proportion of variance in achievement may differ between subjects in schools and in different countries (Sammons *et al.*, 1995). The power of the school effectiveness movement is enhanced because of an associated belief that knowledge now exists about what action is required to make schools effective. Sammons *et al.*'s (1995) list of eleven factors that correlate with more effective school outcomes is well known and, despite the researchers' warnings that their findings are not evidence of causal mechanisms and should be interpreted with caution, their influence on government policies is plain to see. But, as critics of the school effectiveness movement (e.g. Slee *et al.*, 1998) have noted, the model that is being used and recommended to schools is overly rationalistic and takes little or no account of cultural factors at either national or institutional level. One instance of this is the point frequently made in official documents that schools in disadvantaged areas can still succeed and achieve national targets for pupil attainment although there is plenty of evidence about the difficulty this challenge poses, not least because of the bridges that may have to be built between the different cultures of the pupils, parents and the teaching staff. It is as if the proportion of variance in achievement due to factors beyond the control of the school is not given recognition.

Most of the factors that correlate with effective school outcomes have direct implications for teachers (Sammons *et al.*, 1995). Teachers in effective schools are reported to work collegially and to collaborate to achieve shared goals; they have high expectations of their students, teach purposively, monitor student work, give positive feedback, etc. Hargreaves, D. (1995) has proposed a heuristic typology of school cultures in which he identifies four 'ideal types': the formal school culture characterized by pressure on students to achieve learning goals but weak social cohesion between staff and students; a welfarist culture where relations between staff and students are relaxed and friendly but there is little academic pressure; a hothouse culture which pressurizes staff and students to participate in all aspects of school life, academic and social; and a survivalist culture characterized by poor social relations and low academic achievement. He argues that the ideal culture for an effective school is one which balances academic pressure and social cohesion: 'Expectations of work and conduct are high - the principal's expectations of staff and the teachers' of students. Yet these standards are not perceived to be unreasonable; everyone is supported in striving for them and rewarded for reaching them. For both teachers and students, school is a demanding but very enjoyable place to be' (*ibid.*, p. 28). Of course, as he points out, recommendations about an effective school culture are tied to the particular definition of effectiveness that is employed. If effectiveness is judged primarily in terms of academic outcomes then the formal school culture is likely to be preferred. The delicate balance of pressure and support that characterizes Hargreaves' ideal culture is not easy to achieve or sustain. Nevertheless the message that effective schools are characterized by firm leadership, a shared vision and goals and collegial and collaborative relationships among staff who are working to achieve these goals is one that is regularly highlighted in the research literature (e.g. Teddlie and Reynolds, 2000) and has been adopted by policy makers.

Latterly, researchers and writers focusing upon school effectiveness and school improvement have worked to overcome the charge of separateness and build links between these two fields of enquiry. Whereas the criticism made of school effectiveness research was that it did not address how schools could become more effective, the criticism of school improvement work was that it did not take sufficient account of outcome measures, especially pupil achievement. Recent definitions of school improvement show how thinking has moved forward. Gray *et al.* (1999) state that 'An improving school in our study was one which increased its effectiveness over time. In other words, the amount of value added it generated for its pupils would be expected to rise for successive cohorts' (p. 5). Hopkins' definition (1996) also reflects this move: 'school improvement is a strategy for educational change that enhances student outcomes as well as strengthening the school's capacity for managing change' (p. 31). Of course, school improvement is a dynamic, action orientated process which is likely to involve organizational change and challenge the existing school culture. In the final analysis, improvements in teaching and learning can only be achieved at the school level and this is why the teacher is so important. Successive governments have realized that change and school improvement cannot be successfully introduced without the active support of teachers. Specifically, unless teachers are willing to alter their practice in particular ways little or nothing is likely to happen. Yet, as Ouston (1999) has noted, there is little practical advice available for schools about how to encourage staff to do this. She argues that 'Guides to school improvement have a conceptual hole at their centre. They never seem to offer help in answering three key questions, what will you do to improve? How? And why?' (p. 173).

The message that comes across strongly in the literature is that improving schools are ones which have learned to manage multiple change and are moving towards the concept of a learning organization. Clearly, this too requires a radical cultural shift. How does this happen? Fullan (1993) argues that planned change strategies are not the solution because 'reality under conditions of dynamic complexity is fundamentally non-linear' (p. 138). He suggests that learning teachers are the key to a learning organization and that this will require inner learning (intrapersonal sense-making) as well as outer learning (relating and collaborating with others). One means of promoting this is to invest in teacher professional development, widely regarded as a key means of promoting school improvement (Joyce, 1990). Reporting on a study of school improvement Gray *et al.* (1999) concluded that a common theme of schools that were improving more rapidly was that 'they had found ways of facilitating more discussion among colleagues about classroom issues than hitherto' (p. 144). The teachers in Rosenholtz's (1991) moving schools worked in collaborative, learning cultures. Joyce *et al.* (1999) argue for a model of school improvement in which the school is a learning community for teachers as well as students. The micro, school-level cultures that these writers argue are associated with teacher growth and learning are ones in which teachers feel able to experiment and take risks, where collaboration is valued and time is allocated to facilitate shared work, where information is used as a basis for joint enquiry and investigation and where sharing and partnership rather than competition between teachers is encouraged. How are such cultures established? Case studies of schools that appear to be moving in this direction show that changing the culture takes prolonged effort by many people over several years (e.g. McMahon *et al.*, 1996). Despite this, policy makers typically seek quick results. Successive UK governments, recognizing the importance for school improvement of teachers engaging in professional development, have tried to enforce this through legislation. The trend in policy in recent years has been to set a strong regulatory framework for professional development which specifies, through the national contract of service, that all teachers should participate in professional development activities to some extent and, through an annual grant for in-service education, not just the resources available to support professional development but the priority topics for training. Within this framework, responsibility for implementing continuing professional development for teachers (CPD) has been largely delegated to the school level (e.g. planning for five professional development days, spending budgets for in-service education). This strategy, although entirely consistent with the managerialist culture, does not appear to have worked especially well. The mere fact that the government is still seeking new ways of promoting CPD is evidence of this (DfEE, 2000).

THE MACRO-CULTURAL CONTEXT: MANAGERIALISM AND STANDARDS

The wider cultural context for schools in the UK and, indeed, in many other countries is characterized by two complementary forces – managerialism and a drive to raise standards in schools. The defining features of managerialism, also referred to as rational management or new public management (Levačić, 1999; Simkins, 1999; Clarke and Newman, 1997), are a strong central regulatory framework, devolved decision making to organizational level, a focus on measurable outputs and a willingness to rely on quasi-market forces. Levačić (1999) argues that in recent years the British government has increasingly implemented a rational approach to school management. 'The model adopted combines decentralised management of resources at school level with central control of the outputs of schools via a framework consisting of a state specified curriculum, national tests at four key stages of a child's schooling, a national system of school inspection, and open publication of schools' inspection results and test results' (1999, p. 95). One consequence of this, she suggests, has been to strengthen the role of the headteacher as chief executive relative to that of the professional leader.

Levačić's description of the rational approach to school management is entirely consistent with definitions of 'managerialism' developed by writers like Clarke and Newman (1997). Factors that they see associated with the rise of managerialism are: 'doing more for less in pursuit of the holy grail of efficiency; trying to be 'strategic' while juggling an ever increasing number of injunctions and restrictions from central government; managing the problems arising from overlapping, fast changing and often contradictory policy agendas; and struggling to balance all this with living a life beyond the workplace. ... The can do culture of management has a strong preference for practical prescriptions over mere academic analysis' (1997, pp. x, xii).

Simkins (1999) argues that government policies have been designed to create frameworks of incentives which affect the ways in which schools and colleges are managed. First, by manipulating the environment to produce incentives, e.g. introduction of quasi markets and decentralization of decision making to schools. Second, by using government power to determine the broad aims, purposes and structure of the system and to set out performance criteria that individual institutions must satisfy. One feature that Simkins highlights is the central responsibility given to the individual institution in the process of improvement. He argues that managerialism assumes that techniques for achieving better management are knowable and generally applicable to any sector of activity – so managers must be given freedom to manage. Power and Whitty (1999) have suggested that the marketization of education is changing relations within and between schools resulting in the adoption of 'market place values that celebrate individualism, competition, performativity and differentiation' (p. 22). This wider culture of managerialism shapes the environment for primary and secondary schools in England. Schools have devolved budgets, are held accountable for the results achieved by their students and a 'failing' school which fails to demonstrate improvement may be closed. These policies emit very powerful cultural messages from the centre, at least at Schein's levels of artifacts and values.

If managerialism is one powerful influence shaping the macro-educational culture then the government's broad strategy for raising the standard of pupil achievement in schools, which was outlined in the 1997 Green Paper (DfEE, 1997), can be described as a second. The question about how to improve student achievement in schools has been a dominant theme in educational discussion in Britain in recent years among practitioners and politicians. The government has committed itself to an ambitious reform programme which is intended to raise standards in schools. This concern to raise standards is driven in part by the perception that English children are underperforming in core subject areas in relation to those in other countries, though as Brown (1998) has shown in her discussion of the Third International Mathematics and Science Study (TIMSS) data, such international comparisons of performance have to be treated with caution. In many respects the government strategy, which it would argue is informed by educational research, builds on initiatives that were already in place under previous Conservative governments. The systems for monitoring school performance, through analysis and publication of pupil results and through a regular programme of inspection, have been maintained. Literacy and numeracy strategies have been introduced and the importance of ICT in the curriculum is being stressed. Schools are required to set challenging targets for pupil attainment and to monitor their progress in reaching these targets. The problem of underachievement is being addressed on several different fronts: regulation of the curriculum and the assessment of learning; inspection of the quality of management and teaching in the school; tighter control and direction of initial teacher training and, latterly, of teacher professional development. The message that is being reinforced is that all schools, irrespective of their social and cultural context, can succeed. There will be zero tolerance of underachievement (DfEE, 1997). The consequences for schools and individual teachers judged to be underperforming are severe: schools failing OFSTED are put into special measures; inspectors report on the competence of individual teachers; if a school cannot demonstrate improvement it faces closure, and a teacher who fails to improve faces disciplinary measures and possible dismissal. This is a challenging approach which implies that schools can be pressured into improvement. The macro-cultural messages are about target setting and the distribution of rewards and sanctions dependent upon the extent to which targets and goals are achieved. As Jamieson and Wikely argue, in Chapter 9, the extent to which this strategy of raising achievement through a strong regulatory framework matched with tough sanctions on underachievement will foster the collaborative professional cultures that lead to school improvement remains to be seen.

TEACHER PROFESSIONAL DEVELOPMENT AS A MEANS OF SCHOOL IMPROVEMENT

My central argument is that the macro-culture is dominated by two sets of factors – managerialism and standards – and that these are in conflict with messages from research about school effectiveness and improvement. In consequence, the capacity of headteachers and staff in schools to establish a school culture which will promote the school as a learning organization and lead to long-term improvement is constrained. One key indicator of this is the provision of teacher professional development.

The task that headteachers and staff in schools have to achieve is to work within the constraints of the macro-cultural framework while at the same time developing an institutional culture which is supportive of teacher learning and growth. Data gathered in a study of continuing professional development for secondary teachers (McMahon, 1999) indicated how difficult it can be to do this. The quality of school provision for teacher professional development was often adversely affected by two broad factors: first, because managerialism has resulted in much of the responsibility for the provision of professional development being devolved to school level; second, because the standards agenda seems to have resulted in a rather narrow interpretation of the kinds of professional development that are likely to raise the quality of teaching and learning. Schools and teachers are judged on their ability to meet national targets for student achievement, but they have to do this while operating in the quasi market, and this is the dominant message that impacts on the school culture. National standards have been set for the teaching profession (TTA, 1998) but these have not been accompanied by a common entitlement to professional development.

The impact of this macro-culture can be identified in practical and less tangible forms. To cite some specific instances: the data revealed that there were significant differences in the resources available in schools for teacher professional development, not just because of differences in the level of devolved funding but also because some schools were more successful than others in obtaining additional money. Access to advice and expertise also varied as many LEAs had reduced the number of staff in their advisory/ inspection team. Schools in rural areas were additionally disadvantaged in that they often did not have easy access to any higher education institutions and so had to search hard for appropriate consultants to support a school professional development programme. There were considerable variations in the extent to which schools gave priority to teacher professional development and had systems in place for delivering it. Only a minority of schools reported arrangements for job rotation, work shadowing, classroom observation, teacher portfolios, etc. Teacher appraisal, which should have been a key means of identifying individual development needs, had largely ceased to function. Priorities for teacher education and training activities were largely determined by the topics which qualified for funding through the national grant for in-service education and by the need to introduce national innovations (e.g. aspects of the national curriculum) and whole school needs as identified in the school development plan. The bulk of the school budget for CPD was normally devolved to heads of subject areas and was intended to be used to support their teaching plans. While few teachers would disagree with the spirit of this, in practice it meant that individual development needs were neglected unless they were in an area that was designated a school priority. Training opportunities might be available to staff in one subject area but not in others. For example, resources to support professional development were more likely to be available for ICT teachers than art teachers.

The quality of the development experience offered to teachers was often perceived by them as poor and not meeting their individual development needs. Although the five non-contact days/professional development days represent a considerable national investment in continuing development, at least one and sometimes two of these days were regularly used for whole school planning and administrative purposes (e.g. preparing the school development plan). When the day was used for in-service training the focus was typically on a whole school issue (e.g. underachievement in boys) and no differentiation was made between teachers, irrespective of their prior knowledge and expertise. Little time was available for individual training. A great deal of the provision was in the form of short (e.g. half-day or one-day) sessions which meant that little could be achieved beyond raising awareness of innovations (Joyce, 1988). It was very rare for a teacher to be supported by the school to attend a longer, award-bearing course and where teachers were working for a higher degree this was almost invariably at their own expense and in their own time.

The experience of teacher professional development revealed by this data was not unique to the particular schools in the study. Anthea Millett, then Chief Executive of the Teacher Training Agency (TTA), reported in 1997 that research commissioned by the Agency revealed that

> professional development was often ad hoc with insufficient linkage across school development planning, personal development planning and appraisal; there was little consistency in how much schools spent on professional development; very few teachers believed professional development activities had any impact on their work in the classroom'. (1997, p. 5)

Little concern was expressed about this state of affairs; schools were not censured by OFSTED for poor CPD provision for teachers. Even the inspection handbook (OFSTED, 1999) includes only passing references to professional development and then in the context of induction and initial training. The message that impacts on the school culture is that professional development is not valued.

WAYS FORWARD FOR PROFESSIONAL DEVELOPMENT?

There are signs that the macro-cultural messages about teacher professional development are changing. The government has stated that 'High quality in-service training is the key to raising standards through updating teachers' skills and enabling them to keep pace with best practice' (DfEE, 1997, p. 48). It has set itself the task of modernizing the teaching profession and changing the professional culture. 'We need teaching to become a learning profession. Continuing improvement requires a user-friendly, relevant framework for teachers' professional development, allowing access to best practice in teaching and learning and providing opportunities for continuing learning on and off the job' (DfEE, 2000, p. 3). The strategy that is being put in place builds on the work of the previous government and appears to be a combination of pressure and support; providing professional development opportunities which should enable teachers to update their subject knowledge and teaching skills; increasing the provision of teaching resources, especially ICT, but also holding teachers accountable for their success in sustaining and raising the achievements of their pupils. Specific initiatives that have been introduced or are being planned are:

- A professional development framework for teachers which identifies national standards at key stages: qualified teachers; subject leaders; special educational needs co-ordinators; headteachers.
- Opportunities for teachers who are excellent classroom practitioners to be recognized as Advanced Skills Teachers.
- Training for school leadership through the National Professional Qualification for Headship (NPQH) and the Leadership Programme for Serving Headteachers (LPSH); the establishment of a National College for School Leadership.
- Support for teacher action research funded by the TTA.
- New arrangements for appraisal and a system for performance management linked to pay.
- Support for teacher professional development linked to the raising standards agenda.
- The establishment of a General Teaching Council (GTC) for the profession.

The proposals outlined in the Green Paper on Professional Development (DfEE, 2000) seem to promise a new impetus. They herald a commitment to providing time for teachers to reflect on and plan their development. They propose to encourage and fund a wide range of education and training opportunities intended to meet individual as well as organizational goals (e.g. professional bursaries which would make sums of money available direct to teachers; international exchanges and study visits; teacher research scholarships; development portfolios). Professional development is to be influenced by the individual's professional needs and aspirations as well as the needs and priorities of the school and national strategic priorities. This should broaden the CPD agenda and give professionals a voice in determining what is appropriate professional development. These initiatives will surely be welcomed by teachers, particularly if funding is available on anything like an equitable basis. A national focus on teacher professional development will begin to send out a more positive message at the macro-cultural level by signalling that teachers are valued and that investment in their development is worthwhile. This in turn should help teachers to build more collaborative learning cultures within their schools.

However, questions remain about the extent to which a national initiative to support professional development will be sufficient to change the macro-culture. My concern is that these contrary pressures, which reinforce individualism and competition, will be hard to resist. OFSTED inspectors will continue to report on the achievement of individual teachers. Appraisal and performance management systems will make links between the pay and opportunities available for teachers and the achievement of the pupils in their classes. The new performance threshold assessments and fast-tracking systems for able teachers focus upon individual achievement rather than group or collaborative effort. All these factors militate against collaborative joint work in schools.

The composition of the teacher force must also be taken into account. It is known that the teacher force is ageing, more than 40 per cent are aged 40 or more. These teachers will have experienced multiple educational reforms over the past ten years or more and may be reluctant to engage in further change. Early retirement from the profession has been a cause for concern and the difficulty of recruitment into the profession is widely recognized. Senior management posts and headteacher positions are proving more difficult to fill, especially in primary schools. The Teachers' Review Body continues to report concern over teacher workload, motivation and morale (DfEE, 1999), noting recently that 'Many teachers feel under great pressure and the object of excessive criticism' (p. 15). Findings from a small-scale study on the impact of teacher stress on their behaviour in the classroom (McMahon, 2000) indicated that this intensification of workload is likely to have negative consequences for teaching and learning. Teachers reported that their lesson preparation, classroom management and assessment of pupil work all suffered when they were working under undue pressure. The government view is that problems with recruitment and morale will be overcome by the introduction of performance management and pay systems and new approaches to professional development, but this remains to be tested.

CONCLUSION: THE FUTURE OF SCHOOL IMPROVEMENT AND SCHOOL EFFECTIVENESS

Where does this leave the discussion about what might be learned by adopting a cultural perspective on school effectiveness and school improvement? I have argued that the macro-educational culture is dominated by two forces, managerialism and standards, and that, although there is some overlap between the standards agenda and the messages from research on school effectiveness and school improvement, the power of these macro-cultural pressures makes it very difficult for headteachers and their staff to build the kind of learning culture which leads to school improvement, not least because the pressure of the external agenda leaves less room for flexibility at school level. The strength of the cultural perspective on school improvement is that it reminds us that school cultures are not uniform: they differ one from another and cultures differ between subgroups within a school. There is no perfect improvement culture that can be imposed at will.

Furthermore, if learning teachers are fundamental to the existence of a learning organization then a variety of ways of promoting teacher growth need to be explored. The models of continuing professional development that have emerged with the managerial culture are tightly focused on training for specific tasks rather than something that is broader and more open ended. Yet, Little

(1993) has argued that, although training models intended to develop particular skills may work well for technical innovations or particular classroom practices, if used alone they will not help teachers to develop the range of intellectual skills needed for handling the reform agenda. Hargreaves, A. (1995) has been similarly critical of narrow training models of professional development, suggesting that as well as addressing technical competence, professional development should include 'the place of moral purpose in teaching, political awareness, acuity, and adeptness among teachers, and teachers' emotional attachment to and engagement with their work' (p. 126). Eraut (1994) has suggested that professional knowledge cannot be considered independently of how it is learned and used and that it is constructed through experience. Logically it follows from this that their development may well be constrained if teachers have only a limited range of professional development experiences.

Well resourced schools which are judged to be effective might find it easier to build a learning, improvement culture than those which are struggling. Nevertheless, as Schein (1985) and Alvesson (1993) note, the culture of an organization is essentially a pattern of basic assumptions which are built up over time and are difficult to change. Headteachers are themselves products of the culture and will be constrained by it (Alvesson, 1993). Although the espoused values of the policy makers are that teachers are valued and central to school improvement, the symbolic artifacts are transmitting a different message. For instance, although the Teacher Training Agency has funded some teacher research projects, the bulk of the funding for in-service education is allocated to the priorities identified in the government's standards agenda. The introduction of fixed-term contracts for headteachers linked to the achievement of specific objectives is under consideration (DfEE, 1998) and arrangements for the introduction of performance-related pay for teachers have been put in place.

These policies, which go to the heart of individual feelings about job security, seem likely to sustain the current trends and reinforce values and assumptions about regulation, competition and individualism rather than experiment, sharing and collaboration. Less central regulation and more flexibility in provision for professional development are arguably more likely to promote learning organizations; recent proposals (DfEE, 2000) that teachers should have personal learning bursaries, opportunities for study leave, etc. promise a step in the right direction. If these opportunities can be combined with a reduction in the pressures that teachers have been experiencing at work we may see many more schools develop into learning organizations. If individual teacher development is to be a priority and teachers are to be encouraged to select professional development activities that they judge will meet their needs this must be signalled by changes in the messages that are transmitted at the levels of the macro-culture and the school.

REFERENCES

Alvesson, M. (1993) *Cultural Perspectives on Organisations.* Cambridge: Cambridge University Press.

Bolman, L. G. and Deal, T. E. (1991) *Reframing Organisations.* San Francisco CA: Jossey-Bass.

Brown, S. (1998) 'The tyranny of the international horse race', in R. Slee, G. Weiner and S. Tomlinson (eds) *School Effectiveness for Whom? Challenges to the School Effectiveness and School Improvement Movements.* London: Falmer Press.

Bush, T., Bell, L., Bolam, R., Glatter, R. and Ribbins, P. (eds) *Educational Management: Redefining Theory, Policy and Practice.* London: Paul Chapman Publishing.

Clarke, J. and Newman, J. (1997) *The Managerial State.* London: Sage.

Creemers, B. P. M. (1994) 'The history, value and purpose of school effectiveness studies', in D. Reynolds, B. P. M. Creemers, P. Nesselrodt, E. C. Schaffer, S. Stringfield and C. Teddlie *Advances in School Effectiveness Research and Practice.* Oxford: Pergamon.

Department for Education and Employment (DfEE) (1997) *Excellence in Schools.* London: The Stationery Office.

Department for Education and Employment (DfEE) (1998) *Teachers Meeting the Challenge of Change.* London: The Stationery Office.

Department for Education and Employment (DfEE) (1999) *Eighth Report School Teachers Review Body.* London: The Stationery Office.

Department for Education and Employment (DfEE) (2000) *Professional Development: Support for Teaching and Learning.* London: DfEE.

Eraut, M. (1994) *Developing Professional Knowledge and Competence.* London: Falmer Press.

Firestone, W. A. and Louis, K. S. (1999) 'Schools as cultures', in J. Murphy and K. S. Louis (eds) *Second Handbook of Educational Administration.* San Francisco: Jossey-Bass.

Fullan, M. (1993) *Change Forces.* London: Falmer Press.

Gray, J., Hopkins, D., Reynolds, D., Wilcox, B., Farrell, S. and Jesson, D. (1999) *Improving Schools: Performance and Potential.* Buckingham: Open University Press.

Hargreaves, A. (1995) 'Development and desire: a post modern perspective', in T. R. Guskey and M. Huberman (eds) *Professional Development in Action.* New York: Teachers College Press.

Hargreaves, D. (1995) 'School culture, school effectiveness and school improvement', *School Effectiveness and Improvement* **6**(1): 23–46.

Hopkins, D. (1996) 'Towards a theory for school improvement', in J. Gray, D. Reynolds, C. T. Fitz-Gibbon and D. Jesson (eds) *Merging Traditions: The Future of Research on School Effectiveness and School Improvement.* London: Cassell.

Hoyle, E. (1986) *The Politics of School Management.* London: Hodder and Stoughton.

Joyce, B. (1988) *Student Achievement through Staff Development.* London: Longman.

Joyce, B. (ed.) (1990) *Changing School Culture through Staff Development.* Alexandria: Association for Supervision and Curriculum Development.

Joyce, B., Calhoun, E. and Hopkins, D. (1999) *The New Structure of School Improvement: Inquiring Schools and Achieving Students.* Buckingham: Open University Press.

Levačić, R. (1999) 'Managing resources for school effectiveness in England and Wales: Institutionalising a rational approach?', in R. Bolam and F. van Wieringen (eds) *Research on Educational Management in Europe.* Munich: Waxmann.

Little, J. (1993) 'Teachers' professional development in a climate of educational reform', *Educational Evaluation and Policy Analysis* **15**(2): 129–51.

McMahon, A. (1999) 'Promoting continuing professional development for teachers: An achievable target for school leaders?', in T. Bush, L. Bell, R. Bolam, R. Glatter and P. Ribbins (eds) *Educational Management: Redefining Theory, Policy and Practice.* London: Paul Chapman.

McMahon, A. (2000) 'Managing teacher stress to enhance pupil learning' (mimeo). Paper presented at the American Educational Research Association (AERA) Annual Conference, New Orleans, April.

McMahon, A., Bishop, J., Carroll, R. and McNally, B. (1996) 'Fair Furlong Primary School in National Commission on Education', in *Success against the Odds: Effective Schools in Disadvantaged Areas.* London: Routledge.

Millet, A. (1997) 'Tackling a long-standing malaise', *Professional Development Today* **1**(1): 5–8.

Office for Standards in Education (OFSTED) (1999) *Handbook for Inspecting Secondary Schools.* London: The Stationery Office.

Ouston, J. (1999) 'School effectiveness and school improvement: Critique of a movement', in T. Bush, L. Bell, R. Bolam, R. Glatter, and P. Ribbins (eds) *Educational Management: Redefining Theory, Policy and Practice.* London: Paul Chapman Publishing.

Power, S. and Whitty, G. (1999) 'Market forces and school cultures', in J. Prosser (ed.) *School Culture.* London: Paul Chapman Publishing.

Prosser, J. (ed.) (1999) *School Culture.* London: Paul Chapman Publishing.

Rosenholtz, S. J. (1991) *Teachers' Workplace: The Social Organization of Schools.* New York: Teachers College Press.

Sammons, P., Hillman, J. and Mortimore, P. (1995) *Key Characteristics of Effective Schools.* London: Institute of Education, University of London.

Schein, E. (1985) *Organizational Culture and Leadership.* Oxford: Jossey-Bass.

Simkins, T. (1999) 'Values, power and instrumentality: Theory and research in education management, *Educational Management and Administration* **27**(3): 267–81.

Slee, R., Weiner, G. and Tomlinson, S. (eds) (1998) *School Effectiveness for Whom? Challenges to the School Effectiveness and School Improvement Movements.* London: Falmer Press.

Swidler, A. (1986) 'Culture in action: Symbols and strategies', *American Sociological Review* **51**(2): 273–86.

Teacher Training Agency (TTA) (1998) *National Standards for Headteachers.* London: Teacher Training Agency.

Teddlie, C. and Reynolds, D. (eds) (2000) *The International Handbook of School Effectiveness Research.* London: Falmer Press.

Weindling, D. (1999) 'Stages of headship', in T. Bush, L. Bell, R. Bolam, R. Glatter and P. Ribbins (eds) *Educational Management: Redefining Theory, Policy and Practice.* London: Paul Chapman.

Chapter 8

School Effectiveness, School Improvement and the Teaching Profession of the Twenty-first Century

Mike Bottery

INTRODUCTION

School effectiveness research (SER) and school improvement research (SIR) have been dominant if not *the* dominant educational research paradigms on both sides of the Atlantic for some time now. Whilst SIR has a strong and integrated community of academic adherents, SER has probably been more influential with policy makers, capturing their interest and approbation for reasons sometimes other than its intellectual merits, and has thus become pivotal in the development of education policy by political parties of very different ideological hues. This chapter argues that it remains problematic, however, whether either approach, individually or collectively, is sufficient to underpin the practice of a teaching profession which can respond to the challenges of this century. To accomplish this, this chapter will do a number of things. First, it will set the practice of teachers and notions of professionalism within current contexts, describing the kinds of pressures which teachers, education systems and policy makers face, both at the present time and in the future, and examine whether or not current legislation helps to respond to such pressures. It will primarily use the example of education in England and Wales but it will be clear that there are many similarities and parallels with other education systems. Second, it will ask how professionalism should be conceptualized. This is in part driven by those social, political and economic contexts within which teachers work, and will work in the future, but it is also driven by questions concerning the kind of education system and society which are seen as desirable and who has the power and influence to decide what is desirable. Third, the defining characteristics in school effectiveness and school improvement research will be outlined, as will potential clashes and synergies. Further, it will be asked whether these contribute to, work against or add up to the kinds of professionalism teachers will need in the coming decades. Its conclusion is that their combined effects may be necessary but at the present time are insufficient for a fully-fledged professionalism for this century.

POLICY, HISTORY AND THE TEACHING PROFESSION

The tasks for teachers and education systems today are as complex as they have always been. For policy makers worldwide, the principal education and training questions continue to be:

- What kinds of *knowledge and skills* does this workforce need to enable the nation to compete internationally?
- What kinds of *attitudes* do teachers need to inculcate in their students in order to ensure that they work in the manner appropriate to current national and global economic situations?
- How do we ensure that the education system contributes to the development of the chosen or desired *social and political culture*?
- What are the best ways of ensuring that the education system helps to maintain the *legitimacy of the nation–state*?
- What kind of *teachers* do we need in order to deliver these skills and values and this curriculum? Do they need to be a *profession* in any traditional sense of the word?

The answers to these questions have varied, depending not only on different countries' social, political and cultural histories, but also upon the time in a nation's history when these questions were asked. Table 7 provides an example from the history of educational policy in England and Wales, tracing through answers from the nineteenth century, at the height of the Welfare State, during Thatcherite market reforms, through to the new twists given by New Labour and 'New Modernizers' in general. It indicates that whilst the creation of many of the older education systems around the world, such as in France, Germany, the US and Japan, was initially seen as fundamental to the forging of a sense of nationhood, of allegiance to the state above the local, this was seen as of less importance in England (Green, 1997). Because England already possessed a long stable national history, questions of class stability were seen by many of those in power as of more importance. At the same time, altruistic and democratic sentiments ensured that the process of raising not only the level of education, but the age at which the individual left school, involved aspirations and forces which continue to this day. Furthermore, woven into this national garment were some threads, in part derived from a dilettante aristocratic heritage but still held dear by many educationalists, which suggested that education is a good in its own right, worth pursuing irrespective of any precise societal benefits. These same strands are seen in various patterns in different countries and teaching professions worldwide have reflected these diverse trends, though it does still seem fair to say that their role has largely been one

Table 7 Policy agendas in the UK

Education in the UK	C19th	Welfare state	Market	New modernizers	'Theoretically pure' school effectiveness orientation	'Theoretically pure' school improvement orientation	Ideal C21st
Knowledge and skills	Hierarchical/ objectivist. Class-based for most: basic: numeracy, literacy and religious instruction	Largely still hierarchical and objectivist but open to wider spectrum of society and thus enhanced mobility	Consumer-oriented: client wishes enhanced; market standards	That which maintains global competitiveness and services; transnational companies. Some contradictory strands of democracy and hi-tech creativity	Belief in possibility of decontextualized knowledge and skills which is sufficient for external judgements of institutions	Belief in necessity of appreciating the contextualization of knowledge and of the processes of formation; skills developed in and through collegial/ communal approach	Global hi-tech leads to demand for individual flair; 'discourse-aware'; recognition of contextualized knowledge and its provisionality, co-operation and communication skills. Critical citizenry
Attitudes to work	Fixed by factory processes and timetables: know your place in the hierarchy	Still essentially hierarchical and corporatist, but some degree of mobility: promise of career continuity	Flexible, entrepreneurial and inventive; but threat of career change and work fragmentation	The return of hierarchy and control; the continuation of markets and fragmentation; so workers need to accept control policies but implement them creatively	Through decontextualized judgements we can judge worker effectiveness and discipline or reward accordingly	No necessary connection between SIR and national workforce requirements, as contextual and communal judgements lead to idiosyncratic and culturally-based attitudes	Necessary flexibility; but life fragmentation mitigated by voluntary and civic sectors and wealth distribution to offset reduced centrality at work ethic
Social and political aims	Maintenance of social stability and hierarchy. Some noblesse oblige, some philanthropy	Social stability but some market wealth redistribution and modest increased social mobility	Dissipation of social hierarchies, increased personal freedoms and responsibilities. Necessary inequality	Contradictory aims of social control and economic steerage with some strands of democratic participation, devolution and personal innovation	We will categorize, order, judge, manipulate and control because we have the power to 'know'	We need to appreciate the contribution of particular cultures and communities to the creation of individual value judgements	Critical democracy in a global context; communal support; tolerant but principled; symbiosis of duties and rights
Nation–state legitimacy	Threatened by underclass. The use of education to maintain established norms and class divisions	Transferred by class inequalities. Development of society at ease with itself through wealth redistribution and gentle social mobility	Threatened by big brother authoritarian state. Free individuals create society in which market transactions lead to self-interest benefiting all	Threatened by globalization and devolution. Increased control of economic and educational policies leads to co-ordinated defence	We can use our knowledge of schools' effectiveness to control and preserve nation–state legitimacy	School cultures can create stable value environments which contribute to this aim	Citizenship nested at local, national and global levels; loyalty possible at all levels; subsidiarity determines decision locations
Role of teaching profession	Maintenance of epistemological, social and moral hierarchy	Entrusted with choice of materials and methods and knowledge in delivery of broad welfare state aims	Entrepreneurs and sales persons of quality products through marketing techniques to critical and empowered customers	Group servicing controlled and directed education sector; technical–rational implementers within increasingly tightly defined content and quality parameters	To be ordered, judged, manipulated and divided through acquiescence to school effectiveness goals	To focus on, and take ownership of, a change and improvement process located within a dynamic but unique context	'Public' orientation; 'ecologically' aware facilitators of life-long learning; legitimate experimenters internally accountable. Empowerers of others' insights and perspectives

of an inculcation of national sentiment and of social values, skills and knowledge appropriate to the group being educated. In the light of the values which this chapter argues teachers will need in the future, their professionalism has been a restricted one, a circumscription they have generally been happy to accept.

Initial purposes of bolstering nation–state legitimacy were soon added to by many countries, the UK included, shaping their education system to be prime agents – perhaps *the* prime agent – in the creation of workforces with appropriate attitudes. Thus, initially faced by a workforce used to working at home, at their own pace and having only the rising and setting of the sun as a timepiece, the education system ensured that this workforce accepted the demands of the factory system, that time-keeping by bells and hooters was seen as 'natural' and that what they produced would be for someone else and for others' purposes. In so doing they would produce that which was needed to maintain the nation's international competitiveness. Finally, and as importantly, for many nation states this education system could ensure that these workers would be content with their status within society. Schools then were not only concerned with skills, but as importantly with attitudes and values, and these kinds of imperatives on policy agendas have not diminished in importance – nor has the role of the teaching profession in implementing them.

In the latter half of the twentieth century, one of the alleged 'secrets' of the new 'Asian tigers' of Singapore, Taiwan and Korea lay in the manner in which they emulated the earlier practice by Japan and thus developed education systems which have the twin aims of creating very firm bases for national political legitimacy and of being prime engines for economic performance. It is perhaps ironic that since the Second World War, UK educational policies have gone through periods of Welfare State corporatist centrality and of New Right market decentralization before the belief set in, most markedly under New Labour, that these Asian tiger strategies were those which needed to be emulated (see Ashton and Sung, 1997; Bottery, 2000). This led to 'New Modernizer' policies of enhanced central control and direction of not only the economy, but of the education system and of the teaching profession within it. It is doubly ironic in that by the time this realization had been implemented at policy level, some of these Asian successes – particularly Singapore – were having serious doubts about these very same strategies because they failed to produce the flexibility, creativity and inventiveness in workers which were increasingly seen as hallmarks of success in the hi-tech world of the twenty-first century.

TEACHERS IN A GLOBAL TWENTY-FIRST CENTURY

Yet in this new century, education systems – and teachers within them – do not just have the problems of a hi-tech world to cope with. There are other equally pressing agendas which need to be dealt with as well. Whilst the one certainty about crystal ball gazing is that virtually every attempt to describe precisely the conditions beyond the immediate future is almost certainly wrong – and in a period of increasing change this is even more true – yet drawing upon a variety of literature (e.g. Kennedy, 1993; Korten, 1995; McRae, 1994; Naisbett and Aburdene, 1988) there do seem to be certain *trends* which will hold good for some time at least. These are described in Table 8 and developed in the remainder of this chapter. This table also describes many of the current professional realities emanating from these trends, as well as describing some of the skills and values which a profession with a wider consciousness of social and political change will need.

These global changes have led to three interrelated perceptions by policy makers:

- that threats to nation–state legitimacy from forces both greater and smaller than it necessitate it using all its powers upon those things it still remains in control of;
- that in an age of static or decreasing finances, enhanced economic productivity is achieved through the tighter control and direction of the workforce;
- that in an age of increased social change, social instability and fragmentation need to be countered by clearer direction and control of social and moral agendas.

Further, and as noted above, in the UK, but increasingly elsewhere, the major response by governments to such global realities, particularly in the educational sector, has been one of an increase in the centralization of policy making and an increase in the control and evaluation of the implementation of these policies.

However, there is clear and worrying evidence of contradictions between what will be required in the coming decades and the policies currently being implemented. Thus comparing New Modernizer policies and those required for the twenty-first century, four major contradictions are apparent.

(a) *Knowledge and skills.* In a high-tech and fast-changing world, there is an increased need for creative and entrepreneurial individuals, who recognize that what matters is not any one particular body of knowledge but the skills in and access to newly relevant knowledge. Yet an increasingly centralized, directed and content-fixated curriculum, largely determined by what those in positions of authority feel is necessary for global competitiveness, will do little to create a necessarily flexible workforce – and this action has been taken despite the fact that such Stalinist centralization of the command of appro-

Table 8 Global and professional issues in the twenty-first century

Global realities	Professional realities	Professional ideals
	Policy	Socio-political
1. Larger numbers of ageing populations increase tax burden and increase pressure upon welfare services.	• Dominance of centralizing agendas.	• Ecologically aware – need to locate personal and professional practice within societal and global power relations.
2. Increased global competition increases pressure upon levels of welfare state spending.	• Professional incorporation into policies for social stability, desired values and a common morality.	• A public orientation – aligning practice with notions of public good.
3. The market is still seen as the best means of global economic organization but less so nationally.	• Increased influence of business sector concepts and practices in the public sector.	• Professionalism seen as contributory to democratic and citizenship agendas.
4. Transnational companies will continue to expand their power and influence, applying pressure to nation states.	Institutional	Institutional
5. There will be a continued shift of labour to cheaper countries.	• The dominance of managerialist agendas; and attempted incorporation of professionals into these.	• Collegiality but not enforced collegiality.
6. A relative decline in nation–state power, as some is relocated to supranational and regional levels; nation states will attempt to re-assert or bolster their legitimacy by increasing control of those areas in which they retain power.	• Asked to reduce expenditure, and increase efficiencies in welfare state spending.	• Managerial acceptance of social and moral complexity.
	• No time for 'Dionysian' professionals doing their own thing.	• Loosely-coupled for greater innovation.
7. There will be a continued shift in developed countries from heavy to electronic and service industries.	Personal/Pedagogical	Individual
8. There will be changes in lifestyles and increases in related illnesses; new or mutated viral infections will pose increased problems to health services.	• Increased emphasis on client education, client self-help and lifelong learning.	• A commitment to client empowerment.
9. There will be an increased concern over the population, environment and pollution.	• Increased emphasis on the use of information and communications technology (ICT).	• Awareness of the need for others' viewpoints.
10. A continued and increased rate of societal change.	• Increased need for education in health, leisure, the environment and managing stress.	• Seeing themselves as providing opportunities for learning, not as inculcators or discourse manipulators.
		Epistemology/Research
		• Appreciation of the provisionality of 'facts' and research findings.
		• Awareness of the need for judgements to be based on evidence and research.
		• An ability to utilize and marry the evidence from both idiosyncratic encounters and large-scale surveys.

priate knowledge is normally seen as one of the principal reasons for the failure of the Soviet regime.

(b) *Attitudes to work.* In the public sector in England and Wales at the present time, the effects of hierarchy and control combined with the increased fragmentation of work are leading to a demoralized and demotivated workforce (Bottery, 2000). Such hierarchy and control communicate a lack of trust in the workforce and undermine the development of creative and flexible attitudes. Yet for flexibility to work, policies must also be instigated which prevent fragmentation of meaning, and allow for personal work and career narratives to be developed (Sennet, 1998). Added to this, if we are moving into an age of a shrinking or casualized job market, there will need to be a fundamental rethink of the place and meaning of work within personal and social understandings, for if full-time or personally empowering work were to be significantly less of a possibility for a larger percentage of a population, it would be dangerous, personally and socially, not to question the work ethic's centrality. Little of this seems to be contemplated at the present time.

(c) *Social and political aims.* Enhanced control of education is not being attempted solely through an objectivist view of epistemology or of a time-monopolizing legislated curriculum. It stems also from increased attempts at social control and economic steerage, as well as a reduction of citizenship to another form of consumerism: John Major's 'Citizens' Charter' was, after all, little more than a 'Consumer's Charter', providing for the possibility of complaint and redress when services failed to match promises but never seriously envisaging a population which might be involved in the creation and development of such policies. Yet such conceptions – and ultimately such control - run counter to the development of a critical democracy in a global context; to a communal support which is inclusive rather than exclusive; and to a society which recognizes the symbiotic relationship between rights and duties. Whilst there are elements of current legislation which do pay attention to some of this (e.g. DfEE/QCA, 1999), the major emphasis in government thinking seems firmly in other less liberal and democratic directions.

(d) *The role of the teaching profession.* In England and Wales, a whole barrage of legislation increasingly reduces the teaching profession to being a group servicing a controlled and directed education sector, to being technical–rational implementers employed within increasingly tightly defined content and quality parameters.

To take but a few:

(i)   the introduction of the National Curriculum in schools and for initial teacher training;
(ii)   the testing of pupils at 7, 11, 14 and 16 and the publication of the results of most of that testing;

(iii) the use of market mechanisms to ensure that schools gear their efforts to performance on that which is tested;
(iv) the introduction of the National Professional Qualification for Headship (NPQH) to create a model of the headteacher embedded within the adoption of a 'managerialist' approach to institutional management;
(v) the introduction of the highly directed literacy and numeracy hours;
(vi) the redesigned and enhanced roles of both LEAs and governing bodies as overseers of the implementation of government policy in schools;
(vii) the introduction of performance-related pay.

Yet this chapter argues that the role of teachers in a new century should be one:

- where they are aware of, reflect upon and engage with the 'ecological' framework within which they operate – one which would enable them to place their own situation within a wider societal context by understanding the kinds of pressures within and beyond the nation state;
- where they relate their work to a set of 'public' values – how being a member of a public sector organization might place special responsibilities and obligations on them with respect to the development of citizens in a more participative democracy;
- where they recognize – and legislators legitimate – the need to experiment with a variety of policy and implementation options because in a rapidly changing world no one way is going to provide all the answers, even for a short time;
- where, in an age when no one viewpoint can be authoritative, when knowledge bases are necessarily provisional, they need to empower a citizenry to develop their own views, perspectives and means of generating solutions.

Now it should be said that not only are teachers not entirely blameless for the controlled position they find themselves in (see Bottery and Wright, 2000) but an examination of conceptions of professionalism in the UK and the USA over the last one hundred years reveals a mixed history and a lack of preparedness for a demanding role in the future. From professionals being given a mantle by writers like Tawney (1921) and Durkheim (1957) as the much needed conscience of an increasingly business-oriented and value-less world, the literature on professionalism moved to portray them as paragons of virtue, through a concentration on great men of a profession, usually the medical. This picture lasted for some time and was aided by the creation of welfare states in which professionals were largely regarded as unquestioned experts servicing such institutions. It was only with the development of an increasingly unstable and financially troubled Western world that a more questioning literature emerged. This passed through a phase of linguistic self-doubt when the very meaning of the word 'professional' was questioned, with writers like Etzioni (1969) coming to the conclusion that teachers, for instance, only qualified as 'semi-professionals'. However, writers like Collins (1990) then developed a picture of professionals as forming self-aggrandizing occupations, no different from others save in their ability to control and monopolize particular markets – to exercise 'occupational closure'. When one adds to this the politically influential views of Friedman (1962) and Hayek (1973) that societies were best served where market conditions held sway, then the message to the public was clear. Professionals could not be regarded as any more altruistic than other occupations and any advice they might give would be to their own advantage. Professionals currently, then, have a mixed press.

Two things should be added to this analysis. The first is that there seem to have been only three necessary and sufficient criteria for the term:

(a) the occupation has been seen as possessing a specialized and systematic knowledge base;
(b) the occupation has performed what has been regarded as a crucial social function;
(c) the occupation has possessed the prestige and power to maintain occupational autonomy.

The second is that the term 'professionalism' has been very largely *ascribed*, a recognition by others of the need for the performance of particular functions, even if those functions have not necessarily remained the same. The example of the ascription to the professions of a leading moral role in society is one which for many is not centre stage today. Yet the global realities of the twenty-first century, as well as the professional realities which seem to follow from them (see Table 8), demand of professionals that they rethink their role and develop a much wider, more self-critical, more empowering and more political role. Given these kinds of goals, how do SER and SIR impact upon such conceptions?

SCHOOL EFFECTIVENESS AND POLICY DIRECTION

In Chapter 3, Reynolds suggests that there are four propositions which underlie the school effectiveness movement. These are:

(a) that schools have effects upon student outcomes which are independent of any contextual variation;
(b) that these effects can be engineered;
(c) that this engineering can be accomplished by an appropriate use of management systems, rewards and sanctions;
(d) that whilst schools are part of a set of 'nested' relationships, there is nevertheless a sufficient degree of autonomy such that schools can have effects on pupil achievement independent of external factors like social class.

School effectiveness studies then have, broadly speaking, attempted to identify the factors which will produce better schools, irrespective of any particular context. Abstracting from any particular context a list of factors considered essential causes of pupil achievement, the approach suggests that through a battery of managerial techniques, these can be engineered into other school contexts. It will be clear why this model would be appealing to some policy makers. First, it is simple and easy to understand, in outline at least, and in an age of turmoil, with too little time for too much work, a research agenda which suggests simplicity is going to be very welcome. Second, it is linear: it suggests that *a* causes *b* and that there will be no occasions where *b* causes *a*, or where *a* and *b* are interactive. Again, the transparency and simplicity appeals. Third, it suggests that external direction and policy control is not only possible but actually essential and this research agenda suggests that an objective and distanced look at the work of schools can and should be done. Finally, it justifies institutional responsibility for achieving results, for if the answers (i.e. the key factors and the means of inserting them into a school context) are given by policy makers or their representatives to schools as a means of remediating their problems and they fail to do this, then this must be their fault, not that of the policy makers.

Table 7 makes it clear that in England and Wales New Modernizers have adopted a form of policy direction which would welcome SER rather more than SIR, for such a policy approach accentuates already highly centralized norms, whilst also leading to an increased fragmentation of the work situation. Thus, Hoggett (1996) argues that governments have returned to the kinds of policy approaches characteristic of early Thatcherite policies in the public sector, which generated a high output/low commitment workforce. These policies have used four particular strategies:

(i) the enhanced use of markets and competition – now penetrating institutional hierarchies down to the level of the individual. This strategy has led to the adoption of the second of Hoggett's strategies:
(ii) the development of performance management techniques and performance-related pay;
(iii) the continued centralization of policy whilst simultaneously continuing the decentralizing of implementation, and the location of responsibility for the success of implementation at this lower level as well;
(iv) the continued standardization of routines, in particular through the specification of desired outputs and the consequent deskilling of teaching practices.

The SER approach fits such policy direction very well, for:

• it enhances markets and competition through generating the kinds of data from which league tables may be compiled;
• it facilitates centralization of policy and decentralization of implementation, by generating key factors from which policy may be determined, whilst leaving responsibility for implementation to the institutional level;
• it enables the utilization of performance management techniques, by describing context-free factors and thus providing apparently objective output criteria against which teacher performance may be judged;

• by implying that teachers' work is concerned with the implementation of context-free factors, it supports moves towards work standardization and professional deskilling.

SCHOOL EFFECTIVENESS AND PROFESSIONALISM

Furthermore, if school effectiveness research facilitates these kinds of policy agendas, even if unintentionally, it is also going to pose problems for conceptions of professionalism in at least three different ways.

First, the apparent *value neutrality* of much SER allows policy makers to suggest that the application of SER results means that their concerns are purely technical and scientific, and that they can only be criticized on these grounds. Indeed, the very word 'effectiveness' suggests the neutrality of a means to an end. Yet it is perfectly possible to ask 'for what purposes and for whose benefit is something effective?' Hargreaves (1997), for instance, demonstrates convincingly that virtually *any* school culture can be 'effective', depending upon the criteria used to define that effectiveness. Indeed, as Reynolds has noted in Chapter 3 and Chitty (1997) argues

> It is precisely its [SER's] apolitical approach and lack of engagement with sociological and political theory that enables school effectiveness work to be appropriated into the hegemonic project of the Right. (Chitty, 1997, p. 57)

An approach which attempts to extract key factors in order to improve school performance might be extremely helpful in the raising of teachers' professionalism, both from the point of view of the public's perception of the profession and in terms of generating a research-based data bank for improving practice. Yet when such an approach fails to become engaged with value issues, it may do as much harm as good, for it may end up producing findings for policy agendas which profoundly damage those 'ecological', 'public' and 'empowering' professional activities suggested in Tables 7 and 8. Moreover, because SER is so apolitical, it implicitly suggests a concept of professionalism which is also apolitical. In so doing, anyone embracing such a paradigm may fail to realize the necessity of incorporating these kinds of concepts into future conceptions of professionalism.

Second, perhaps *the* fundamental assumption of SER is that it is possible to extract key factors from situations and that there is a genuine linearity of causation which allows this. The assumptions within this perspective are also potentially very damaging to an extended view of teacher professionalism because the assumption of linearity of causation provides policy makers with the justification for assigning blame to implementers. Yet the relationship between context and school is normally not linear, but 'relational, dynamic and interactive' (Angus, 1993, p. 342), as schools influence as well as are influenced by their situations. In Rutter *et al.*'s celebrated study (1979), for instance, it is not clear if the good schools produced good students, or whether the good students produced good schools. The reality is that change is hugely complex and, as Fullan (1999) argues,

the link between cause and effect is difficult to trace ... change (planned or otherwise) unfolds in non-linear ways ... paradoxes and contradictions abound. (p. 4)

which means that linear accounts are almost certainly going to be too simplistic and are going to mis-describe the situation. As Fullan continues

It is one thing to see an innovation up and running; it is entirely another matter to figure out the pathways of how to get there in your own organisation. (p. 14)

Thus, policies which utilize such a linearity to ascribe praise and blame and a professional expertise which fails to recognize the problematics of reversible causality are both going to be built on very shaky foundations.

Furthermore, and perhaps more importantly, such an approach may radically mis-describe the learning process and thus significantly distort educators' views of what professional practice amounts to. Silcock (1993), for instance, argues that the key factor in pupil – and hence school – effectiveness is not *teaching* but *pupil learning*. Silcock – heretically from an SER perspective – suggests that learning often happens, or fails to happen, in a manner which is independent of the teaching that takes place, and that whilst teachers should do their best to provide the conditions which facilitate learning, they cannot guarantee it. This points to a radically different approach to professionalism, for as Silcock argues, if it is the state of the learner which guarantees learning, then

providing an opportunity to learn requires particularly sensible and flexible ways of dealing with the widely differing circumstances learners introduce into classrooms. (p. 18)

Now perhaps this apparent exclusion of teachers from the learning process may go too far. As Hopkins *et al.* (1997) argue, there is clear evidence that the use of appropriate *teaching* strategies can dramatically increase student achievement, and that the goal needs to be one of helping teachers

[to become] professionally flexible so that they can select, from a repertoire of possibilities, the teaching approach most suited to their particular content area, and the age, interests and aptitudes of their students. (p. 268)

On both accounts, though, professionalism, instead of being conceptualized as that of the expert who researches an international data bank to identify the critical factors missing from a particular situation, and then similarly searches through a bank of managerial strategies to ensure their input, is now conceptualized very differently. Now instead of being fixated at the institutional level, a different concept of professionalism recognizes the idiosyncratic nature of each learning encounter between teacher and pupil, the indissoluble contextualization, the dynamism, non-linearity and inherent messiness. This is not, of course, a professionalism which will appeal to policy makers bent on simplicity and greater centralization – but it may well be a more accurate picture of the learning process and a firmer foundation for school improvement.

Third, as Fay (1975) and Grace (1998) argue, any SER-type approach may reduce the vision of the research community from a critical one, a questioning of ends as well as means, to that of policy science, where the role of researchers becomes one of recommending to policy makers the technically best course of action needed to achieve a particular goal chosen by those policy makers. And this will involve a 'taming of the academy' (Ball, 1998, p. 73), for now educationalists are no more than technical advisers for paradigms and policies decided elsewhere. They are no longer involved in the activity of asking what role education should play in the creation of the good society or what that society might look like. Instead, they can only advise on the best technical means for creating any kind of society policy makers want. They have in effect emasculated themselves. What is created, Ball argues, is a new kind of academic activity – 'policy entrepreneurship . . . the proselytizing and, in some cases, the sale of the "technically correct answers" ' (*ibid.*).

The value neutrality of SER, its linearity, its assumption of the centrality of the teacher rather than the learner and its reduction of the research community to policy entrepreneurs, steers the profession away from ecological or public visions, from the development of a critically aware citizenry and from being able to marry the evidence of the idiosyncratic encounter with that of the large-scale survey. It undercuts precisely those qualities of professionalism in education which should form its defining features in the twenty-first century.

SCHOOL IMPROVEMENT RESEARCH

School improvement research has a number of distinct characteristics (Stoll, 1996), which many would see as strengths, which make it clearly very different, even oppositional in approach, to school effectiveness research. Thus,

- because it has a focus on process, it is better able to interrogate the process of change in schools than SER, for change is never simple, never one-shot, never to be fully understood by the cross-sectional approach;
- linked to a focus on process is an orientation to action and to an appreciation of schools' on-going development; schools are not cadavers waiting to be dissected by researchers but dynamic and evolving and SIR, better than SER, appreciates these qualities;
- if a school is to improve, those within the institution need to be involved and take ownership of the change and improvement process, and SIR has a much greater emphasis on school-selected developmental priorities than SER, which tends to see a school as a site for external researchers to compare with other such sites;
- whilst school culture may be an important factor for SER researchers, in that backward mapping may lead to the conclusion that a particular kind of school culture is necessary for the creation and maintenance of an effective

school, yet this may fail to appreciate that school culture can be an idiosyncratic and not necessarily replicable set of characteristics, requiring a multifactorial approach which SIR researchers are more likely to understand and embrace;

- because of this idiosyncratic nature, because of the need to delve deep into the nature of organizational functioning, in-depth case studies, qualitative and naturalistic data gathering may be much the more effective instrument for determining how a school 'ticks'. Once again, SIR is much more open to such an approach than SER.

Thus the movement now celebrates

> *bottom-up* school improvement, in which the improvement attempts [are] 'owned' by those at school level, although outside school consultants or experts would be allowed to put their knowledge forward for possible utilization. It celebrate[s] the *lore* or practical knowledge of practitioners rather than the knowledge base of those who [have] conducted research. (Reynolds, 1997, p. 252)

From the point of view of developing the teaching professional, it might be argued that this is a vast improvement on school effectiveness approaches, for it appreciates the school context, the dynamic nature of school functioning, the multi-factor nature of any improvement, the need for a fine-grained approach and for an understanding of a school's evolution. Schools, SIR advocates would maintain, are not some pedagogic machine, whose parts can be welded together from bits found in other (successful) pedagogic machines. This metaphor, they suggest, is not only inappropriate, it is actually damaging. A school, they would claim, is more like a living organism and just as you can't graft the leg of a cheetah onto an alsatian to make it run faster, so you can't graft one particular factor into a school and expect it to make dramatic improvements. You have to work with the nature of the school and improve that and to understand that you have to understand the nature of the organism. This, I believe, was Reynolds' point (1997) when he argued that ineffective schools are not simply a deficit example of effective schools. They are schools in their own right, with their own characteristics, produced by 'interpersonal problems, projections, defences and the like . . .' (p. 257) and to improve such schools one must start from their nature, their culture and the combination of elements within them.

So far, perhaps, so good, but the criticism by metaphor is a little too neat. Whilst schools are not cars or computers, neither are they cheetahs or alsatians. If the machine metaphor radically underestimates the cultural singularity of each school, the organismic metaphor radically overstates this. If the one, at its extreme, would argue that anything can be transplanted from one school to another with a minimum of problem, the other, at its extreme, would argue that each is its own measure and that points of comparison are not only invalid but impossible. By *that* route one then develops a solipsism which is as profoundly damaging as any advocacy of unthinking transfer.

SCHOOL IMPROVEMENT RESEARCH AND PROFESSIONALISM

The danger of this is that SIR's strengths can then turn into its weaknesses. Thus,

- a focus on process can too easily lead to an inattention to an improvement of outcomes. Yet without attempts to measure the impact of changes in improvement programmes upon student outcomes, there can be little genuine progress towards *improving* the learning experience of students, clearly a crucial aim of any educational professional;
- a focus on action and development can all too easily lead to the neglect of distance, objectivity and reflectivity and, from there, to the belief that *doing* is a good in itself. Yet, clearly again, unreflective action can lead one down all sorts of roads, produce all kinds of outcomes, which a calmer, more objective, more studied moment would prevent;
- a focus on school ownership can all too easily lead to a disparagement of insights or expertise which are not generated or located within the school context; yet whilst the internal view is vital, it is greatly strengthened by the outsider who provides a comparative focus or critical overview, who sets action in context and asks whether there are other ways of achieving aims;
- a focus on school culture can lead to a belief in its uniqueness and the inutility in examining other organizations, which, as mentioned above, can lead to a solipsism which excludes the valuable outside contribution or which prevents the attempt to unpick the relationship between factors and assess their respective strengths and the quality of the relationship between them;
- a focus on qualitative and naturalistic research can lead to the disparagement of the quantitative, of the utility of the wider picture, of the benefits of an appreciation of trends and patterns.

These weaknesses can easily turn into a professionalism which, in its own way, is as limited as that which might derive from an exclusively SER approach. This can be seen by referring to Hargreaves and Goodson's (1996) discussion of the three kinds of professionalism. The first form, classical professionalism, is one which does not directly relate to SIR, being the kind where teachers attempt to model themselves on the legal and medical professions and, in not fitting too well, leads to an attempted professional*ization* rather than a true professionalism. However, the two others have direct relevance. Thus, the second form, flexible professionalism, is based upon the embedding of expertise and practice within local teacher communities rather than upon scientific enquiry. This conception runs the risk of insulating the local from the influence of the wider picture. Indeed, as Hargreaves and Goodson argue, it numbs them

> against their capacity to feel committed and to actively engage with bigger social missions of justice, equity and community beyond their own workplace. (p. 11)

A final form of professionalism, practical professionalism, is located in the practical knowledge and judgement that teachers have of their own work. It draws heavily on notions of 'reflective practice' (Schon, 1983). Its essence lies in the ability to exercise judgement when situations are full of uncertainty – the 'swampy lowlands' of professional practice. Yet the usefulness of such reflection depends upon not only the quality of who is reflecting but what each individual actually brings to the reflective process, and such exclusivity may well prevent reflection upon wider ecological issues. This is what Schon tends to suggest in his writing and was also found by Wright and Bottery (1997) in a study of the views and priorities of school mentors. It will be clear that SIR approaches, if over-emphasized, could lead to a combination of flexible and practical professionalism which excludes other, wider commitments necessary for a teaching professionalism. So whilst those contemplating viable and acceptable forms of teacher professionalism need to be aware of the pitfalls of SER approaches, they need to be similarly critical of SIR.

THE BENEFITS OF RAPPROCHEMENT

There remain large differences between school effectiveness research and school improvement research in terms of their purposes, scope, the metaphors by which they conceive the organization and its inhabitants and the tools which they feel are most appropriate for investigation. Yet it is clear that there is much that one set of researchers can learn from the other, to the ultimate benefit of the teaching profession and education as a whole. Perhaps the most fruitful way to conceptualize their respective contributions is to address the potential *synergy* between the two approaches. Thus Table 9 suggests that the way forward may be to take the best from each.

Attempted rapprochement between SER and SIR (e.g. Gray *et al.*, 1996) and suggested in Chapters 2 and 3, betokens a potentially fruitful alliance which could have considerable beneficial impact upon notions of professionalism. It might generate a similar approach to that proposed in Chapter 9 by

Table 9 The potential synergy of school effectiveness research and school improvement research

SER	SIR
1. A focus on outcomes	A focus on process
2. A focus on comparative evidence	A focus on the individual school context
3. Single factor focus	Multi-factor focus
4. A broad-based approach	A fine-grained approach
5. Data for reflection and decision making	Data for action and development
6. Cross-sectional approach	Longitudinal/evolutionary approach
7. Quantitative orientation	Qualitative orientation

Jamieson and Wikely who, in response to the standard SER model described above, propose a 'contextual model'.

'Good practice' for teachers, then, changes from learning how to engineer standard factors into particular schools via managerialist techniques, to a practice which uses these same schools as sites of critical reflection in the making of intelligent contextual judgements which are then communicated elsewhere for similar critical reflection. A recognition of the strengths and weaknesses of each approach and of the use of intelligent argumentation in finding a balance between the two approaches seems the most fruitful way forward. So whilst, for instance, SER can be too context-free, a too rigid adherence to SIR can lead to systems becoming too decentralized. As Fullan remarks:

> since new ideas are crucial, and since the education system is traditionally weak at accepting and spreading new knowledge and practices, a deliberate system of stimulating innovation is required. (Fullan, 1999, p. 58)

Professional practice can be enhanced by a critical but tolerant melding of both approaches.

BRINGING SOCIETY BACK IN

Yet this will still be insufficient as a model of professional practice for educators in this century, for what is lacking from both approaches is a wider societal dimension. If SER has been guilty in the past of depoliticizing professionals through focusing its attention on the technicalities of context-free factor implementation, SIR has a tendency to depoliticize professions through still focusing almost exclusively on the traditional teaching and learning dimensions of professional practice. Yet this is an age in which educationalists need to be critically aware of the policies that shape their practice, not only for their own sake but for their clients as well. Whether educators like it or not, theirs is an area of *political* activity and this continues to be a recognition largely neglected by the profession at the present time. Thus, in a series of qualitative interviews with teachers in LEA, voluntary aided, grant-maintained and private schools (paralleled by interviews with professionals in similar positions in hospitals in the public and private sector), the present author (Bottery, 1998) found that these professionals exhibited a dangerous mixture of overwork and disinterest towards the reasons why legislative and professional changes had come about, and what their reaction should be with respect to these changes. Crucially, they saw their 'job' as one centrally concerned with either 'the kids' or 'the subject'. For these professionals, for both personal and practical reasons, a wider vision of their role was simply not an option. They saw their job, both before and after the deluge of legislation of the last fifteen years, as that of teaching pupils their subject matter as well as they could (or in hospitals, almost exclusively, with treating the patient). Objections were primarily concerned with the speed, the lack of consultation and the lack of co-ordination between different parts of recent legislation, as well as the fact that some of it was poorly thought through. Relatively little was said about the actual nature or function of the legislation, nor of the effect it would have upon them and their role within the larger community.

Yet the teaching profession may have set itself up for such demotion well before this. In research which has spanned most of the last decade, Bottery and Wright (2000) uncovered evidence strongly indicating that little of the in-service training of school staff develops in them a wider conception of their role. Few attempts within such in-service development were made to generate an understanding of the 'public' nature of their job. Nor was there much to suggest the conscious development of an 'ecological' understanding of their situation. Instead, what strongly emerged was a pre-occupation with the mechanics of implementation, a concentration upon in-service training and development largely devised to enable teachers to do a better job in the classroom or to facilitate the management of school resources for implementation. Of course, there is nothing wrong with this *per se* – indeed, there is much to commend it. Yet when the evidence gathered suggests that this seems to be *all* that is happening, has happened or is being planned for the future, then it would seem that it is not just government legislation which is driving the teaching profession to the neglect of these wider issues but rather that there is something endemic to the culture which leads it as a profession to neglect them.

CONCLUSIONS

This chapter then has argued that in the coming decades, it is crucial that the teaching profession develops the following qualities to a much greater extent than it has done so far. In *epistemological and research terms*, the teaching profession needs to have a greater awareness of the need for judgements based on genuine research and evidence, which marries the idiosyncratic with the large scale, and yet which nevertheless appreciates the provisionality of facts and findings thereby generated. In *individual terms,* the teaching profession needs to see its role more clearly as one of client empowerment, which would involve a much greater awareness of others' viewpoints, as well as an understanding that their job is not about the inculcation of learning but about providing opportunities for it. In *institutional terms*, the teaching profession needs to develop a collegiality which is not enforced and which recognizes the need for a degree of loose coupling, in order to reflect the social and moral complexity of education and society, as well as thus enhancing a greater degree of innovation. This has clear and critical implications for the use of current 'managerialist' approaches and of current approaches to conceptions of leadership.

Finally, in *socio-political terms*, the teaching profession needs to be more 'ecologically' aware, to be able to align its practice with notions of public good, to contribute to the development of greater democracy and active citizenship. Not only must it avoid manipulating educational discourses to suit its own purposes, it must be able to point out when other power groupings attempt this as well.

If these qualities are accepted as real and desirable, SIR tends to come out rather better than SER, but even this approach would be insufficient. At an epistemological level, SER tends to adopt a more objectivist position than SIR, which has induced policy makers to interpret its findings in non-problematic ways. Furthermore, whilst SIR might be comfortable with an approach which advocates a belief in client empowerment, the use of other stakeholders' viewpoints and wide opportunities for learning, an SER approach might find this more difficult, predicated as it seems to be on top–down approaches.

Similarly, in institutional terms, whilst SIR approaches actively promote collegial aims, SER seems to imply the need for a form of directive and controlling managerialism which is very much at odds with the qualities listed above. However, it is at the socio-political level that both seem to be inadequate. SER either ignores this dimension of teacher professionalism or runs directly counter to it by opening itself up to appropriation by centralizing policy makers who would have little desire for a profession with these characteristics. SIR, whilst perhaps more philosophically inclined to such a view, does not however normally include such concerns within its purview. Both then need to attend to the social and political context within which educators work, for neglect of this dimension leads to the real possibility of professional emasculation and of profound damage to society's democratic foundations.

REFERENCES

Angus, L. (1993) 'The sociology of school effectiveness', *British Journal of Sociology of Education* **14**(3): 333–45.

Ashton, D. and Sung, J. (1997) 'Education, skill formation and economic development: the Singaporean approach', in A. H. Halsey, H. Lauder, P. Brown and A. S. Wells (eds) *Education, Economy, Society*, pp. 207–18. Oxford: Oxford University Press.

Ball, S. (1998) 'Educational studies, policy entrepreneurship and social theory', in R. Slee, G. Weiner and S. Tomlinson (eds) *School Effectiveness for Whom?*, pp. 70–83. London: Falmer Press.

Bottery, M. (1998) *Professional and Policy*. London: Cassell.

Bottery, M. (2000) *Education, Policy and Ethics*. London: Cassell.

Bottery, M. and Wright, N. (2000) *Teachers and the State*. London: Routledge.

Chitty, C. (1997) 'The School Effectiveness Movement: origins, shortcomings and future possibilities', *The Curriculum Journal* **8**(1): 45–62.
Collins, R. (1990) 'Market closure and the conflict theory of the professions', in M. Burrage and R. Torstendahl (eds) *Professions in Theory and History*, pp. 24–43. London: Sage.
DfEE/QCA (1999) *Citizenship (National Curriculum for England)* London: Stationery Office.
Durkheim, E. (1957) *Professional Ethics and Civic Morals*. London: Routledge and Kegan Paul.
Etzioni, A. (1969) *The Semi-Professionals and their Organization*. New York: Macmillan.
Fay, B. (1975) *Social Theory and Political Practice*. London: Allen and Unwin.
Friedman, M. (1962) *Capitalism and Freedom*. Chicago: University of Chicago Press.
Fullan, M. (1999) *Change Forces: The Sequel*. London: Falmer Press.
Grace, G. (1998) 'Realizing the mission: Catholic approaches to school effectiveness', in R. Slee, G. Weiner and S. Tomlinson (eds) *School Effectiveness for Whom?*, pp. 117–27. London: Falmer Press.
Gray, J., Reynolds, D., Fitz-Gibbon, C. T. and Jesson, D. (1996) *Merging Traditions: The Future of Research on School Effectiveness and School Improvement*. London: Cassell.
Green, A. (1997) *Education, Globalization and the Nation State*. London: Macmillan.
Hargreaves, D. A. (1997) 'School culture, school effectiveness and school improvement', in A. Harris, N. Bennett and M. Preedy (eds) *Organizational Effectiveness and Improvement in Education*, pp. 239–51. Buckingham: Open University Press.
Hargreaves, A. and Goodson, I. (1996) 'Teachers' professional lives: aspirations and actualities', in I. Goodson and A. Hargreaves (eds) *Teachers' Professional Lives*. London: Falmer Press.
Hayek, F. (1973) *Law, Legislation and Liberty* vol. 1. London: Routledge and Kegan Paul.
Hoggett, P. (1996) 'New modes of control in the public service', *Public Administration* vol. 74, Spring, pp. 9–32.
Hopkins, D., Ainscow, M. and West, M. (1997) 'School improvement – proposition for action' in A. Harris, N. Bennett and M. Preedy (eds) *Organizational Effectiveness and Improvement in Education*, pp. 261–70. Buckingham: Open University Press.
Kennedy, P. (1993) *Preparing for the Twenty-first Century*. Toronto: Harper-Perennial.
Korten, D. (1995) *When Corporations Rule the World*. London: Earthscan Publications.
McRae, H. (1994) *The World in 2020*. London: Harper-Collins.
Naisbett, J. and Aburdene, P. (1988) *Mega-Trends 2000*. London: Sidgwick and Jackson.
Reynolds, D. (1994) 'School Effectiveness and quality in education', in P. Ribbins and E. Burridge (eds) *Improving Education: Promoting Quality in Schools.* London: Cassell.
Reynolds, D. (1997) 'Linking school effectiveness knowledge and school improvement practice', in A. Harris, N. Bennett and M. Preedy (eds) *Organizational Effectiveness and Improvement in Education*, pp. 251–61. Buckingham: Open University Press.
Rutter, M., Maughan, B., Mortimore, P., Ouston, J. and Smith, A. (1979) *Fifteen Thousand Hours*. London: Open Books.
Schon, D. (1983) *The Reflective Practitioner*. New York: Open Books.
Sennet, R. (1998) *The Corrosion of Character*. New York: W. W. Norton and Co.
Silcock, P. (1993) 'Can we teach effective teaching?', *Educational Review* **45**(1): 13–19.
Stoll, L. (1996) 'Linking school effectiveness and school improvement: issues and

possibilities', in J. Gray, D. Reynolds, C. T. Fitz-Gibbon and D. Jesson (eds) *Merging Traditions: The Future of School Effectiveness and School Improvement,* pp. 51–74. London: Cassell.

Tawney, R. H. (1921) *The Acquisitive Society*. New York: Harcourt Brace.

Wright, N. and Bottery, M. (1997) 'Perceptions of professionalism by mentors of student teachers', *Journal of Education for Teaching* **23**(3): 235–52.

Chapter 9

A Contextual Perspective: Fitting School Round the Needs of Students

Ian Jamieson and Felicity Wikely

INTRODUCTION

This chapter challenges one of the central orthodoxies of much school effectiveness and school improvement work – namely that schools should strive to become more consistent environments for pupils and teachers. It reviews the arguments for consistency; the success of centralized systems and the 'mirroring' of factors of effectiveness at the different levels of organization and examines the evidence which seems inconsistent with this thesis, for example, the differential performance of boys and girls in some schools and of certain ethnic groups in some school environments. Whilst not suggesting that 'consistency' theories should be rejected in all circumstances, the chapter argues that the motivation of students is the key factor which needs to link school organization and school context. Drawing on organizational literature the analysis concludes that effective schools are most likely to be those which are able to differentiate their structures, strategies and policies for different groups of pupils and different learning tasks.

THE CASE FOR CONSISTENCY

There is an important range of studies that consider international comparative data on schools, or school system performance, in order to advance an argument about the importance of strong, consistent systems of schooling for effective schools. A theoretical case is made by Stringfield (1995) when he examines the organizational features of 'high reliability organizations'. These are organizations that are purported to meet their goals to a high, consistent standard. Examples include electric power grids and air traffic control, and, in a slightly different category, McDonald's. Stringfield attempts to elucidate the 'secret' of these organizations. He broadly concludes that it is because they have, amongst other things, a single, clear and widely accepted purpose or goal and a strong formula or system of doing things, which can be implemented in a variety of different sites (contexts) with predictable outcomes.

This theoretical argument is supported by others using comparative education data (Reynolds *et al.*, 1995; Green, 1997). In an ambitious project, the International School Effectiveness Research Project, Reynolds and his colleagues are studying the effectiveness of schools in nine countries representing different educational traditions, with a particular focus on mathematics. The preliminary findings are very much in support of the 'strong system' model. They conclude, 'overwhelmingly, what strikes one about the effective school is how predictable their day-to-day life must be for their students and their teachers, in the sense that their goals are clear, their routines are well organised, and their mutual interactions stable and productive' (p. 26). Reynolds' position is further exemplified by a review of international surveys of educational achievement commissioned by the British government (Reynolds and Farrell, 1996). These surveys of the International Association for the Evaluation of Educational Achievement (IEA) and the International Assessment of Educational Progress (IAEP) began in 1960 and again have focused largely on mathematics and science with some modest work on literacy. In an independent analysis of the recent IAEP studies in science and mathematics (IAEP, 1988; IAEP, 1992) Green comes to similar conclusions and comments in particular on the wide dispersal of scores for both the UK and US 'with the bottom twenty-five per cent doing particularly badly in both these countries' (Green, 1997, p. 288). In addition to re-analysing IAEP data, Green presents the results of his collaborative study with Steedman (Green and Steedman, 1993) on the comparative performance of six countries on national qualification attainment. This was defined as the qualification taken at the end of compulsory schooling and at the end of upper secondary education. Qualifications were compared using a benchmarking of standards process.[1] Green and Steedman showed that countries which achieve higher standards in education and training, like Germany, France, Japan and Singapore, would appear to have one fundamental thing in common: 'as nations they place great emphasis on educational achievement, engendering high educational aspirations amongst individual learners' (p. 290). This success is achieved with systems which are relatively highly regulated, i.e. the state tends to prescribe teaching styles, materials and modes of assessment. Green (1997) is not slow to note the irony that it is the UK and US systems 'which traditionally pride themselves on their concern for the individual student, which seem to leave so many without hope or self-confidence, whereas in some other systems, which are often characterised as less humanistic because of their more regimented and uniform nature, fewer students are so marginalised' (p. 293).

In addition to these large-scale studies, Reynolds and Farrell also review work emanating from the UK National Institute for Economic and Social Research (Prais and Wagner, 1985; Bierhoff and Prais, 1995; Prais, 1995).

Although the review begins cautiously, acknowledging methodological problems with many of the studies, Reynolds and Farrell make reasonably clear assertions of the rather modest comparative performance of UK children, especially in mathematics, although less so in science, and the long tail of low achievement. Their explanation follows the previous pattern: the strong, system level variables are hypothesized to lead to more effective performance.

Taking a micro, as opposed to a macro, perspective Creemers (1994) also identifies consistency as being an important factor of effective schools. In his proposed model of educational effectiveness he suggests that individual elements at classroom level (quality of instruction, curriculum, grouping procedures and teacher behaviour) are all important factors in raising pupil achievement. He argues for the need for a high degree of integration of these factors to produce a consistent approach in achieving the goal of improved performance. Creemers also argues that consistency is an important, cross-level factor and needs to be displayed not only between classroom-level elements but across the school and context (by which he means system) level (Creemers, 1994). For example, he states that at the system level there needs to be a policy focusing on evaluation, with a national testing system which is consistent with each school's policy and system of evaluation which in turn is consistent with the evaluation of the curriculum, grouping procedures and teacher behaviour at the classroom level. In other words effectiveness is achieved through a consistent approach at all levels. Scheerens and Bosker (1997) call this repetition of effective characteristics at different levels 'mirroring'. They acknowledge that in creating models of effectiveness they have to simplify the purpose of schools, but argue that productivity is the key criterion by which schools should be judged. All other outcomes they suggest are essentially support functions. It is perhaps this over-simplification to fit the model that we would argue over-emphasizes the role of consistency.

However, these arguments suggest that at the system, school and classroom level there is evidence that consistent practices which fit with school effectiveness precepts are likely to lead to strong academic performance. At the school level this has led to a view that schools should strive to provide consistent and similar experiences for all of their students; consistent from school to school, classroom to classroom, teacher to teacher. The arguments are powerful in the UK, both empirically and ideologically. 'Teachers [have a] tenacious commitment to the principles of universalism and individualism. Assertions such as "we treat them all the same" and "we respond to the individual needs of our children" constitute professional tenets which are incompatible with policies that are designed to address the needs and interests of an entire group of pupils defined in terms of their race, gender or class' (Troyna and Carrington, 1990, cited in Hatcher, 1998). The idea of the common school where children were treated equally was one of the driving forces of the comprehensive school movement in the UK just as the community school served some of the ideological ends of nation building in the US. We have also seen that there is certainly enough evidence to mount a *prima facie* case that some of the more successful countries in terms of academic achievement adopt strong elements of the common school model, at least in the early years. Associated with this position is the argument, most often associated with David Reynolds, that the policy of differentiation as practised in many US and UK classrooms is far too complex and difficult for most teachers to handle. Many teachers who do so find it exhausting and it leads to burnout (rates are certainly much higher in the US and UK than most other societies). Reynolds argues that there are secure routines for teaching a variety of subjects, tasks and age groups that render such differentiation unnecessary.

This is a powerful theoretical position which has often been too easily dismissed by its critics. However, it has three basic problems. On the one hand, we would argue that in many areas not enough is known to implement robust, reliable systems for teaching most children successfully. In other words, 'evidence-based teaching'[2] is not uniformly possible, at least not in the US and UK, or certainly not yet. However, it could be argued that the more we carry out good, quality, educational research on programme effectiveness, the more this objection might be met. The second problem relates to implementation. In examining the implementation of leading effectiveness programmes in the US, Stringfield notes a catalogue of known implementation problems beyond the original successful site. He writes that 'the research teams found almost no examples during the first year of the program which was fully implemented, well integrated into the whole school's program, and clearly institutionalized' (Stringfield, 1995, p. 74). There are many possible reasons for this which are well documented in the educational 'change' literature: they include the fact that teachers who regard themselves as professionals are unlikely to follow sets of procedures unless they have had some hand in their development. Reezigt, Guldemond and Creemers (1999) also encountered problems when they set out to test the validity of their consistent classroom model by re-analysing a longitudinal data-set using multilevel analyses. They found that although classroom and school-level factors had some effects on student achievement these were by no means stable across subject areas or different cohorts of students. They analysed clusters of factors using their concept of consistency (the balance of factors enhancing effectiveness) and found that levels of consistency within schools and between teachers did not appear to correlate with student levels of achievement. The model put forward by Creemers in 1994 had an in-built assumption that factors, or groups of factors, would have the same effect on student achievement in different subject departments and on different student outcomes. The re-analysis showed it was hard to find stable effects at the classroom and school level. The only stability they found was at the student level. Reezigt *et al.* explain this as a problematic research design although Sammons *et al.* (1997) suggest 'that an overriding interest in school-level factors had led to some important features of teachers' collective practices and interactions being simply ignored or under-valued' (p. x).

It would also not be fair to imply that there is total agreement on the data of international educational achievement, nor its explanation. In a trenchant critique of the work of Reynolds and Farrell, and to a lesser extent that of Prais, Brown (1998) argues that much of the information in international league tables 'is often too technically flawed to serve as an accurate measure of national effectiveness' (p. 33). Even in its own terms, Brown attempts to show that, in the case of the UK at least, the results are much more complex than had been asserted by Reynolds and Farrell. For example, she argues that where the UK curriculum matches the international tests and is given prominence by the national curriculum and schools, the UK performs comparatively well. She also contests the view, at least for mathematics, that the studies show that the UK has a long tail of low achievement. Goldstein (1997) makes a similarly vociferous argument when he questions the methodology of many inter-national comparative effectiveness studies. He cites Creemers *et al.*'s 'International School Effectiveness Study' (1996), which used small numbers of non-randomly selected schools within each country and made no proper adjustment for intake achievement. Goldstein suggests that such research offers very little that is meaningful to the field of school effectiveness. Finally, Brown argues that there is no evidence to suggest that teaching methods have an effect on aggregate country performance. She quotes, with approval, the SIMS longitudinal study of eight countries which concluded: 'all we can safely say (we hope) is that students do experience different types of instructional arrangements cross-nationally and that the influence of these arrangements generically appears to be weak relative to such matters as prior learning and the contents of learning opportunities during the course of study' (Burnstein, 1992, p. 278).

We would wish to argue that there is an equally strong case against what we are calling a 'consistent' approach which stems from research focused on learning rather than teaching.

THE CASE AGAINST CONSISTENCY

Although educators have always been aware that individual differences amongst students present them with a challenge, in most places and in most times, actual instructional practice has remained basically unchanged. But it is possible to trace two intellectual origins of this force for differentiation.

The first focuses on learning styles. This can be traced through the work of Witkin *et al.* (1977) – field dependent/field independent; Hudson (1979) – convergent/divergent thinking; Pask (1976) – holist/serialist learners. More recently the work of Kolb (1984) and his four learning styles (diverger, assimilator, converger and accommodator) has become more prominent in teaching circles. Another tradition emanates from research on intelligence with the collapse of the view that this was a single univariate construct. The work of Howard Gardner (1993) and his seven different intelligences has a high profile in education, although not in mainstream psychology where the triarchic model of Sternberg (1984) has significant experimental evidence in its support. Both of these traditions feed systems which are ideologically and culturally disposed towards differentiation. A great many teachers in both the UK and US would like to agree with Entwistle (1991) when he argues that teachers should take account of the range of learning styles in their students and recognize that their own learning style is likely to be reflected in their teaching. The difficulty is that there have been very few attempts in either the US or the UK to translate these academic insights into proven pedagogic strategies.[3] More generally this is the difficulty with many of the undoubted advances in what one of us has called the 'new cognitivism' (Jamieson, 1996). It is very difficult to see how these insights can be easily integrated into the system of mass schooling current in either the UK or US.

Another argument for differentiation comes from work on subject discourses. The work of Whitty and his colleagues (Whitty *et al.*, 1994) serves as a good illustration of this line of argument. In a study which discovered the relative failure of cross-curricular work to permeate the subject curriculum of secondary high schools, Whitty *et al.*, drawing on the work of Bernstein, argued that schooling can be seen as an inculcation into the very different discourses of the various ways of seeing and making sense of the world through (school) subjects. Different clusters of subjects are quite different one from another and require different attitudes, behaviours and activities on the part of pupils. It also follows that pedagogies and, indeed, classrooms themselves should ideally look quite different for different subjects. Such observations do not on the face of it fit well with the homogenizing tendencies built into much of school effectiveness thinking.

Finally we would argue that another major difficulty in both the UK and US is the problem of pupil motivation – a relatively neglected topic in school effectiveness studies. The low performing 'tail' in the UK and US is evidence enough of significant problems for many pupils. In one of the largest US studies, Steinberg (1996) argues that around 50 per cent of high school students have 'disengaged' from school by the age of 12–16. This is not the place to disentangle all the complex reasons for this state-of-affairs but the reasons are by no means only to do with the state of schooling. First, we can identify significant socio-economic inequality in both the UK and US which produces, particularly in the inner cities, a class of disenfranchised people who almost form an underclass. This tends to be quite different from many of the more successful, educationally achieving countries that are marked by a much greater degree of homogeneity in social, cultural and economic terms. Second, neither the UK nor US has managed to create either a culture or a set of institutional practices that support educational inclusivity for the whole population. Green (1990) argues that this is because of the ideology of neo-liberalism in both countries and because of the way in which the nation state, and its view of education, emerged. Third, as Green (1997) again shows, there is much less of a connection between educational credentials and employment opportunities in the UK and US than in many other countries.

The school effectiveness view of this issue can take several forms. Because there is often so little discussion about motivational problems, there seems to be a tacit assumption amongst some writers that school populations are relatively homogeneous or at least can be treated as such for teaching purposes. This is not a wholly unreasonable assumption in many areas of this country where a combination of the housing market, parental choice and the advent of marketization policies have created schools where children from certain backgrounds cluster (Lauder *et al.*, 1999; Gewirtz *et al.*, 1995). Selective schools also, almost by definition, have much less of a problem and policies in both the UK and US to create 'magnet schools' specializing in certain aspects of the curriculum also push in the same direction. What does appear to be agreed is the complexity of judging whether or not a school is effective when considering the variation in pupils by such factors as ethnicity, gender, ability, etc.

The literature on gender and performance is particularly significant here. As Arnot *et al.* (1998) argue, 'the ways in which pupils are grouped, the ways in which their work is assessed, the curricula they encounter, the teaching styles they experience, the role models they are offered, the expectations teachers have of boys and girls and the ways teachers reward and discipline them can all affect the size and nature of the gender gap' (p. 90). They suggest that schools will only be able to respond if they are aware of the possibilities and monitor the progress of particular groups in order to be able to intervene appropriately and sensitively. None of these recommendations would imply a school-wide consistent approach, in fact quite the opposite. They and others (e.g. Murphy and Gipps, 1996) argue that even if schools did offer a consistent approach it is likely to be perceived and experienced differently by different groups of students. Murphy and Gipps discuss the possibility that boys and girls may need different pedagogies and that to address the issue of under-achievement of either boys or girls research suggests there is a need to look at the knowledge base of the subject as well as how it is taught. They argue that schools need to supply a range of strategies, materials, content, teaching styles and classroom arrangements for different groups of pupils and different subject areas. Similar arguments have been made by Brown *et al.* (1996) and Stringfield (1995).

Gillborn and Gipps (1996) paint a similarly complex picture for differential performance when considering ethnicity. Indian pupils tend to achieve better than other South Asian pupils and also better than their white counterparts in the same urban areas in the UK. In most areas Bangladeshi pupils, who often experience high levels of poverty and low levels of fluency in English, are lower achievers than other South Asian groups. Gillborn and Gipps (1996) point out that regardless of their ethnicity children from economically advantaged homes do better than those from more disadvantaged homes and studies carried out outside London show that children from the loosely termed 'white' group still leave school with the best qualifications. Post-sixteen the pattern changes again and ethnic-minority children, particularly those of Asian background, tend to stay on in education longer than their white counterparts and by the age of eighteen Asian children are the most highly qualified.

Brown *et al.* (1996) and Thrupp (1997) make a similar case for social class in their work on the effects of school composition. They found that schools with predominantly middle-class pupils were using different pedagogies from those with predominantly working-class pupils.

Finally, there are school factors themselves: there is persuasive evidence to suggest that these are a factor in the poor motivation of some pupils. We would argue that the managerialist model of school improvement with its emphasis on target setting and performance management creates a model of the learner which strips them of their social identities, cultures and experiences and in doing so can be highly demotivating. Of course most pupils tolerate the practices of schools and teachers and relatively few openly resist. Even the resisters are not necessarily all from the lower socio-economic groups, although resisters do tend to be associated with groups of children. Such children react to being labelled in negative ways, to poor, unstimulating teaching and to school practices which depower them. As Berends (1995) has observed, 'Cross-sectional studies have noted that academic performance is positively associated with student behaviour and attitudes such as attentiveness, effort, interest, motivation, industry, responsibility and involvement' (p. 341).

If one accepts that the motivation problem is a serious one in a large number of UK and US schools, then the question is whether the rather Tayloristic 'one best way' model of some of the effective school proponents is likely to be successful or whether, as we contend, schools need to adopt a hybrid model which incorporates many factors of the effective schools model and also manages to adapt itself to different groups of children. Our thesis is that through these apparently conflicting positions, it is possible to discern a model of effective schooling that is consistent with the many studies we have about teaching and learning and effective schooling. We believe further that such a model is likely to be sufficiently robust that it can accommodate a widening of the goals of schooling beyond conventionally measured academic attainment.

A CONTINGENCY MODEL OF SCHOOL EFFECTIVENESS

The first element of such a model accepts much of the evidence about effective schools insofar as this is relevant to the management of learning. In other words it accepts that schools which organize all or most of the following features of the management of learning effectively and consistently have fulfilled many of the necessary conditions for success. Our list would certainly include most of the things on the usual 'lists' which abound in the 'effectiveness' literature. It is almost certainly the case that having clear goals which are shared with learners; maximizing time on task; keeping accurate records of pupils' strengths, weaknesses or progress; giving frequent and systematic feedback to pupils on academic and social 'performance'; creating a safe and secure environment; and having high expectations of pupils are likely to contribute to effective learning at school.

These are generally necessary but, almost certainly, not sufficient conditions for effective schooling. Not doing these things will severely inhibit a school's or teacher's ability to produce academic achievement but it need not be fatal. It is possible for schools which do few of the above to perform well in absolute terms if they have attracted able middle-class students. As Bourdieu has shown, schools are often very successful with those whom they do not have to teach how to learn because they have acquired many of their skills in their own social milieu. At the individual teacher level there will always be teachers in the charismatic 'Dead Poets Society' mould who can be successful despite breaking all or most of the rules.

So what needs to be added to these 'necessary conditions' to make them sufficient? We believe that the answer has to centre around the importance of student motivation. By working with this idea it is possible for the school effectiveness movement to engage with its critics and encompass the context within which schools operate. And if they do this they will find themselves almost inevitably moving away from the somewhat 'Fordist' concept of the 'effective school' with its striving for a consistent set of procedures, routines, structures and goals which are the same for every child.

Our thesis is that unless students are engaged with school and motivated to learn, then the school effectiveness strategies are unlikely to be very effective, although of course this will vary with the ability and cultural capital of groups of pupils. It is significant that the relationship between measured IQ and academic achievement is relatively modest (Featherman, 1980). This is because ability needs to be harnessed to motivation to succeed if it is to deliver. In order to motivate and engage students, schools need to adapt themselves to some of their needs and interests, which are often mediated through their subcultures. In practice this will mean schools and their teachers 'striking a deal' with groups of students about schooling. The essence of this deal must be based around the idea of mutual respect and will almost certainly involve trade-offs on both sides. We believe that a key finding from much of the literature on secondary/high schools suggests that schools will not succeed unless children are treated as adults and their dignity respected (for a recent good example see Rudduck, Chaplain and Wallace, 1996). We hypothesize that in those schools where the performance of girls has significantly improved (and this is not uniform, strongly suggesting a school effect), it is because girls are being treated differently by their teachers. Such differences are likely to include: expectations about performance; more girl-sensitive curricula; greater respect for the abilities of girls. Similarly, we strongly suspect that those UK schools that perform well with non-white ethnic groups do behave significantly differently with those groups. In criticizing school effectiveness research for using an 'abstract universalist model of the learner – deracialized, degendered, declassed', Hatcher (1998) cites the work of Nehaul (1996) and Sewell (1997), who in research with Afro-Caribbean students showed that if schools are to raise the levels of achievement of these pupils they have to address issues of race not only in their organization but also through the curriculum. They argue that the curriculum cannot be assumed to be neutral and if disaffection and lack of motivation are to be overcome there has to be a discussion of the present curriculum and whose points of view it legitimizes and whose it rejects.

This approach need not rule out a certain 'bounded consistency'. A 'contract' between various groups and the school will only work well if it is adhered to reasonably consistently by the teachers. But this is a long way from the homogeneous 'one size fits all' model. There is also enough evidence to suggest that schools need to work routinely with groups of students, not with individuals. Schools are composed of subcultures of students (Bradford Brown, 1990; Brown, 1987) and the effective school is likely to be one where the dominant school culture is one where hard work and academic success are rewarded or, at least, not derided (Epstein, 1983).

We believe that this position is supported by recent research in the field. Sackney and Walker (1999), in a study of a group of Canadian schools, argue that a key variable for success is 'trust', i.e. authentic, open relations between members of the school community, such that 'clear (talked about) teaching and learning goals were agreed by students, parents and teachers' (Sackney and Walker, 1999, p. 17). Their model was of the school as a learning community, a place marked by 'gemeinschaft' relations, where agreements were negotiated between key actors (teachers, students and parents). This finding is supported by Chapman (1998) quoted in Little *et al.* (1999), who demonstrates that procedural rules for incorporation of students, e.g. the setting up of a School Council or parent–school contracts, can be ineffective, even counterproductive. What counted was substantive involvement in key decisions, where substantive engagement was defined as 'cognitive, behavioural and affective'.

Teachers are obviously crucial to the deal which needs to be struck with various groups of students, indeed teacher motivation and engagement is the other side of the coin of pupil motivation and engagement. Just as students are unlikely to be motivated to work hard if they see that they have to conform to an unyielding model of work tasks and school organization, so teachers are unlikely to give of their best if they are presented with a teacher-proofed model of teaching. Teachers' capacities to be motivated to work hard and do their best for their students depends partly on whether they can relate to the students in the school. The operation of the labour market for teachers helps here. The inner city, for example, tends to attract teachers who have some commitment to students from these social contexts; black teachers tend to be attracted to those areas where there are concentrations of black children. Our model has clear implications for teacher recruitment and selection, as well as induction in the culture of children in the school if this is 'foreign' to them.

This model of the 'effective school' is one where the school has adapted some of its practices to embrace some of the interests and values of the young people who attend. Although there might be one guiding principle here – respect for many of the values of the students and respect for their dignity as individuals – in practice this could look quite different in different schools. And the more heterogeneous the school population the more complex this could be (imagine a co-educational UK school with sizeable groups of Asian, Afro-Caribbean and white students). Our thinking has been developed from our experience of secondary education and we accept that a different model may be more appropriate at the primary (elementary) stage although similar principles may apply particularly in considering the key role played by parents in the early stages of school. But certainly as children grow older and move to the secondary high school, the potential for conflict between the young people asserting their sense of self and their culture and the monolith of the school grows in importance.

Not only do effective schools need to adapt to young people but schools also need to give greater recognition to the needs of individual subject disciplines inside the school: the discourse of science is quite different from the discourse of English and this needs to be recognized organizationally by the timetabled pattern of the day, organization of teaching areas, etc. (Whitty *et al.*, 1994). None of this is necessarily to deny the importance of what Reynolds (1998) calls 'an applied science of teaching', i.e. a codified set of routines for teaching various subjects to various ages. The difficulty with this position, which he seems to barely acknowledge, is the uncertain status of much of this knowledge and, in particular, the inconsistent findings of much research on particular strategies (the Reading Recovery Scheme (OFSTED, 1993) is a good modern example). Researchers like Stringfield (1995) are inclined to argue that this is because of implementation problems. Others are more inclined to lay the blame at the feet of the research community itself and blame poor research design. Whilst accepting that both the above factors may be important in particular cases, we are more inclined to indict a failure on the part of schools and teachers to engage and motivate students. Like the curriculum, teaching routines are not context-free technologies that can be applied uniformly whatever the context of schooling.

There is a significant support for this position in the organizational literature which has been curiously ignored by the education community, despite some obvious parallels. It is tempting to see a shadowy Tayloristic model in some of the school-effectiveness writing. There are 'experts' who have discovered the best way of teaching certain subjects; it is 'science' (cf. Reynolds' 'applied science of teaching') and the 'workers' are to be instructed in these new models. At the level of the organization classical management theory was built on the Taylorist conception of the 'one best way' which bequeathed us a set of apparently universal management and organizational principles. Such a model largely ignored the context within which organizations worked. Of course some models of schooling assert that this is how schools ought to be, that is, because the school embodies the distillation of certain sets of values, then it is right in principle for children to adapt to them. Once this socialization model is partly abandoned for one that places a much greater stress on academic performance measured in a standardized way, then a model which ignores context looks very vulnerable. In organization theory this led to some version or other of contingency theory. In this model, how an organization should be structured and organized depends on the context in which it finds itself. In a classic early formulation Burns and Stalker (1966) showed that organizations operating in very stable environments could work well with rather bureaucratic, mechanistic structures, whereas this model proved to be very difficult for organizations working in fast-changing, dynamic markets like electronics or fashion; here a more organic structure fitted best. Further interesting developments by Lawrence and Lorsch (1969) showed that it was wrong to see firms as homogeneous structures, although they recognized the strain towards consistency in all organizations. Lawrence and Lorsch argued that sub-units of organizations are likely to have different environments and therefore require specific structures and management in order to be successful. This important study concludes with the view that a crucial problem for organizations is finding a balance between differentiation and integration.

In its original formulation (Pugh *et al.*, 1969), contingency theory seemed to be asserting that organizations need to strive for an almost mechanical 'best fit' between organization and environment. This proved too crude a model, not least because the data threw up too many 'rogue' organizations which did not fit the model. An important modification was made by Child (1984) in his introduction of the notion of 'strategic choice'. He argued that the dominant coalitions in organizations have some latitude in choosing in what sorts of environments to work and what sorts of structures to build.

This contingency model reflects the ideas provided in Chapters 4 and 6 and it also fits our emerging model of effective schooling very well. It recognizes the need for schools to adapt to their 'environment' (effectively their students); it posits the notion of 'best fit' between environment and school – in our terms striking a deal between the needs and interests of the young people and those of the school and its teachers; it recognizes that school managers can exercise a certain amount of strategic choice both over the sorts of young people that the school will accept/retain and over the structure and culture of the school itself. In other words it recognizes the importance of the concept of agency, both on the part of young people and their teachers – a concept that has sometimes been lacking in some school effectiveness research.

CONCLUSION

This chapter began by outlining the case that can be made for a model of the effective school with its powerful routines of organization and teaching. There is little doubt that if this could be made to work in a wide variety of contexts then it would be a very significant achievement. The irony is that it has become deeply embedded in the educational politics of two societies, the UK and US, where the conditions are amongst the least good for its successful implementation. It is not that the model is in essence misguided: far from it, we agree that many of the central principles of school effectiveness are praiseworthy and are part of the armoury of effective schooling. If most children came to school with a keen desire to learn, either for intrinsic or extrinsic reasons, and with a broadly shared cultural heritage and cultural capital, then we would have a powerful model. But these conditions do not hold in either the UK or US: both are multicultural societies with huge disparities in income and wealth. With so many children living below the poverty line and a clear inner-city underclass in both societies it is not possible for schools to have simple goals like academic achievement, they have also to attend to the social and the subcultural.

School improvement is faced with a much more difficult job than merely implementing the model of effective schooling. The organization and structure of the school and teaching strategies have to be adapted to the clients of the school, its students. This is a process of active negotiation, a dynamic process full of compromise. It gives teachers an active role in adapting their school and their teaching strategies to the point where young people become committed and motivated to achieve. The results of soundly based school and classroom effectiveness work need to be seen as providing useful scaffolding and supportive structures in situations which are generally marked by messy complexity. Once students and staff are 'engaged', then the effectiveness models can be worked on to provide routines that are more likely to produce achieving students. The urgent research task, for both teachers and the research community, is to discover which elements of the models can be safely adapted to circumstances and which are key elements which must not be changed because they are the key causal mechanisms of effective performance. For policy makers we suspect that the key issue is to realize that the policies that might lead to effective schooling for all may be inconsistent with policies concerned with the importance of the common school for citizenship.

NOTES

1. 'For each country the major national [i.e. state-recognized qualifications] were selected and benchmarked against UK levels. Judgements about levels of qualifications were made by subject experts drawn from each of the countries and through analysis of syllabuses, test criteria and examination papers' (Green and Steedman, 1993).
2. Evidence-based teaching is a term analogous to 'evidence-based medicine', i.e. that movement which requires strong research-based evidence for the efficacy of particular procedures (teaching routines).
3. For notable exceptions see Bell (1991) in the UK and Guild and Garger (1985) in the US.

REFERENCES

Arnot, M., Gray, J., James, M., Rudduck, J. with Duveen, G. (1998) *Recent Research on Gender and Educational Performance*. London: The Stationery Office.

Bell, G. (1991) *Educating for Capability*. London: Royal Society of Arts.

Berends, M. (1995) 'Educational stratification and students' social bonding to school', *British Journal of Sociology of Education* **16**(3): 32.

Bierhoff, H. J. and Prais, S. J. (1995) *Schooling as a Preparation for Life and Work in Switzerland and Britain*. London: NIESR.

Bradford Brown, B. (1990) 'Peer groups', in D. Feldman and G. Elliott (eds) *At the Threshold: The Developing Adolescent*. Cambridge, MA: Harvard University Press.

Brown, M. (1998) 'The tyranny of the international horse race', in R. Slee and G. Weiner with S. Tomlinson (eds) *School Effectiveness for Whom? Challenges to the School Effectiveness and School Improvement Movements*. London: Falmer Press.

Brown, P. (1987) *Schooling Ordinary Kids*. London: Tavistock.

Brown, S., Riddell, S. and Duffield, J. (1996) 'Possibilities and problems of small-scale studies to unpack the findings of large-scale studies of school effectiveness', in J. Gray, D. Reynolds, C. T. Fitz-Gibbon and D. Jesson (eds) *Merging Traditions: The Future of School Effectiveness and School Improvement*. London: Cassell.

Burns, T. and Stalker, G. M. (1966) *The Management of Innovation*. London: Tavistock.

Burnstein, L. (1992) *The IEA Study of Mathematics III: Student Growth and Classroom Process*. Oxford: Pergamon.

Child, J. (1984) *Organisations: A Guide to Problems and Practice*. London: Harper and Row.

Creemers, B. P. M. (1994) *The Effective Classroom*. London: Cassell.

Entwistle, N. J. (1991) 'Cognitive styles and learning', in K. Marjoribanks (ed.) *The Foundations of Students' Learning*. Oxford: Pergamon.

Epstein, J. L. (1983) 'The influence of friends on achievement and affective outcomes', in J. Epstein and N. Karwait (eds) *Friends in School*. New York: Academic Press.

Featherman, D. (1980) 'Schooling and occupational careers: constancy and change in worldly success', in O. Brien and J. Kagan (eds) *Constancy and Change in Human Development*. Cambridge, MA: Harvard University Press.

Gardner, H. (1993) *Frames of Mind: the theory of multiple intelligences*. London: Fontana.

Gewirtz, S., Ball, S. and Bowe, R. (1995) *Markets, Choice and Equity in Education*. Milton Keynes: Open University Press.

Gillborn, D. and Gipps, C. (1996) *Recent Research on the Achievement of Ethnic Minority Pupils*. London: OFSTED.

Goldstein, H. (1997) 'Methods in school effectiveness research', *School Effectiveness and School Improvement* **8**(4): 369–95.

Green, A. (1990) *Education and State Formation*. London: Macmillan.

Green, A. (1997) *Education, Globalisation and the Nation State*. Basingstoke: Macmillan.

Green, A. and Steedman, H. (1993) *Educational Provision, Educational Attainment and the Needs of Industry: a review of the research for Germany, France, Japan and the USA and Britain, Report No. 5*, London, NIESR.

Guild, P. and Garger, S. (1985) *Marching to Different Drummers*. Alexandria, VA: ASCD.

Hatcher, R. (1998) 'Social justice and the politics of school effectiveness and improvement', *Race, Ethnicity and Education* **1**(2): 267–89.

Hudson, L. (1979) *Contrary Imaginations.* London: Methuen.
International Assessment of Educational Progress (IAEP) (1988) *Science Achievements in Seventeen Countries.* London: Pergamon.
International Assessment of Educational Progress (IAEP) (1992) *Learning Mathematics.* New Jersey: Educational Testing Services.
Jamieson, I. M. (1996) 'The Role of Compulsory Schooling in Economics and Industrial Development'. Plenary address to CEDAR Conference, University of Warwick, April.
Kolb, D. (1984) *Experiential Learning: experience as the source of learning and development.* Englewood Cliffs, NJ: Prentice-Hall.
Lauder, H., Hughes, D., Watson, S., Waslander, S., Thrupp, M., Stratdee, R., Simiyu, I., Dupuis, A., McGlinn, J. and Hamlin, J. (1999) *Trading in Futures: Why Markets in Education Don't Work.* Buckingham: Open University Press.
Lawrence, P. R. and Lorsch, J. W. (1969) *Developing Organizations: diagnosis and action.* Reading, Mass.: Addison-Wesley.
Little, G., Highett, N. and Rogers, T. (1999) 'Ways of knowing'. Paper presented to the International Congress for School Effectiveness and Improvement, San Antonio, Texas, January.
Murphy, P. and Gipps, C. (eds) (1996) *Equity in the Classroom: towards an effective pedagogy for girls and boys.* London: Falmer Press.
OFSTED (1993) *Reading Recovery in New Zealand: A Report from the Office of Her Majesty's Chief Inspector of Schools.* London: HMSO.
Pask, G. (1976) 'Styles and strategies of learning', *British Journal of Education Psychology* **46**(2): 128–48.
Prais, S. J. (1995) *Productivity, Education and Training: an international perspective.* Cambridge: Cambridge University Press.
Prais, S. J. and Wagner, K. (1985) 'Schooling standards in England and Germany: some summary comparisons based on economic performance', *Compare* **16**(1): 5–36.
Pugh, D. S., Hickson, D. J., Hinnings, C. R. and Turner, C. (1969) 'The context of organisation structure', *Administrative Science Quarterly* **14**(1): 91–113.
Reezigt, G., Guldemond, H. and Creemers, B. (1999) 'Empirical validity for a comprehensive model on educational effectiveness', *School Effectiveness and School Improvement* **10**(2): 193–216.
Reynolds, D. (1998) 'Teaching effectiveness: better teachers, better schools', *Research Intelligence* No. 66: 26–9.
Reynolds, D., Creemers, B., Stringfield, S. and Teddlie, C. (1995) 'World Class Schools: a preliminary analysis of data from the International School Effectiveness Research Project'. Paper presented to European Conference on Educational Research, University of Bath, September.
Reynolds, D. and Farrell, S. (1996) *Worlds Apart? A Review of International Surveys of Educational Achievement Including England.* London: OFSTED.
Rudduck, J., Chaplain, R. and Wallace, G. (1996) *School Improvement: What Can Pupils Tell Us?* London: David Fulton.
Sackney, L. and Walker, K. (1999) 'Learning Communities for Effective Schools'. Paper presented to the International Congress for School Effectiveness and Improvement, San Antonio, Texas, January.
Sammons, P., Thomas, S. and Mortimore, P. (1997) *Forging Links: Effective Schools and Effective Departments.* London: Paul Chapman.
Scheerens, J. and Bosker, R. (1997) *The Foundations of Educational Effectiveness.* Oxford: Elsevier Science.
Steinberg, L. (1996) *Beyond the Classroom.* New York: Simon and Schuster.
Sternberg, R. J. (1984) *Beyond IQ: A Triarchic Theory of Human Intelligence.* Cambridge: Cambridge University Press.
Stringfield, S. (1995) 'Attempting to enhance students' learning through innovative

programs: the case for schools evolving into high reliability organizations', *School Effectiveness and School Improvement* **6**(1): 67–96.

Thrupp, M. (1997) 'The school mix effect: how social class composition of a school intake shapes school processes and student achievement'. Paper presented to the Annual Meeting of the American Educational Research Association, Chicago, April.

Whitty, G., Rowe, G. and Aggleton, P. (1994) 'Subjects and themes in the secondary school curriculum', *Research Papers in Education* **9**(2): 159–81.

Witkin, H. A., Moore, C. A., Goodenough, D. R. and Cox, P. W. (1977) 'Field-dependent and field-independent cognitive styles and their educational implications', *Review of Education Research* **47**(1): 1–64.

Chapter 10

School Effectiveness and School Improvement: Future Challenges and Possibilities

Nigel Bennett and Alma Harris

INTRODUCTION

This book has presented a range of perspectives upon school effectiveness and school improvement research. Its basic premise is that organizational theory and organizational analysis can contribute to the development of both fields and, by doing so, provide a basis for more fruitful collaboration. To conclude this book, we offer some final thoughts on some of the issues, challenges and possibilities facing both fields. However, before embarking upon this analysis it is important to reiterate the major achievements of the school effectiveness and school improvement traditions. In a number of significant ways, both fields have informed and reformed approaches to the study of school performance and development. In particular, the school effectiveness research field has:

- Challenged the idea that schools make little difference to the life chances of pupils;
- Focused attention on what schools are able to achieve;
- Emphasized pupil attainment as the basis of judging effectiveness;
- Exposed and examined differential effectiveness within schools;
- Provided a basis for diagnosing a school's effectiveness;
- Encouraged and enabled schools to think more critically about their performance.

Similarly, the school improvement research field has made important contributions to the theory and practice of school-level change. In particular it has:

- Endorsed the centrality of teacher development in school development;
- Emphasized the classroom as the focus of educational change efforts;
- Demonstrated the importance of differential strategies for school-level change;
- Identified a number of important levers for school-level change;

- Highlighted the importance of using research findings to inform practice;
- Refocused attention on the importance of school culture and context.

Such contributions stand as a major and lasting credit to those researchers who have worked in both traditions for the last twenty years. Their work has continued to place a spotlight on the issue of variable school performance and has consistently demonstrated that schools make a difference. It has also resulted in a wide range of initiatives aimed at assisting schools to improve in order to maximize learning outcomes for all students.

MOVING FORWARD?

The chapters in this book have tried to point to issues and approaches that might produce a stronger basis for connecting together the school effectiveness and school improvement traditions. From these chapters it is possible to draw out a number of themes that illustrate some of the limitations that persist across both fields. These themes relate to critical questions highlighted in this book and include:

- What goals or criteria are used as the basis for differentiating between effective and ineffective schools?
- How do we measure schools' relative achievement of these goals or attainment of these criteria, so that the more effective can be distinguished from the less effective?
- How do the features of effective schools (which distinguish them from ineffective schools) contribute to their effectiveness?
- When those within the school improvement field try to promote 'better' practice, how is that practice defined and how does it produce better results?

Each of these themes demonstrates the potential importance of 'problematizing' the issues surrounding the two fields, despite David Reynolds' claim (p. 27) that the strength of the school effectiveness movement lies in its refusal to do this.

First, there is the issue of defining 'effectiveness', which establishes what is seen as good and bad practice and provides the direction for improvement efforts. Most definitions of effectiveness are based upon comparing students' academic achievement. From the very outset, school effectiveness writers have focused on a very limited number of pupil achievement scores. In the USA and the Netherlands, for example, they have tended to measure achievement scores in English and mathematics tests, while in England and Wales the focus has been on GCSE and key stage test results.

This can result in a focus on improving overall test scores at the expense of those children with non-standard 'special needs', especially when the measure of effectiveness has been some kind of benchmark, such as the percentage of children gaining '5+ GCSEs at grades A to C' used in England and Wales. The result can be *less* effective provision for those unable to reach this benchmark, as their needs are ignored while teachers concentrate their attention on the others.

But the question then becomes how to prevent this narrow focus? This does seem difficult without challenging far more explicitly the ways in which educational effectiveness is defined and measured. As Mike Bottery points out in Chapter 8, school effectiveness writers have focused their attention on means, not ends.

Second, there is the issue of taking the ends of organizational action as predefined or imposed. This has implications for the kinds of means that are seen as appropriate. Defining the goals can also lead to definitions of 'good practice'. A narrow definition of goals is likely to produce a narrow rigidity in approaches to teaching and learning which becomes articulated as orthodoxy. Government-generated literacy and numeracy strategies are introduced into primary schools, extended into secondary schools, and then used as the basis for a plan to 'overhaul teaching methods and provide recommended lesson structures and extension work' (TES 2001, p. 3). An emphasis on the measurable becomes a justification for ignoring less measurable but equally important outcomes of schooling, such as citizenship and sporting or musical achievement. It is interesting to note that in Great Britain, politicians who until recently have emphasized key stage scores and GCSE results are now expressing concern about the apparent deterioration of young people's performance in these other fields.

Along with this danger of a narrowly defined orthodoxy, school effectiveness writers have been criticized by opponents of the movement (e.g. Slee *et al.*, 1998) for proposing a simple traditional relationship between teaching and learning. Partly because of the failure to move beyond correlational association to seek causal evidence, there is a tendency to equate changes in teaching with improvements in learning.

The chapters by Jamieson and Wikely (Chapter 9) and by Bottery (Chapter 8) both reassert the emphasis upon individualism and ask why consistency across all settings is seen as a desirable aim. They suggest that individual requirements might be better met by a more flexible view of the teaching–learning relationship. The same point can be made in relation to Reynolds' discussion of possible ways forward. He talks about clinical audits to identify 'well' or 'ill' schools, without acknowledging that, like all medical models, they are essentially normative impositions of a way of thinking about schools. Kuhn (1970) has highlighted some of the dangers of this approach. He shows how a historical understanding of science reveals an uncritical acceptance of 'normal science', which leads to theories and models being stretched to accept more and more conflicting data, until such time as a new set of models takes over.

Third, an uncritical acceptance of externally defined and interpreted measures of effectiveness does not help schools become more effective unless we are told that these measures of effectiveness are what schools have to follow. In Chapter 9 Jamieson and Wikely comment, as part of their appeal for individuality, on the need to negotiate outcomes with students, to treat them with dignity and to recognize the central element of motivation if students are to achieve in terms that the school is allowed to recognize. This crucial point recognizes a far more complex association between teaching and learning than is to be found in the simplistic linear model that appears to underpin much school effectiveness writing. It can also be extended to address a fundamental omission of much of the school improvement field, that of achieving a sufficient motivation on the part of the staff to take part in the changes that are being proposed or negotiated through the school improvement intervention (Bennett and Harris, 1999). Agnes McMahon's discussion of the individuality of school cultures, in Chapter 7, emphasizes this point.

Finally, an issue that has been acknowledged by recent writers on school effectiveness (Sammons *et al.*, 1997) and school improvement (Harris, 1998, Harris and Hopkins, 2000) concerns whether the school is the appropriate unit of analysis. Research by Sammons *et al.* (1997) highlights the existence of differential effectiveness across and within different subject departments. Recent work by Harris and Hopkins (2000) has emphasized differential teacher effectiveness and the importance of the classroom as the unit of change.

Such arguments suggest that to analyse pupil achievement school by school is to overlook much closer influences on individual pupil performance. It also suggests that the school is not the proper unit of analysis for 'improvement' activities but that interventions need to target much more precisely the 'ineffective' areas within each school (Harris, 1998). In Chapter 7, Agnes McMahon raises a further question about the concept of the school or department as a unit of analysis. She draws on the concept of the learning organization (Garratt, 1987; Senge, 1990), which postulates an inherent orientation towards reflective practice and a willingness on the part of individual members to regard their own actions as open to scrutiny and reconsideration (Schon, 1983; Osterman and Kottkamp, 1994). This approach to considering how one might increase school effectiveness opens up the importance of subcultures within the organization (Meyerson and Martin, 1987) but in doing so it raises the question of whether these subcultures match up with formal structures such as departments. It also strengthens Nigel Bennett's emphasis on seeing organizations as dynamic rather than static entities and reintroduces the idea of power as a resource flowing between participants, whose distribution varies according to the setting.

One approach to analysing practice that has questioned the extent to which subcultures are structurally defined is that of Wenger (1998), who has postulated the concept of 'communities of practice'. This idea may have considerable value to both the school effectiveness and school improvement movements, since it provides an analytical approach that simultaneously accommodates the uniqueness of individual schools and the universality of educational systems. It also draws upon concepts of structure, culture and power that are also centrally important within this book.

Wenger (1998) suggests that individuals derive their understanding of their work from the community of practice within which they carry it out. The members of the community have a shared understanding of the work and individuals are drawn into the community by a process of learning where the boundaries are situated which define the collection of tasks which make up the practice. One becomes a member of the community by a combination of participation in actions and what Wenger calls 'reification' – investing particular activities with a status of reality. Part of the process of becoming a member is a form of apprenticeship – Wenger refers to it as 'legitimate peripheral participation' – through which one both learns the tasks and develops a sense of one's status within the group.

Wenger introduces two important points. First, everyone is a member of more than one community of practice. Teachers, for example, are part of a wider community of teachers, which defines certain aspects of behaviour as legitimate, whilst also being members of a school. Further, teachers are simultaneously members of a school and a department, of a department and a classroom. Through this multiple membership individuals transact the expectations of one community of practice into others and also develop their understanding of the expectations of neighbouring and related communities of practice through their perception of the others' actions. Teachers interpret those broader expectations through their individual and group participation in specific organizational contexts – classroom, school corridor or hallway, departmental office, staff room, etc. – and may behave quite differently in each, for each is a part of a particular school community practice. This approach incorporates children explicitly into the analysis: children behave differently when visitors are in the classroom or when they are with a teacher they like or respect. They are part of school communities of practice.

Different communities of practice, even within the same organization, may have quite different perceptions of what counts as 'best' or even 'good' practice. Wenger (1988) illustrates this by reference to the different interpretations of a newly designed computer form by its designers and its users. Bennett (1991; 1995) found that English teachers' perceptions of 'best practice' teaching differed quite sharply from those of science teachers and this produced quite different perceptions of the 'proper' role of the head of department. Such an analysis suggests that the imposition of consistency in the pursuit of imposed goals or outcomes may be difficult to achieve and may not be a sound aim for school improvement consultants.

Much of Wenger's (1998) analysis could be interpreted as the manifestation of subcultures within organizations. But an important difference is that Wenger suggests that the participation, reification and negotiation between community members that must be a part of such activities creates a range of understandings of practice that influence the ability of communities to change in two crucial ways. The first derives from practice being conceived as the combination of participation and reification. This suggests that any change proposed has to link in some clear way with existing practice, and that any over-radical change simply will not be understandable and will therefore cause, at least, significant problems. Second, Wenger suggests that individuals derive their identity from their membership of, and participation in, communities of practice. Consequently, simply to operate on the basis of 'the school' or even 'the department' as a unit of analysis is to ignore these potentially profound meanings which individuals invest in their day-to-day actions. This suggests that a more negotiative, more flexible and less directive approach to determining the criteria for assessing school effectiveness is required and that over-radical change efforts are likely to produce major difficulties for those expected to participate.

CONCLUSION

This discussion draws on a range of arguments made in this book and suggests that despite the very real achievements of the school effectiveness and school improvement, certain limitations persist. Without attending to these short-comings, it is suggested that a synthesis between the two fields will remain elusive. The fact that school effectiveness research sees schools as similar and stable entities which can be brought to a consistency of practice and school improvement views them as individual and potentially dynamic entities persists as a major point of difference. It is our view that organizational analysis provides alternative ways of viewing schools and could address such fundamental differences. Its emphasis on structural, cultural and political analysis, we suggest, has the potential to provide school effectiveness and improvement research with the opportunity of a closer theoretical relationship.

While attempts have been made to generate theories of school improvement (Hopkins, 1996) and school effectiveness (Creemers, 1994), further work remains. We suggest that organizational theory may assist this development by offering school effectiveness and school improvement researchers a new and shared set of analytical frames or perspectives. To date, school effectiveness and school improvement research has produced a significant reorientation of thinking about what educational systems can do and what might be expected of them. However, as Ouston (1999) among others has demonstrated, there is still little to explain how changes might be brought about to improve schools and what changes work more effectively than others. This is still relatively unchar-ted territory.

The argument presented in this book is that an alternative theoretical grounding could enable researchers in both fields to provide a more powerful set of strategies for securing school effectiveness and school improvement. By using perspectives from organizational theory and management theory we suggest that the possibilities for a closer relationship, both theoretically and practically, between school effectiveness and school improvement are enhanced. It would lessen the danger of the two movements being dismissed as the academic equivalent of the emperor's new clothes. More importantly, by seeking to establish greater synergy between both fields we move a step closer to ensuring that every school makes the maximum difference to the learning and achievement of every student.

REFERENCES

Bennett, N. (1991) 'Change and continuity in school practice: a study of the influences affecting secondary school teachers' work, and of the role of local and national policies within them', Unpublished PhD thesis, Department of Government, Brunel University.

Bennett, N. (1995) *Managing Professional Teachers: Middle Management in Primary and Secondary Schools*. London: Paul Chapman Publishing.

Bennett, N. and Harris, A. (1999) 'Hearing truth from power? Organizational theory, school effectiveness and school improvement', *School Effectiveness and School Improvement* **10**(4): 533–50.

Creemers, B. P. M. (1994) *The Effective Classroom*. London: Cassell.

Garratt, B. (1987) *The Learning Organization*. London: Pan Books.

Harris, A. (1998) 'Improving ineffective departments in secondary schools: strategies for change and development', *Educational Management and Administration* **26**(3): 269–78.

Harris, A. and Hopkins, D. (2000) 'Alternative perspectives on school improvement', *School Leadership and Management* **20**(1): 9–15.

Hopkins, D. (1996) 'Towards a theory for school improvement', in J. Gray, D. Reynolds and C. T. Fitz-Gibbon (eds) *Merging Traditions: The Future of Research on School Effectiveness and School Improvement*. London: Cassell.

Kuhn, T. (1970) *The Structure of Scientific Revolutions*. Chicago: University of Chicago Press.

Meyerson, D. and Martin, J. (1987) 'Cultural change: an integration of three different views', *Journal of Management Studies* **24**(6), pp. 623–47.

Osterman, K. and Kottkamp, R. B. (1994) 'Rethinking professional development', in N. Bennett, R. Glatter and R. Levačić (eds) *Improving Educational Management Through Research and Consultancy*, pp. 46–57. London: Paul Chapman Publishing.

Ouston, J. (1999) 'School effectiveness and school improvement: critique of a movement', in T. Bush, L. Bell, R. Bolam, R. Glatter and P. Ribbins (eds) *Educational Management: Redefining Theory, Policy and Practice*, pp. 166–77. London: Paul Chapman Publishing.

Sammons, P., Thomas, S. and Mortimore, P. (1997) *Forging Links: Effective Schools and Effective Departments*. London: Paul Chapman Publishing.

Schon, D. A. (1983) *The Reflective Practitioner: How Professionals Think in Action*. London: Maurice Temple-Smith.

Senge, P. (1990) *The Fifth Discipline*. New York: Doubleday.

Slee, R. and Weiner, G. with Tomlinson, S. (eds) (1998) *School Effectiveness for Whom? Challenges to the School Effectiveness and School Improvement Movements*. London: Falmer Press.

Times Educational Supplement (TES) (2001) 'Heat turned on Secondary staff', 26 January: 3.

Wenger, E. (1998) *Communities of Practice: Learning, Meaning and Identity*. Cambridge: Cambridge University Press.

Index

The index covers the main text, but not preliminary pages or reference lists. Headings categorize effectiveness research, improvement research and organizational theory for schools, the principal subjects of the book. **Bold** type within a sequence of page numbers indicates a more significant section; an 'f' after a page number indicates inclusion of a figure; a 't' indicates inclusion of a table.